I0450685

MARCHING TO AN ANGRY DRUM

C. G. MITCHELL

Writers Club Press
New York Lincoln Shanghai

Marching to an Angry Drum

All Rights Reserved © 2000 by C. G. Mitchell

No part of this book may be reproduced or transmitted in any form or by any means, graphic, electronic, or mechanical, including photocopying, recording, taping, or by any information storage retrieval system, without the written permission of the publisher.

Writers Club Press
an imprint of iUniverse, Inc.

For information address:
iUniverse, Inc.
2021 Pine Lake Road, Suite 100
Lincoln, NE 68512
www.iuniverse.com

All names of individuals used in this story are fictional and any resemblance to persons living or dead is purely coincidental. Any slights of people, places, or organizations is unintentional.

ISBN: 0-595-00144-0 (Pbk)
ISBN: 0-595-75810-X (Cloth)

Printed in the United States of America

DEDICATION

This book is dedicated to the hundreds of thousands of gay and lesbian servicemen and women who have served, and who are serving in silence as members of the armed forces of the United States.

Many have sacrificed their lives for their country, and many have had their lives destroyed. To these honorable men and women this country owes a debt of gratitude, an apology, and finally, full recognition for their unselfish and loyal dedication to the military, and to this nation as a whole.

Acknowledgements

To Robert P Stanley for his support and continuous encouragement.

To all those individuals who have given me friendship, love, support, and encouragement, I am deeply grateful.

INTRODUCTION

Many of the events, situations, and characterizations portrayed herein are essentially true. I have attempted to utilize my personal experiences and associations with the many gay men with whom I had the pleasure to serve with while I was an active member of the United States Army.

A further goal in writing this book was to dispel the many stereotypical myths associated with gays in the military. It was my intention to bring forcibly to the attention of the reader that gays and lesbians have suffered greatly from the many and unwarranted purges that were and continue to be perpetuated by the biases and prejudices of the intolerant and misinformed. It is an indisputable fact that gays and lesbians have served heroically, bravely, and honorably; many have forfeited their lives in the service of their country. It is likewise an undeniable fact that the only difference between gay men and lesbians and their heterosexual counterparts is that of sexual orientation, and nothing more.

I am reminded of the epitaph of the late
Leonard Matlovich
A gay Vietnam veteran
*"When I was in the military they gave me a medal for
killing two men, and a discharge for loving one."*

CONTENTS

Chapter 1

Vince sat by the pool slowly sipping on the beer that he had poured over an hour ago. It was one of those perfect evenings, warm with a gentle breeze, lit by a thousand stars and a brilliant moon—a perfect time for reflecting on the past and wondering of the future.

"Hi, Vince," Gary said as he entered through the back gate. "Looks like I'm the first one here. Steve went to pick up Paul and I guess he'll be picking up Bill at the same time. Where's Harold? I thought he'd be staying with you."

"He was welcome to stay, but Niki and Maria asked if he'd stay a few days with them. I expect him to arrive at any moment. He said he was going to stop off and pick up a few things at the store, then he'd be right over. Why not help yourself to a drink in the meantime."

"Thanks, Vince. You don't mind if I fix myself a screwdriver, do you?"

"No, have anything you want Gary. You didn't have to ask. I'm sure you know that by now."

"Yeah, I knew I didn't have to ask but I was just making conversation, I guess. Hey, here comes Steve, Paul, and Bill right now."

"Hi, Vince, I see that Gary beat us here. Has Harold arrived yet?"

"Not yet, Steve, but we expect him at any time now. Make yourselves at home while I go in to get us something to munch on," Vince said as he got up and made his way through the sliding glass doors and into the house.

"Hey, Gary, do you mind turning on a little music while we get ourselves a drink?"

"Anything in particular, Steve?"

"No, just something soft and easy. Boy, you couldn't find a more perfect evening, could you?"

"Nope, don't think you could. Hey, here comes Harold. Looks like he bought out the store."

Harold was almost six-feet, with very dark brown eyes. His features and build were similar to that of an All-American athlete—somewhat rugged yet quite handsome. His hair was medium brown with a military style crewcut. His brother, John was slightly smaller in height and build and there was no question that they were related. Aside from a noticeable birthmark on Harold's neck, they could almost pass as twins.

"Hi, guys. Gee, it's great seeing all of you here tonight. Where's Vince?"

"Inside getting something to snack on," Gary answered. "By the way, how's Niki and Maria? You could have brought them along, you know."

"Yeah, I know, but they said they'd rather stay home tonight, but to give their love to everyone."

The next few hours passed rather quickly with the conversation centering around John.

Finally, it was time for everyone to go, leaving only Harold and Vince behind.

"You know, Harold," Vince questioned. Every now and then I heard someone mention John and David—almost like they were always together. When I asked who David really was, Gary said, 'Ask Harold, he's John's brother.'

"Who was David, Harold? What I mean is, I really don't know anything about him other than what little I know already. I never heard John mention him before."

After a long moment of silence and deep reflection, Harold began. "He loved him, Vince." Again Harold paused. "I mean—he really loved him. Perhaps in every way that one can love. I don't know; but nonetheless, he loved him probably more than his family, his friends, more than God himself. He never forgot him, and talked often of him when we were alone."

"Well Vince," Harold continued, I guess I'd better start from the beginning. As best I can remember, it went something like this:

"They met in '49, the Army. Yeah, '49, when John first met him—David that is. John and I joined together and shipped off to Fort Riley, Camp Funston, in Kansas. We were both kids. John was just seventeen, and me, a year older. Full of life, excitement; you know—adventure. I could never forget it. It took John about three weeks to finally convince Mr. Alan at the Children's Home to let him join. It was only after I agreed to join up with him that he gave his approval. We spent ten years in that home. I don't know if John ever told you about it.

"John was an orphan after our mother died, but I still had my father. John's father was killed in an auto accident when John was three. We were half brothers, you see—different fathers, same mother. That's why we don't have the same last names, and that's why we ended up in The Home.

"Let's see now, it was May 6th that we reported to that recruiting station in Detroit along with a number of other men. After a brief period we were ushered into a rather large room and lined up in three rows for a physical examination. We had already finished with our written tests and marched before the psychiatrist, who was primarily interested in weeding out anyone he believed to be homosexual or anyone with deviant behavior—whatever that meant.

There were a number of officers and enlisted men in uniform standing around. Finally a sergeant with gray hair who looked to be in his early forties introduced himself as Sgt. Maple.

"First off, if you're shy or bashful, you'll soon get over it. There's no place for modesty in this man's army. Now I want each of you to strip off everything but your shorts. If you have no shorts then I guess you'll just be naked."

Sure enough there were about ten guys who stood there naked as jay-birds, and those of us who wore underwear did all we could to control ourselves from laughing.

"Dr. Spitzer will check each of you for heart or lung problems. When he stands in front of you, you will turn your head to the side so as not to breathe directly into the doctor's face. After listening to your heart with the stethoscope he will listen to your chest and ask you to take some deep breaths, then let them out. Next, I want each of you to open your mouths wide as you can so that the dentist can check your mouth, tonsils, gums and teeth."

Following the heart and lung exam, we stood there with our mouths wide open and it was all we could do to control drooling, as swallowing was almost impossible with your mouth in this fixed position for any length of time.

"Now I want everyone to drop his shorts and when the doctor stands in front of you he will examine your penis and testicles, after which he will be checking you for hernias. When he presses his finger near your testicles you will be directed to turn your head to the side and cough. He'll also be pressing on your abdomen to check out your liver, kidneys and spleen."

After some minor discomfort the doctor finished with his examination and we were ready for the next part of our physical.

"Next I want everyone to remain with their shorts pulled down. Each of you will bend over and spread the cheeks of your butt. The doctor will pass by each of you and check you for hemorrhoids. Then you can pull up your shorts and prepare for the final part of your examination. Those of you who didn't wear shorts may pull up your pants, and I'm sure you'll be wearing them in the future."

One of the officers had each of us first stand, then take turns sitting on a chair to have our feet checked for any possible deformities or disease. After this we were put through a number of exercises such as forward, sideward and backward bending along with knee exercises. Fortunately, all of us passed and we were now ready to take the oath.

After we were officially sworn in we were taken into the dining area for lunch. All of us were then given a three-day pass before we were to report back.

Three days passed rather quickly and after returning from pass we assembled in the same room where we had recently been sworn in. After all were accounted for, we were bussed to Grand Central Station to board the train bound for Fort Riley, Kansas. God, were we excited. Neither John nor I had ever been on a train, and never away from The Home for any length of time."

Again he paused, as if almost projecting himself backward in time.

"Hey John—I mean soldier. Can you beat that, you're a soldier now. And so am I, for that matter. Wait until they see us in our uniform, we'll knock 'em dead, I bet."

"You're right about that, Harold. We'll really look great. Wonder what all our friends and the kids at school will think when they see us—in uniform, that is?"

The day before we left for camp, Mr. Alan, Miss Tingsley, several other counselors, along with some of their friends, as well as ours, all got together for our going away party. I remember how both John and I got a carton of cigarettes from Mr. Alan. It was a real surprise to us, as we didn't know that anyone had the slightest idea we had started smoking. Along with the cigarettes we each got about $15 in cash—quite a bit of money back then. The Home's kitchen did the cooking and I think it was one of the most memorable parties that we ever had.

The following morning we arrived at the railroad station where we joined about forty other guys whom we were sworn in with. The excitement was electric and you could feel its current as it flashed throughout the group.

At long last we boarded the train which would arrive at Fort Riley early the following morning. A corporal was in charge and after a roll call we were all assigned to seats which were later made into bunks. There were two guys to a seat, which meant one guy took the top bunk and two shared the lower. I was seated in front of John with some guy named Bruce. Let's see now, Bruce had the waviest reddish-brown hair I've ever seen on a guy. He was about five foot-ten. He couldn't have been much shorter than I was and I would say he had an average build. From a woman's point of view he had to be quite attractive, as most women were crazy about him. At least he claimed they were.

John was seated with David. Yeah, that's where he first met him.

David was—well, a good-looking Italian from New York, with olive skin and thick dark hair. A little over six foot. I could almost compare him to those classic sculptures of a Roman god. He was a really nice guy, and lots of fun—a pleasure to be with. As it turned out, David and John were to share the lower bunk together.

I have to laugh when I think about it, as they had to sleep head to foot and fully clothed. I guess this was the Army's way of justifying the necessity of bunking two guys together in the same bed.

This was the first time that John and David would be so close to one another and although nothing happened between them, I'm sure that neither one of them managed to sleep that night.

The trip was great, good food, good conversation, and good company. Have you ever sat in a dining car with the train rocking gently back and forth? I can remember how our coffee cups occasionally rattled on their saucers as the countryside passed by the windows. Strange how you remember those little things. As for the club car—we were all too young. Most of the day was spent just talking, telling jokes, laughing, and playing cards.

When we finally turned in for the night we were lulled to sleep by the soft clicking sounds of the wheels passing over the tracks.

At last we arrived at our destination, Camp Funston, Fort Riley, Kansas, home of the Tenth Infantry Division. It was early May and raining—one of those light and misty rains, warm and invigorating.

Once again the corporal gathered us together and after accounting for everyone, we were promptly ushered into a large building and given coffee and donuts. They called this place the Mess Hall, and it would be in a building much like this that we took our meals every day. You know, I heard a lot about how bad that Army chow was. I must be nuts, but I liked it. I even liked that shit on a shingle, which turned out to be creamed hamburger or chipped beef on toast.

It was after we arrived at Company 'E,' and more or less settled in, that Cpl. Bannish entered the barracks to give us our first taste of Army life.

Cpl. Bannish was a rather slightly built guy with a pleasant enough manner. His light brown hair was thinning a little and he couldn't have been any older than nineteen, if he was that old. He was obviously from down South somewhere—just where, I never did know.

"All right, men," Cpl. Bannish began. "I am one of your platoon cadre. The cadre are the ones in charge. When I say fall in, I want each of you standing at attention at the foot of your bunks, and in front of your footlockers," as he pointed to what looked like a trunk at the foot of each bed. "OK? "

"Yes, Corporal," we all yelled in unison.

At this point Cpl. Bannish indicated that as a member of the cadre he was responsible for the barracks as well as for us, second only to Sgt. Bragg, who was to be our platoon sergeant. Sgt. Bragg, as it would turn out, was a man probably in his mid-thirties, lean and thin, with a rather weathered face and sharply pointed nose.

"Your first sergeant is Sergeant Price," Cpl. Bannish continued. "Your platoon leader is Lieutenant Hall, and the company commander is Captain Hasselman. You'll recognize the captain when you see him. He's the one with the two silver bars. He's in his thirties, guess that's one of the reasons why they call him the old man. It might be a little complicated right now, but you'll soon get the hang of it, and by the way, these cans are for butts. Not your butts—cigarette butts, that is. The latrines and showers are located on the first floor at the front of the barracks. Everyone takes a shower every day and I don't want to see anyone playing drop the soap. You'll have a lecture on bathing later on. Every day one of you will be assigned to latrine duty. This means that you will be responsible for keeping the toilets, sinks, showers, floors, and mirror as clean as they can possibly get. Once a week someone will be assigned to shine the brass fixtures until you can see your face reflecting from them—so much for latrine duty.

"Next, you are responsible for checking the bulletin board every day for special assignments or announcements. If you are assigned to latrine or KP duty, it'll be posted there. Failure to check the bulletin board daily will result in demerits. You will find the demerit system posted on the bulletin board. While I'm on the subject, the Company bulletin board is located outside the Company Commander's office, and you're responsible for checking it every day as well.

"I want you to pay careful attention to all the bugle calls as they will let you know what is happening and when.

"I'll start with first call. This will be the first thing you hear in the morning. Sort of a warning that the next call is about to be sounded. That would be Reveille. Reveille means rise and shine.

"But a word to the wise, you had better get your asses up and out of bed if you know what's good for ya.

"The next call you'll hear is Assembly. By the time you hear Assembly you should have used the latrine, shaved, brushed your teeth, dressed, and made yourself ready for roll call.

"Following Assembly the bugler will sound To the Colors. This is when the flag is raised and everyone will stand at attention and salute until the flag has been raised.

"Mess call comes next and is played three times a day. Like the name implies, this is the time that we go to the mess hall for chow.

"Other bugle calls are Fatigue, Drill call, Recall, Church call, Mail call and Retreat.

"Last we end the day with Tattoo which means that you will get ready for bed and turn out the barrack lights.

"The final call of the day is Taps.

"By the way you might want to remember the words that were written for Taps.

Day is done, gone the sun,

From the lake, from the hills, from the sky.

All is well, safely rest, God is nigh

So much for bugle calls. You'll catch on soon enough.

"When lights go out at night, I don't want to hear about anyone making a tent out of their sheets and rattling the springs. The only hard-on better be a piss hard, the only man in your bunk had better be just you—if you know what I mean. No women in the barracks at any time, and that's about all I have to say on this subject. By the way, payday is once a month and as recruits you will receive seventy-five dollars a month. So that you can purchase some of the things you will need, each man will receive a partial pay in a day or two." He then continued to brief us on other do's and don'ts, as well as on our initial duties as new recruits.

Later that day we were assembled in front of the barracks and marched to the cadence of Hup two three four as we made our way for a regulation GI cut. Each man in turn sat in the chair while the barber pressed his huge fat belly hard against the poor guy waiting to be shorn. I honestly think he got some sort of sexual or sadistic pleasure as he removed his victim's hair right down to the scalp. When he got done with us, we looked like bald old men with young men's faces. Stripped of individual identity we took the first step in discarding our civilian lives.

After we left the barber we were marched off to an old warehouse to be issued uniforms, the next step in molding us into soldiers. It was evident that it would take a lot more practice before we got the hang of marching together as a well-disciplined unit.

Upon entering the building, we all stripped down to our shorts, were measured, and issued uniforms. Would you believe that even the undershorts were a regulation olive green—baggy boxers that not many guys would want to wear, much less be seen in. For the most part we would wear a work uniform that they called fatigues. Oh yes, they also issued us a helmet with liner, backpack, sheets, pillowcase, a blanket, a spade, and a barracks bag, which was a long canvas bag large enough to hold all our personal belongings. Rifles would be kept locked up and issued later on.

From here it was back to the barracks to unload our gear.

"OK, men, take a fifteen minute break, but be sure to use the butt cans if you smoke. After break, I want you to police the company grounds. When I say police I mean you'll be picking up any cigarette butts or trash. When you're finished with that, you'll head off down to lunch. After you're finished eating you'll form up outside for a class on the UCMJ, which stands for the 'Uniform Code of Military Justice.' The UCMJ now replaces the Army's old 'Articles Of War.'"

Time flew quickly by and soon it was dinner; time off and early to bed with the sound of taps as it flowed softly across the camp. Our first night there and it felt good—not lonely, not sad, but good.

The following day, we were awakened rather early in the morning to the sound of the bugler at reveille. "I can't get 'em up, I can't get 'em up, I can't get 'em up in the morning"—something like that. One of the Company cadre was busy making sure that everyone was up, making his bed, and washing up in preparation for breakfast. As I think about it now, I almost have to laugh, as I recall three or four men in the showers with several guys sitting bare ass on the open toilets oblivious to the others nearby. Privacy was a luxury not to be found here. Others no older than seventeen or eighteen were standing there by the sinks attempting to master the manly art of shaving. Several of the guys were using soap mugs and shaving brushes to create a lather as they attempted to copy the bygone days of their fathers and grandfathers. One guy even tried to prove his mastery of shaving with a straight razor at the risk of cutting his throat. Most of what got shaved off was the peach fuzz they wanted to think of as hair. You have no idea how many guys came from this ritual with small pieces of toilet paper plastered here and there on their faces, in an effort to stop the bleeding.

First thing in the morning, after roll call was taken, morning report and calisthenics were to be our daily routine.

Following breakfast our whole company was marched off to the division parade grounds where we were told to form a single line stretching the width of the field.

"All right, men," Sgt. Price yelled at the top of his voice, "you'll be getting down on your hands and knees and picking up every cigarette butt you can find. If it don't move, pick it up. All I want to see is assholes and elbows. Do I make myself clear?"

"Yes, Sergeant," we all yelled back, as we took up the required position. This degrading task proved to be almost a daily routine, and actually it wasn't so bad considering some of the many other options.

After we finished picking up everything but the grass we were hurried off to breakfast at a running pace. If you didn't have an appetite before, you sure had one by then.

Following breakfast it was back to the barracks for a class in personal hygiene.

"Listen up, men, If you don't know by now, I'm your platoon leader. My name's Sergeant Bragg. Take a good look at my face and don't forget it. You'll be seeing me every day. Right now I'm here to give you some instruction in personal hygiene. From the looks of it, some of you need it, and others don't know what it is. To start with, I want everyone brushing their teeth every day. You'll be getting a class on dental hygiene later on by the dentist.

"Next is bathing. I don't want to hear of anyone not taking a shower every day. A whore's bath is when you fill your helmet with water and bathe with it. This will do when you're in the field and that's the only bath you can get. Now getting back to bathing, while you're in the shower, you'll wash your hair—what little you have—then scrub every inch of your body until you're squeaky clean, and that means asshole, dick, and balls. Those of you who are uncircumcised will skin it back and keep it clean. We're not running a cheese factory here, you know. Any man who neglects to bathe will wish to God he had after his buddies forcibly drag him into the shower and scrub every inch of his body with those large brushes we use to scrub the floors. We call this a GI shower and believe me, if you've ever had one, you'd never want one again.

"Every man is expected to shave every morning. I don't give a damn if you don't have a single hair on your face, you'll shave until one grows in, and continue shaving after that.

"I suggest you purchase a good deodorant from the PX. The PX stands for Post Exchange—that's where you can buy things. I want you looking good and smelling good. Your uniform along with your underwear and socks will be free of odors and remain clean at all times. Your shoes, boots, and brass will be cleaned and polished every day.

"Bed linens will be changed once a week and along with your bunk, your footlockers will remain clean, orderly, and ready for inspection. So much for personal hygiene, have I made myself clear?"

A resounding "Yes, Sergeant" was echoed across the room.

"After I leave, Corporal Bannish is going to show you how to make your bunks. When he gets done showing you, I want you to practice until you get it right. You'll know you've done it right when you can drop a dime on it and it bounces back.

"Demerits will be issued for failure to comply with Company rules. The number of demerits you receive will determine your punishment.

"Not bathing or having body odor will cost you twenty pushups and ten laps around the Company grounds at full speed.

"Bad breath or not brushing your teeth will result in twenty pushups. If you have bad teeth, you'd better speak up now or get ready for sore arms from the pushups I promised.

"Improperly made bunks will bring you twenty pushups for each time you continue to make it wrong.

"A dirty uniform will get you written up in addition to twenty pushups and twenty laps around the Company grounds. Always remember this, your uniform represents the United States Army, and how you wear it represents you as a soldier, and you as a man."

After Sgt. Bragg was finished and left the barracks, Cpl. Bannish commenced with instructions in bed making. When he was finished, each man took to the task with such intensity that you would think it was the most important task on earth.

For the first week, Harold recalled, we continued to be oriented to our daily routine along with classroom, lots of marching, and short order drill. Oh yes, each of us had blood drawn to check our blood types and I can't forget getting those shots. My arm was sore for days. We were all issued M-1 Garand rifles and instructed to memorize the rifle pledge. Let's see now, I think it went like this.

This is my rifle, there are many like it, but this one is mine. My rifle is my best friend, without it I am useless. Together we are the defenders of our country. Strange how I can remember that after all these years.

Later that week each of us received two dog tags, which hung on a beaded chain. These tags contained your name, serial number and blood type. We were required to wear them around our neck at all times. In a way receiving them seemed to be the final proof that we were no longer civilians but had become soldiers in this man's Army.

One day in our second week, Cpl. Bannish called us together after returning to the barracks. "OK, men, I got good news for you. Tonight after dinner you can all go where you want, so long as you don't leave the base. Each man will receive partial pay so that he'll have some money to spend. You can visit the PX, the Enlisted Men's Club or the Base Theater. The uniform will be fatigues, and I expect all of you back in the barracks before taps." Needless to say, this news was greeted with loud yells of excitement.

As different groups went off together and John and I were about to leave, David came up, put his arms around us and said, "How 'bout me joining you guys?"

"No problem," I said. "Come on."

Strange how John and David never seemed to have much in common until they got their first pass. John was always sort of a loner—sort of shy, while David, on the other hand, was outgoing and made friends easily.

Let's see now. Bruce and I, David and John all headed for the PX where in addition to buying cigarettes at a dollar a carton, we bought those Tenth Division patches and shoulder pins. We also bought some Kiwi shoe polish, a blitz cloth to polish our lapel and buckle brass, toothpaste and brush, a sewing kit, and some other things we were told we must have. After returning to the barracks, we carefully locked away our treasures then hurried out again. I remember walking around the parade grounds hoping for passing officers to practice our saluting on.

Finally, we were off to the Enlisted Men's Club together. None of us up to this point had ever done much in the way of drinking so the 3.2 beer was more intoxicating than we could handle. Were we drunk, or was it only in our minds? At any rate, after about four beers we all staggered back to our barracks long before taps had sounded. Some of the men went promptly to bed while others played cards and joked around.

We had one guy named Bishop who really got drunk and passed out in bed the moment he hit it. I still have to laugh when I think about it. About four or five guys from the platoon upstairs came down and poured water all over his ass and onto the cot so he'd think he pissed the bed when he awakened. A couple other guys had filled condoms with water and tossed them out the windows upstairs onto some unsuspecting guys just returning. If it wasn't practical jokes it was occasional arguing, fighting, wrestling, or grab-ass, which was soon broken up with little to no injuries reported. Boys will be boys, so they say.

I can still remember Sgt. Price with his rifle training class.

"OK, men, fall in. Today we're going to spend the first half of the day at the barns learning how to assemble and disassemble the M-1. Garand rifle. Pay careful attention, as you will all be required to perform this task with your eyes closed. You can practice that tonight. The second half of the day will be about the carbine, the B.A.R. and the .45-caliber pistol. Along with the bayonet, and grenades, these are the four basic weapons you will be required to master. Oh yes, there is the 1903-A3 Springfield rifle—good for sniping. Older than the M-1, but really accurate. Like I said before, when you get back to the barracks, I want you to start practicing what you learned today with your M-1's. You better learn it, and learn it good. If you remember nothing else, remember this. This is not a game. It's kill or be killed, and you better be the best damned killers we've ever trained. Do I make myself clear?"

"Yes, Sergeant Price," we all yelled out as loud as we could.

The next evening we were assigned to a number of places around the base. With empty rifles at the ready, we were prepared to defend our turf and challenge any and all comers bold enough to venture onto our path. We walked guard two hours on, with two hours off to rest, before going back out and walking guard duty again.

"Don't let anyone pass unless they're properly identified. You will say 'Halt, who goes there.' I don't care if it's the Company Commander. He must identify himself, or he doesn't get by. Is that clear?" Sgt. Bragg asked, as he dropped us off at our prearranged posts. Aside from the interrupted sleep, guard duty wasn't all that bad.

The following week the entire company was assembled for rifle practice at the range.

"Today we'll be firing on the range. Everything you've learned up to now about your weapon is important; but actually firing it is what it's all about," Lieutenant Hall said, as we waited to board the nearby trucks.

After a few preliminary instructions, we boarded the trucks and proceeded to the firing range. It was rather hot the day we made our way
down the dusty dirt roads, and as the truck in front stirred up the fine gray
dust, you could actually taste it as it settled on your face.

On arrival at the range we left the trucks and assembled for further
instructions.

"May I have your attention, and you'd better be paying attention if you
know what's good for you. I'm Sergeant Dressler. I'm in charge here at the
rifle range. If you have any questions you'll address me by calling out
Sergeant, and raising your hand. Now, before we get started I want to go
over a few important rules. First, you never, and I repeat, never point your
weapon at anyone or anything other than the target, is that clear?"

After everyone yelled out "Yes, Sergeant" as loud as they could, Sgt.
Dressler continued. "Each of you will have your turn on the firing line
and each of you will have your turn in the pits raising, lowering, and
scoring the targets. The first thing you will do is assure that your weapon
is set on safety. Next, when I say 'load,' you will remove one clip of
rounds and place it into the chamber. Next, I will say 'ready on the right,'
then, 'ready on the left,' followed by 'ready on the firing line.' When
everyone is ready, I will say 'targets up.' You will now aim at the target
and be ready for the next command, which will be 'commence firing.'—
You will continue to fire until I say 'cease fire.' When I announce 'cease
fire' I don't want to hear one single round fired after that. Is this clear to
everyone here?"

Once again a loud "Yes Sergeant" indicated that everyone understood
the directions.

"OK, next, I want the first group of men on the line and ready to fire."
With this said, John and David took up the prone position facing the targets and waited for the first command.

"Once again, before we start, I want to remind you that your weapon
is never to be pointed at anyone, or anything other than the target unless
you want your ass kicked good and hard. Oh, yeah, almost forgot. You're

not alone here; we do have snakes. I've never seen one on the firing range, but I have seen them down in the pits. Most are non-poisonous but some of them are. Just remember this, snakes are more afraid of you than you are of them. Move away from them; but never, never jump up. It would be better to be bit than it would be to get shot. Now that everyone is ready, load." On the command of commence firing, those on the firing line took aim and started firing at the targets as they zeroed in their sights on the bull's-eye. The distinctive sulfureous odor of the ignited gunpowder would be something we would never forget.

When we finished on the line, we were marched off to the pits where we entered a long, deep trench and took up positions next to our assigned target. As the next group commenced firing we were reminded to keep low of the target and never under any circumstances raise our heads above the pit. As the bullets came whizzing by we didn't need to be reminded again.

I got a marksman's badge while John and David somehow managed to earn the right to wear the attached word expert to their badge—the highest rating you could possibly earn for proficiency in marksmanship. Wow, were we ever proud. It was the first thing looking like a medal that we could actually pin on our chests.

It seemed like quite a few weeks, Harold went on, before we finally got our first off-base pass. We all showered and put on our dress khakis after we had first carefully checked that we had correctly sewed on the Tenth Division patch to our upper left sleeve. Next we put on our shoulder pins, our marksmen's badges, and checked our lapels to be certain that the brass US and crossed rifles were correctly and evenly placed.

I remember how each man seemed to migrate to the latrines to stand admiringly before the mirror, positioning and repositioning their caps in an effort to bring about the most effective military look a soldier could possibly have. Shoulders back, chest out, stomach in. There was no doubt, we were the best-looking soldiers on the base, if not in the whole damned army.

Afterward we boarded the base bus and proceeded to Junction City—yeah, that's the name. The guys called it Junk Town—I don't know why as it seemed OK to me. Well, we headed for a bar. The name sure fit: The Hole in the Wall. It was one of the smallest bars in town. We ordered soda with a twist of lime—to make it look like a real drink.

I got tied up with one of the locals, for lack of a better word, while David and John sat there drinking and talking. They just seemed to click. They laughed a lot, and seemed to have a great time, just sitting there together. After that, well, they were just the best of friends. Almost insep-arable; when you saw one, you saw the other. They went on pass together, drank together, fended for each other, and just never seemed to tire of this relationship. As for me, well, I had my friends and John had his. But we always had time to talk about the good times, as well as the bad.

Can't remember many of their names now—the guys we were with in Basic. Let's see now, there was Johnson, that skinny redhead with the bad complexion and the pointed nose from New York, who never smoked or drank and lent money at $3 interest for $5 borrowed. A real asshole, no one liked him, but near the end of the month most guys used his services. It wasn't legal, but if you needed him, you wouldn't tell. That's how he got by. It wasn't exactly easy living on the $2.50 a day that the army paid us, but somehow we managed. Some guys even sent money back home.

Garrett slept about three bunks down from me. A great card player, sort of on the quiet side though. The thing I remember most about him was his considerably pitted skin as a result of years of severe acne. He was always conscious of it, I'm sure. No doubt that was the reason he was always so quiet, and except for the card games, he stayed more to himself. By the way, he had one of those really deep Southern drawls, sometimes hard to understand. It was just as well he didn't talk much.

Beside Bruce and Garrett, I guess the only other guys that I had much to do with were Bill Standish and Jay Green, both from Detroit.

Standish had a somewhat medium build, greenish colored eyes and sandy hair; and he always had a pleasant smile. He was quite handsome and completely in contrast to Green whose face was always reddish, round and puffy-looking, which gave his eyes a squinting look. This was punctuated with double chins, which could only further detract from the way he looked. His chest showed early signs of breast development, and the term 'love handles' could hardly apply in this case, as his belly far exceeded the acceptable inch or so of fat. A beauty he wasn't, so how could he help but be the company clown. He could keep you laughing, no matter what. Boy, could he remember the jokes. With all said and put aside—I liked him.

John and I had both known Standish since we were kids; and as for Green, we'd known him for about as long.

Oh yeah, there was one other guy. Who could forget Dickson, another guy from down South? I would say he was no taller than five foot five, and rather thin with narrow hips and a rather small waist. Now who would ever have believed it; he had the biggest dick any of us had ever seen. We called him big dick Dickson, or dickhead—out of envy, I guess. I think he liked to get in the shower just to show it off. Let's be honest, I don't think there was a guy in the platoon who wouldn't have wanted to be born with something like that. If you used it right, you couldn't help but be the most popular guy on base. No wonder he was a little dense—I think all of his blood went to his dick, leaving not quite enough for his brain.

One morning the Company was assembled and we were marched off for training in gas attack. Sergeant Bragg gave the lecture.

"There are three basic types of gas that we worry about." Immediately, someone to the rear of the building answered, 'farts.'

"No, wise-ass—not farts," Sergeant Bragg continued. "First we have mustard gas which not only burns your skin but also burns out your lungs. Second, we have chlorine gas—really raises havoc with your breathing and if you're exposed too long, it can kill you. Lastly, we got tear gas—burns the hell out your eyes. Oh, yes, could be all kinds of biological gases to give you diseases that either knock you out of the fighting, or kill you—

if you don't get it by shrapnel, bayonet, land mine, incendiary bombs, or a bullet first. Something to think about, isn't it?"

Boy, he's a cheerful one, I remember thinking.

We all took turns entering a small room with gas masks on, and then, on command, we removed them just long enough to get a good whiff of the chlorine gas that was tossed in—Jesus, what an experience that was. David must have taken a few extra breaths of chlorine and John tried frantically to get him into the fresh air and breathing normally again. You know, as I look back, I think that was my first indication as to how close John was becoming to David. After we thought we had recovered from this first attack, we were sent back into that room without our masks. The doors were closed and a tear gas bomb was tossed in. It didn't take long before we were clawing at the doors, which a corporal seemed to take his time to open. With tears streaming down our faces we rushed into the open air with the smoke of the bomb clinging to us as we ran. Thank God they didn't spray us with mustard gas or we'd never have survived.

One day we were marched off to the barns for a first aid lecture. A corporal who had been a medic in WWII would conduct the class.

"My name's Corporal Larks, but that's not important here. The important thing is first aid and how well you remember what you're taught. First, I want each of you to pair off with the guy sitting next to you. One guy will get down on the ground and turn over on his belly. The other guy will straddle him and start artificial resuscitation after I've demonstrated it here up front."

"Oh, shit, wouldn't you know, I just got Green to partner up with," Turner said. "The son of a bitch had better not sit on me while I'm down, or I'll kick the shit out of him if I ever get back up again." Everyone roared with laughter as they took up the required position.

After the corporal was satisfied that we had mastered this somewhat simple task, he continued with his instruction.

"Next, we have snake-bite. What do you do if you're bitten. Anyone have the answer?"

"Yeah, suck out the poison, unless you're bit on the dick. Then you have someone else suck it out for you," one of the men answered. Again, roars of laughter, which seemed to perk up those guys who were nodding and those who were asleep.

"OK, wise-ass, for that you'll give me twenty pushups while I continue. However, you're right about sucking out the poison, although we have a snake-bite kit for that. We also have antivenom to counteract a poisonous bite. If given right away you should be OK In the meantime try applying a tourniquet to keep the poison from traveling throughout the body. This is done in conjunction with suction and remaining still and keeping calm. Now don't get bit by a cobra or some other exotic snake, as we don't have antivenin for that.

"What do you do for a sucking wound, and I don't want another wise-ass with an answer to that?"

No one seemed to know the answer, we didn't care, or we were just too tired to bother. After a moment of silence, the corporal continued with verbal instructions and hands-on demonstration of the sucking wound technique.

Lastly, after we were almost lulled asleep with greenstick, compound, compression and simple fractures, Cpl. Larks ended the class, with instruction on heat stroke, sun prostration, and almost every conceivable wound he could think of.

The following day while we were back at the barns, a Lt. Fogg presented a class in venereal disease.

"All right men, listen up. I'm about to talk about your favorite subject—screwing." This remark brought about loud laughter, embarrassed smiles, and several men were seen reaching for their crotch.

"By now you must think we're training you to be cloistered monks. By that I mean that the reason you're not getting any is because there's no women around to give it to. Also, we want you to avoid unmarried sex and keep yourselves clean of VD. I could go on for hours on the subject of

VD, but this short movie will save a lot of time and get the message across a lot better than I could do by just talking about it."

At this point, the large doors to the barn were closed and the movie was projected on the screen.

Let's see, there was gonorrhea, syphilis, herpes, crabs, and several other long names we never heard of. This was followed with the correct procedure for performing the short arm inspection, which involved skinning it back and milking it down. If a thick purulent discharge was squeezed from the penis, and it burned like it was on fire, you were infected with VD and should report to the dispensary for treatment. If your crotch kept itching like mad and scratching never brought you relief, no doubt you had the crabs and only the medics could offer relief. Wasn't it enough that we refrained from sex this long, being satisfied only with wet dreams or taking care of ourselves when we thought no one was watching, and we should have been sleeping instead of playing around?

After lunch, it was back to the barracks for that dental class Sgt. Bragg had promised.

"Good afternoon, men, I'm Captain Paris, the base dentist."

The corporal here will pass out samples of toothpaste and a toothbrush to each of you. I've brought along several posters and a movie, which the corporal will show when he's set up. In the meantime I want to stress the importance of brushing and the use of mouthwash for good dental hygiene.

Mouthwash kills the germs and freshens your breath.

"When the movie is over the corporal and I will check each of you for dental caries, after which you will line up by the latrine so that we can observe as you brush your teeth over the sinks. Does everyone here brush daily?"

"Yes sir," Standish answered. "I see Green brushing the hair from his teeth every morning." Even the dentist roared with laughter from this joke at Green's expense.

"Now, I'm not one for toothpicks. They damage the gums. What I suggest is that you get a spool of the finest silk thread you can find, cut off a piece, and pass it between your teeth after brushing to get rid of food particles and plaque. Plaque hurts your gums. Pay attention to the corporalas he demonstrates this procedure."

It's a good thing none of us had some awful disease, as the dentist and his assistant placed their mirrors from one mouth to another, only taking time to briefly wipe it off with the same alcohol pad used on everyone else. This was almost like kissing by proxy.

Immediately after the visit by the dentist we were quickly escorted to the local chapel where we would be introduced to the various base chaplains. There was one Protestant, one Catholic, one Jewish and an Episcopalian who professed to go either way. I was never one much for church and my religious convictions remained much in doubt. At any rate, sitting there for a couple hours was probably much more tolerable than marching around in the hot sun. If it was a choice between church and a lot of other things, I guess I'd have to opt for the chapel.

At last it was time for dinner and after washing our hands and faces, we dashed to the mess hall like we'd never seen food before. Roast beef, potatoes, celery and carrots with chocolate cake for desert—God, did it taste good. I was really getting into that army chow and so were a lot of others. After dinner it was back to the barracks where we practiced field stripping our rifles. This entailed taking them apart and putting them back together again. Next, with a ramrod, patches and oil we cleaned our rifles and put them away. Lastly, we polished our boots, straightened our area and prepared for whatever tomorrow would bring.

Finally, it was early to bed for some much-welcomed sleep. There was no doubt we would be up long before dawn and ready for another day.

From the first day of training, we would practice the following commands: *To the right—March, To the left—March, To the rear—March, Forward—March, Quick—March, Route step—March and Oblique right & left—March.* We also practiced short order drill, which involved the use of our weapon: shoulder arms, present arms, Port arms, Inspection arms, Parade rest, and Attention. In addition to this routine daily training we would attend more classes, and learn many new things.

One afternoon shortly after lunch, we were marched off to what looked like a parade ground, to practice hand-to-hand combat and bayonet training. After the order to count off was given, those with the even numbers were lined up on the right and those with the odd numbers to the left. When this was accomplished, you were paired off with the man in front of you. Wouldn't you know, I got the biggest and strongest man in the platoon. David and John got even matches, and Green got the smallest and probably weakest guy in the whole company. I had to laugh—it was like a sow wrestling a chicken. I guess I shouldn't have been surprised, but Green took the worse of it while his partner walked away unscathed.

After a couple hours of different holds and blocking methods, karate chops, and other defensive maneuvers we were reassembled into ranks to await our turn with bayonet practice.

"The first ten men, line up here," Sgt. Bragg ordered, "and prepare to fix bayonets. When I give the command to charge I expect you to move out fast while at the same time giving one of those rebel yells you've seen in the movies. That should scare the hell out of the enemy. When you approach the target I expect you to go for the heart with a thrust and jab. If there's no questions, then get ready to move out." With this said, the order was given to fix bayonets and charge. We couldn't have sounded worse than those rebels from the Civil War, even though we were a little short on stabbing. The second time around we made the grade of killers.

The following week we were marched off to the obstacle course, where we were to perform a number of tasks that Lt. Hall told us we might encounter one day. Sgt. Price took charge while the Company Commander and platoon leaders watched from the sides.

"All right men, I want you to form up in back of me. When I give the command move out, the first line will get down prone on the ground and start crawling toward the end of that barbed wire that you see stretched out a couple feet from the ground. I want you to stay so close to the ground that it would look like you're making love to it. They will be firing live ammunition directly over your heads. Lift up your head and you're a dead man. As you're crawling toward your destination you will see roped off circles. Stay clear of these, as periodically we will be setting off charges within them. Does everyone understand me? Do I make myself absolutely clear? Come on, let's hear it loud and clear."

"Yes, Sergeant," the men yelled back as they took up the required position.

When the command to move out was given, we clung as close to the ground as we could while the sound of machine guns announced the bullets flying over our heads. Half crawling and half dragging, we inched our way to the other end where we continued to crawl away from the site long after the firing had stopped. After successfully making our way to safety, we were ready for the next event.

"Once again, on the command of move out, I want the first four men to run and fall on that barbed wire while the rest of you use their bodies to step over the wire and get to the other side. I don't want to see anyone stepping directly on the backs of these men. You'll be stepping on their butts when you do it. OK now, move out."

As fate would have it—you could hardly call it luck as I was one of the chosen few who got stepped on. Anyway, with only a couple scratches we made it through this part of the course.

We climbed over high fences, swung on a rope across a muddy pond, Bruce fell in and was followed by David—what a mess. Thought they would never dry out, but they did. Green couldn't make it on the horizontal ladder and had to go back three times before they gave up on him and sent him on to practice the two man carry. After we finished the course, we fought a mock battle in a makeshift town.

We thought the cadre had forgotten about fire training, but they didn't. One week later we were taken away for a lesson in fire fighting. An old brick building was set ablaze while each of us in turn manned the fire hose in an attempt to put it out. After this we were instructed on the use of water and chemical extinguishers. Oh yes, "Don't smoke in bed" were the closing remarks of the day—no doubt the best advice we would carry away from this class.

One weekend, while on pass, David, John and I decided we would go swimming in the river. We all stripped down to our shorts and proceeded to step in. Cripes, it was all mud. Our legs sank down so deep it was all we could do to pull ourselves free. We all had leg cramps for fifteen minutes or so. Do you know we were fools enough to try it a second time with exactly the same results?

Another time we had passes to Salina, Kansas, where we visited an Episcopal boy's farm. One of the priests took us over to see the pigs. I have to laugh each time I recall the group of us standing there and looking in, as though we were enraptured by the sight of those pigs wallowing in the mud.

David got stung on the lip by a bee, and John was beside himself worrying that David's throat might swell and choke him. It didn't; aside from some swelling and discomfort, it only proved to be a minor inconvenience.

Just one more thing before I forget. One night I had the strangest dream. David, John, Bruce and I were all riding in this car when we suddenly approached a small town. There was a billboard on the side of a hotel advertising "Lucky Strikes." We parked the car and went into the hotel. In the lobby were about six chairs and a couple of spittoons, a large potted plant, and a small enclosed area at the end of the room for registration. The place looked like something out of an old western movie. We asked the guy for rooms and John said he wanted to share with David. I stayed with Bruce, who chose to sleep on the floor while I took the bed. The reason I mention this at all is that, by whatever strange coincidence, all this actually happened later on. They call it déjà vu, I think. Someone we met in Junction City had a car, and that's how we got to that town in the first place. The dream was even true to the point when John ordered cantaloupe at a nearby restaurant where we had breakfast together. Strange, isn't it?

Time was finally drawing to a close with our training, and we had one last task to perform. Would you believe, a twenty-mile hike with a steel helmet and liner, rifle, and full field pack. As I recall this came to 65 pounds that we had to carry. It was really hot that day and Capt. Hasselman had each of us put two salt tablets into our canteens. It tasted like hell at first, but after a while you could hardly notice it. The road was hot and dusty, much like it had been that day we were on the truck heading for the range. Every now and then we were allowed to take a fifteen-minute break. Most of us just collapsed by the roadside where we were allowed to light up and smoke. This was also the time when you could move farther from the road to take a leak. If I had to make that hike today, I think it would kill me. When we finally arrived at our destination, the captain's wife was there to give us coffee and donuts—no doubt as our final reward. When we had rested a while, we were assigned partners to share pup tents, which we pitched on the bivouac grounds nearby. An exercise in throwing grenades made heroes of those who made baseball their life's ambition and losers of those who did not.

Following dinner, which was brought in by a truck, we were informed that we were to fight a battle. Two clips of blank ammunition was issued to each of us with precautions on their use. We were divided into two groups called the Blues and the Reds. Bruce and I were assigned to the Reds, while John and David were assigned to the Blues. When the sun had set and it was sufficiently dark, the battle began with the cadre deciding if you lived or died, and who the winners would be. To the yells of Geronimo, the Blues attacked with a vengeance. The Reds lost, but it was a hell of a lot of fun losing. Except for our fear of snakes, we really enjoyed being there in the woods, playing war games, telling jokes, laughing, and camping out with our friends.

Thank God we were hauled back by truck and didn't have to make that journey again. This final hike and bivouac in the woods was about the last thing we did in closing out our basic training and earning the title of soldier.

At last it was over, and as the Regimental Band played various marches, we paraded across the field to celebrate our graduation. The Commanding General was present and saluted as we passed in review.

The Regimental Commander gave a brief speech as we came to attention and pretended to hear what he said. We could hardly wait until the top brass had left, and we were marched back to our Company for lunch.

With the formalities now over, we were no longer recruits and had automatically reached the rank of private. On return to our barracks each of us received a new assignment, changed into dress uniform, and took off for a weekend of fun. This time it was Kansas City, and we had far more reason to celebrate than we had ever had before.

John, David, and I, as well as all our friends were transferred to the 25th Field Artillery Battalion, Fort Riley. From our understanding we would remain there until such time as we received a permanent assignment elsewhere. As it turned out, we were to stay there throughout the remainder of the year, celebrating Christmas and New Year's together on the base, and it was not until March of 1950 that we finally received orders to proceed to our new assignments.

Chapter 2

Transfers: Warm weather here we come. Fort Ord, California, and the nearby Presidio of Monterey—God, it was a dream come true—something like out of the movies. This was to be one of the most beautiful places I had ever seen. As I have already said, we'd never been away before, except to Kansas for Basic. Best yet, David, John, and Standish got the Presidio, while Bruce, Green, and I, as well as some of the other guys from our company, got Fort Ord. We would be next-door neighbors, so to speak.

The Presidio was located on top of a hill adjacent to Pacific Grove. It had a long history, and was already quite old when the Army started using it for the Army Language School. After being shown to their barracks, both John and David were assigned to the maintenance detail. They would be responsible for cleaning the offices, latrines, and the officers' quarters. Sort of a shitty job, but better than a lot of places they could have ended up at. Standish lucked out; he got furniture refinishing because he said he'd done it before. Actually he hadn't, but he was quick to learn. We thought it was a crappy job at the time, but it really wasn't so bad.

The next year or so was great. San Francisco, here we come, with the fisherman's wharf, and those hills, restaurants, clubs and bars, China

Town, the Golden Gate Bridge, and of course the ocean, which we quickly came to love. You had to see it to believe it. By now I had a couple of new running buddies, but David and John were as steadfast as ever. Sometimes when we were alone, John used to tell me how David lifted his spirits and just made him feel good. Then he'd go into their many exploits together. I was glad for John, for as I said, he was always sort of a loner before and didn't make friends too easily. God, I can remember it almost as clearly as if it was yesterday, Harold added, as he leaned back in his chair and momentarily closed his eyes. After a few moments of deep reflection he continued to put memories into words, but this time as though he were an observer and a participant rather than himself.

"Hey, David. Did you ever see such big geraniums in your life, they're so big they look like orchids? And look at the size of those snails. God, they're huge. I bet they're the kind they eat. I think they call it escargot. Can you believe that people actually eat them? I sure wouldn't—how 'bout you and me going into town? It's a nice walk down the hill, and I've never been around the ocean before. I hear they got one of those fishermen's wharves in Monterey, just like they got in San Francisco," John said as he lit up a cigarette.

"Yeah, I can hardly wait to get into town myself, John. How's 'bout you and me just grabbing a bite here, and then heading out. Maybe after payday we can eat in town."

"Sounds good to me, David. By the way, one of the guys on the base told me there's a nice little church in town that's pretty old. If we have time I'd like to see it. OK?"

"I'm not one much for church, but if you want to, it's OK with me. You know, your brother's at Fort Ord, and we got to get hold of him pretty soon. If we don't spend too much time in town, we can hitch a ride to the fort. It's not far, you know."

"How about tomorrow, David? There's so much to see, I don't think we'd have time for anything else."

As David and John made their way down the hill from the Presidio into town, John couldn't get over how beautiful the various plants along the roadside were.

"Look at those," pointing to a group of flowering bushes. "I think they're about the prettiest things I've seen yet. What do you think, David?"

"Yeah, not bad, John," David said, as he put his arm around John's shoulders.

Almost instinctively, John started to pull away from David, but somehow, the touch of David's hand upon his shoulder didn't feel wrong, or bad, but rather reassuring, friendly, and right. It made him feel a closeness to David that he hadn't felt before. At this point, John moved closer to David, and they continued their walk down the hill and into town.

As David and John reached the water's edge they noticed a small ship to their left. While slowly making their way toward it, they occasionally stopped to pick up a shell or some other object that interested them at the time.

"Look, David, it's some sort of Navy ship. See the flag they're flying?"

"Guess you're right about that, John."

"Hey, soldiers. How's 'bout comin' aboard and see how the Navy lives. My name's Gary, what's yours?"

"I'm David, and this is John. Sure, why not, we'd like to come aboard." Neither John nor David had ever been on anything larger than a rowboat, and to them this ship looked like a destroyer. "Do you stay here all the time, or are you just here for now?"

"We're like the 'USS Never Sail.' I've been here for about six months and we've only gone out about four times. Yeah, this is our home base—if you want to call it that."

David and John followed Gary onto the ship and into the galley where a couple other sailors were cleaning some of the largest crabs that they had ever seen.

"Where'd you ever catch them?" John asked as he moved in for a closer inspection.

"Right here, off the ship. We use traps. We're making a salad. Want some?" Gary said. "And by the way, this is Dale, and that's Steve."

"Hi, I'm David and this is John. Yeah, that salad sounds great. I don't want to sound greedy but you got anything else to go with it?"

"Sure, why not. We're having stew. We got more than enough. By the way, you guys from Fort Ord?"

"No—the Presidio. We just got here, and this is the first place we've seen so far, since we came into town. I'm glad we ran into you, now we got some new friends already," David said as he sat down at the table.

"Hey guys, this crab is really great. I've never had it before. Who made the stew? Nothing like that Army chow we get. This stuff's got flavor," David remarked as he accepted a second helping. "Who does the cooking?"

"Well, we all sort of help, but mainly Dale is the cook," Gary answered. Dale was about five foot six inches tall and more than a little on the chubby side. It was evident that he liked his own cooking, or anyone's cooking for that matter.

"You guys play cards?" Gary asked as he started cleaning off the table.

"Sure, how about hearts?" John answered. "I'm not too good at cards, but we learned to play it about a month ago, back in Kansas where we were stationed last."

"Hearts is fine, we play it a lot," Steve said as he started to shuffle the cards. Steve looked to be no older than 15 or 16, with an innocent-looking baby face, but he was actually the same age as John. "I got a friend at the Presidio," Steve said as he started to deal out the cards. "His name is Paul. Paul Sabastian Perry. Now how's that for a name. When you guys get back to the base, why not look him up. He's really a nice guy."

"Yeah, we'll do that," John said as he rearranged his cards to start playing. "What's he look like?"

"He's over six foot, blondish hair, blue eyes, and rather good-looking." Steve suddenly became embarrassed as his face took on a flushed look; and almost as if trying to correct himself for saying too much, he continued, "like one of those actors you see in the movies. You can't miss him. He's really a swell guy. You'll like him."

David and John played cards for the next two hours or so before realizing how late it was getting. "Hey guys, we better be getting back, it's getting late, and we want to get a look at town before we head back to the base," David said. " And by the way, the chow was great and you're sure some swell guys. If you don't mind, we'll come back again."

"Come on back anytime," Gary said. "Glad we met you guys."

David and John made their way down the main drag, briefly taking in everything they saw. On the way back, it was already getting dark as they started up the hill toward the base.

"Those sure were some swell guys on that ship. We were lucky to run into them. I bet they know a lot of great places to go," John said, as he moved a little closer to David's side.

Suddenly David took John's hand and after holding it briefly, he once again placed his arm around John's shoulder. Like before, it felt good to have David this close to him—like it was a perfectly normal thing to do. It felt honest and right. After all, John thought, isn't David my very best friend. Shouldn't friends be this close? I think so.

Around eight the next morning, David and John were taken to a small room in a nearby building where they were to meet ten other guys in the maintenance detail. It was now two days from payday, and everyone was broke. Getting paid once a month was rough.

"Boy, could I do for a cig," David said, after introducing himself and John to the group.

The tallest of the men was smoking some sort of strange brown cigarette—something between a cigarette and a cigar.

"How 'bout trying one of these," he said. "I roll 'um myself."

David accepted the smoke without hesitation. There was no doubt about it, this guy had to be Steve's friend, Paul Sabastian Perry. He sure fit the description.

"Do you have a friend off base named Steve?" David asked. "If so, he said we should look you up."

"Yeah, I'm Paul—Paul Perry's my name. If you know Steve, you're a friend of mine. By the way, I roll these cigarettes from butts I find. Roll 'um up in this brown paper towel. Have one, they're a little strong, but it works.

"Here's another cigarette for your friend. I'll show you how to roll 'um yourself."

Corporal Spencer was in charge of the group, and he gave out the assignments. David got assigned to cleaning the officers' quarters, while John got assigned to cleaning some offices as well as latrines.

At one of the offices, sitting at a nearby desk, was an older woman, probably in her early fifties. "Hello, young man. My name's Maria. What's your name?"

"John English—short for John Earl English."

"Well now. Glad to meet you, John Earl English," the woman said in her soft and friendly voice, punctuated with a foreign accent. "Maria is just part of my name also. It's actually Maria Anastasia Romanov Nevsky. You can call me Maria if that's easier for you. That's what they call me here at the office. My husband was a general in the Russian army, that was before the communists took over. Now he teaches the Russian language here, and I was fortunate enough to get a job here in this office."

"Excuse me, Maria, but wasn't Romanov the name of the Russian czar?"

"Yes, you're right. It was the name of the czar. I was his cousin. After the revolution, my husband and I escaped to this country, and we ended up here."

As John finished his chores and was about to leave, Maria turned to him and said, "Stop by to visit anytime, I'd be pleased to have your company."

"You'll be seeing a lot of me, I guess, Maria. I'm assigned to cleaning this office every day."

"That's good, John Earl English. We shall see each other again tomorrow; I'm sure we should have much to talk about," Maria said, as John prepared to leave.

That evening, David and John left on pass as soon as they finished their dinner. This time they did not stop off at the ship, but instead headed straight into town. As they got about halfway down the block, much to their surprise they ran into Harold and the others.

"Hey, John, we were just on our way up to see you. I bet it's a lot easier finding you at the Presidio than it would be for you to find us at Fort Ord," Harold said as he gave John a friendly pat on the back. "Nevertheless, how about you guys meeting us at the main gate at the fort tomorrow—say around six, and we'll show you where we're staying? And by the way, we got a really great club on the base. No 3.2, but real beer this time."

"Sure, Harold, we'll be there, so be sure you're there too," John said, as he stopped to look into a nearby window of the pawnshop.

Suddenly, as John was still looking in the window, someone came up behind him, grabbed him by the butt and said, "How about a piece of ass, soldier." John jumped so fast that he almost hit the glass. Wouldn't you know, it was Green—still the clown.

"One thing's for sure, you still got life in you," Green said as he quickly backed off. "I got three bottles of wine, four packs of cigarettes, and some paper cups in this bag. Aren't you glad I'm 21? Let's drink it down on the beach. No one will see us down there, and we found the perfect spot on the way to town."

"Gee, thanks a lot, Green" David said. "But no more ass grabbing, at least for tonight. OK?"

"OK, no more tonight," Green said as he reached over and gave David a quick pinch on the chest.

It wasn't long before they all made their way to the beach and opened the first bottle of wine. It was a cheap wine, but no one in the group had enough experience with drinking to know the difference. As the day wore on everyone decided to return to his base and that they would meet again tomorrow.

The following evening David, John, and Standish made their way to Fort Ord. Harold was there waiting for them at the gate so that they wouldn't miss seeing him.

"Hey, big brother," John said as he grabbed Harold's arm in a gentle shaking motion. We're here, now how about showing us the place, and by the way, where's Green and the others?"

"Oh, they're going to meet us at the barracks. We'll all go to the club together. I wanted you to see the barracks first, so you'd know how to find it again."

It was about a fifteen-minute walk, and after finally arriving at the barracks, everyone was there as planned.

"OK guys, we're all here so let's start heading for the club," Bruce said, as he moved toward the door.

"Lord, this is a big place," John remarked, as he sat down at a table and ordered a round of beers.

"If you think this is big," Green cut in, "you haven't seen anything yet. Wait until you see this broad sitting up there with her back to us. Like, shit—she's got the biggest tits I've ever seen. I gave her my Saint Christopher's medal and told her if she let someone rub it, it would give her good luck. She let me rub it twice. She's a little dense, I think, so I'm sure I'll make out. Now, she's got a girlfriend who's really bad news, I tried it with her, but she said if I tried it again, she'd cut my dick off. If you thought ass grabbing was bad, try having your dick cut off."

Harold reached across the table, and placed his hand on John's. "Where you guys going this weekend? It's payday, you know."

"Yeah, we know," John answered, "Standish has a cousin in San Jose, and he's taking David and me to visit him. Where you going, Harold?"

"Like they say, 'San Francisco, here I come.' Bruce, Green, and I are taking off as soon as we can. We'll let you know how it was when we get back—and you guys can let us know about San Jose. OK?"

After a few more drinks and about ten of Green's latest jokes, Standish, David, and John staggered aboard the base bus and headed back to town from where it was just a short walk back to the base.

The following morning, David and John were sitting in the mess hall with Standish and a few other guys.

"The Eagle shits today," Roberts said, as they finished breakfast.

"What do you mean by that?" David answered. "I never heard that expression before."

"How long you been in this man's army anyway? It means payday. We get paid today. Where you going for the weekend?"

"I'm not sure yet, maybe San Jose. Standish has a cousin there, and he knows lots of places to go. Yeah, John and I will probably go with him," David said, as he started to get up from the table."

After breakfast, John got busy with his cleaning, saving Maria's office for last.

"Well, hello again, John Earl English. Now where do you think you'll be going for the weekend?"

"San Jose, Maria. Do you know any good places to see there?"

"I'm really not familiar with San Jose, but you'll be fairly close to Santa Cruz," Maria said as she sipped at a cup of tea she had prepared on a small electric burner she kept not far from her desk. "They have a beautiful beach there. Why not go swimming?"

"We just might consider it—that is, if David and Standish want to go."

"Did you actually know that Rasputin guy when you were in Russia? I hear he was sort of mad, and controlled the czar," John remarked as he emptied the wastebaskets.

"Oh, yes. I have seen him many times, but he was always quite charming, but a real womanizer so far as I could see. As for his being mad, I've heard that said, but I don't know if he was really all that bad. There was a conspiracy to get rid of him, you know. It was political. I'll tell you more about it another time, it looks like you're ready to go. Oh, by the way,

John, if you ever feel you'd like to talk to someone, confidentially that is, you can be assured of my absolute confidence."

"Thanks a lot, Maria I appreciate that, and that story about Rasputin was really interesting. I'd like to hear more about him later on," John said, as he hurried to leave for the day.

It was Friday, and John, David, and Standish left for town the moment they finished work.

"Let's see if we can hitch a ride together. I see lots of other guys doing it. We can save us some money this way. If we have to split up, we'll all meet at the Greyhound—it shouldn't be hard to find. OK?" Standish said. "I'll call my cousin as soon as I get in. He's expecting my call."

David and John stood at the side of the road together, while Standish walked about a half block down the way. A number of cars went by before one finally stopped and picked up Standish first. It was another twenty minutes or so before David and John hitched a ride.

John sat up front, while David sat in back.

"Where you guys bound for?" the driver asked. He was an older man, a little heavy, and in need of a shave.

"San Jose," John said. "You going that far?"

"Well, it depends on you guys," he said as he placed his hand on John's leg.

David was leaning forward on the back seat, and the moment he saw the man touch John's leg he suddenly reached over and smacked the man's hand away. "Listen, you son of a bitch, if this is what you mean by 'it depends on you,' you can let us out right now. Don't you ever touch him again, or I'll knock the shit out of 'ya."

The driver quickly pulled the car to the side of the road, and, as he apologized for his actions, David and John got out. The man couldn't drive away fast enough.

"Let's have a cigarette, John. You got a light, my lighter's not working. What did you make of that bastard trying to put the make on you with me in the back seat? I was so goddamned mad, I could've killed him. If anyone is going to put their hands on you, it had better be me," David said, as he put his arm around John's waist.

"Gee, thanks David, I feel the same way about you—but I'm sue you guessed that by now." Just then another car pulled up and this time it was a man and his wife. As luck would have it, they were also on their way to San Jose. David and John climbed in and took their place on the back seat. The man had lived in Detroit once, so they had plenty to talk about for the remainder of the trip.

The man let them out at the entrance of the bus station, and the moment they walked in they were met by Standish, who was sitting on a bench near the entrance.

"What took you guys so long?" Standish said jokingly. "I mean, like I've been here a half-hour already."

"You wouldn't believe it but this is what happened," David said as he then commenced to give the details of their first ride.

"If you think that's something, wait until you hear what happened to me. This guy picks me up, and just like with you, he had his hand on my leg before we were five miles down the road. You guys got to learn how to play the game. I put him off until we were about six miles out of town. About this time he was really getting impatient, so I promised to give him a blow job once we got into the city. Jesus, did he step on the gas, and we arrived before I could think of another thing to say. It was me that got cussed out this time, when I left without so much as a kiss goodby. Take my advice: As long as you can fight them off, or talk your way out of it, you'll get where you're going every time."

"We'll keep that in mind next time," David said. "Hope you don't get in so deep someday that you can't get out of it, and by the way, I can take care of myself. I just didn't like it, seeing him try that on John with me sitting right there in the back seat. Did you get hold of your cousin yet?"

"Yeah, I'll have to call him back. Let me make a quick call, and he should be here within fifteen minutes. He said he had a surprise for us.

Some place to go, but he wouldn't say where. Said we could get served there, so I guess it's a bar. Wait a minute, here he is now."

"This is my cousin Art, I told him all about you guys," Standish said as they climbed into the car. "We can stay at his place for the weekend. He has a really swell house not far away. First we'll stop off to eat somewhere, then we'll have a few drinks at his place. Oh, by the way, Art, this is David, and this is John. Now what's say we get going?"

After stopping off briefly for a hamburger, it was only a short ride before they pulled up in front of Art's house.

"What kind of work do you do, Art?—to have a place this nice. Jesus, it's nice," John said, as he and the others left the car and made their entrance into the house.

"I own a karate school and a florist shop. I've been in business for about eight years now. Got started when I was just twenty years old, so if you're good at math you should be able to figure out my age."

"Hey, this is great," John said as he took a sip on the drink that Art had made for him. "What is this thing? It sure tastes good."

"A Singapore sling. You've never had one before?" Art asked as he handed one to David.

"No, never. Actually, I've never had a mixed drink before—only a little wine and some beer at the base," John answered as he continued to sip on his drink.

"Well, the trick to it is not to drink too fast. Mostly just hold the drink in your hand, especially when you're out somewhere—like tonight. We'll stop for coffee on the way to the club. That way we won't get too drunk."

Later that evening after stopping for coffee at Mr. Joe's, they all arrived at "Madam's Place," just outside of town. "Here we are, guys, this is the surprise I promised you. Now I want everyone to behave themselves and we won't be noticed—not too much, that is. Next time bring something to wear other than those uniforms. Oh, not that they don't look great on you guys. It's just that they might look too great, if you know what I mean—and you don't, but you will."

Art requested a table back in a corner with poor lighting. "You can see quite well from here, and you won't be so conspicuous while you're drinking. Now let's see, how about a double orange juice Screwdriver? That's vodka with double orange. Lasts longer, so sip on them and enjoy the show. I know the owner so there's no problem with you being served."

Suddenly, a spotlight focused on the stage and from behind the curtains there emerged one of the most beautiful women that John or David had ever seen—other than at the movies.

"Hey, guys, isn't 'he' something," Art said as he put his arm around his cousin's shoulders.

"You mean that she's a 'he'?" David said, as a big smile came across his face.

"Come on, guys, relax. Put your arm around John, David, and just take in the show. By the way, quit calling me Standish. You can call me by my last name on the base, but off base, it's Bill. OK, guys?"

"Sure, Bill," David said as he took Bill's advice and placed his arm around John's waist, thinking this was less noticeable than his arm around John's shoulder.

"Hey, Art, how come you were never in the service? I did my math, and figuring that you went into business when you were twenty, you wouldn't have had much time for the service," David said, as he kept his eyes glued upon the stage. "And, by the way, what ever made you go into the karate and flower business?"

"Well, I guess the best way I can answer all your questions briefly is to say that there are three things I love most in life, that's fighting, flowers, and men. Now that shouldn't be too hard to figure out, should it? Miss Lemons is up next. When you see her, you'll know how she got the name—smallest tits of any of them. I guess it's sort of her trademark. You know, as small as he is, he's one hell of a fighter. He's been taking classes from me for several years. Now, by the way, how you guys like the show?"

"It's really great. Not bad at all. Never knew they had shows like this, and those guys really look like women. You know that comic one, they call

Miss Sassy Nasty, she sure had me roaring—and look, she's coming over to our table right now," John said as he ordered another drink.

"Art darling, and where did you ever find these luscious creatures? Been hiding them on me, haven't you? Mind if I join you? I won't be back on stage for another half-hour."

"Sure, Sassy, you can sit next to my cousin. His name's Bill, and that's David and his friend John over there."

"My, John, you have the most beautiful deep brown eyes I have ever seen. Real bedroom eyes if I ever saw some. Brown hair—I like brown hair and I like crew cuts. And those lips of yours sure are made for kissing, I bet you're really wild in bed. Correct me if I'm out of place, but a handsome man is a handsome man, and he deserves to be complimented once in a while. How tall are you?"

"I'm five foot-seven," John answered, a little embarrassed by the questions and compliments.

"And David, what I wouldn't give for a man like you, in fact all three of you soldier boys are just about the most perfect specimens I have ever seen. God, you know I almost forgot what I came over here to tell you. You know Miss Barbara Boobies, don't you, Art? Well at any rate he was attacked by four guys as he left the club last night. They broke his leg, and really beat the hell out of him. I just want to warn you that someone saw them outside again tonight. God, be careful."

"You don't need to worry about us, Miss Sassy," John said. "We had self-defense back in Basic. Learned a little karate, just enough to take care of ourselves, I guess.

"How 'bout letting David and me take care of them guys. What do you say about that?"

"It's OK with us, but save one for Miss Lemons, Barbara was his friend," Harold said. And then he added,

"If you can't take 'em on, I'm sure Bill and I can lick the hell out of 'em. Shit, I'm looking forward to it. Like I said, there's nothing I like more than a good fight."

"Be careful, boys, and don't any of you get those beautiful faces scarred—I couldn't stand it. I got to go now, I follow Miss Joy Stick. But drop by any time. Like I said, you're the most beautiful guys in the club—and that goes for you too, Art, even if you're not in one of those sexy uniforms."

As Art got up to visit the john, he said, "Thanks, Sassy, but if anyone can take care of themselves, we can."

The show lasted another hour, and when it was over everyone finished their drinks and headed for the door. As they stepped outside, just as Sassy had said, there they were—four of them waiting over by the side of the building. Suddenly they strolled up to Art and remarked, "What you Army sissies doing here? I hope you know how to fight, because we're really going to break you up bad." As he started to take a swing, Art grabbed his arm and tossed him over onto his back. At this point the three others quickly came forward.

"They're all yours, guys," Art said, as he stepped aside.

David gave a jumping kick to the stomach of the first guy, knocking him to the ground. This was quickly followed up with another kick to his face putting him permanently out of the running. At the same time, John took out one of the others with a solid punch to his face, knocking him out instantly.

Miss Lemons came running out when she heard the commotion. "That son of a bitch—that one there, he's the bastard that broke poor Barbara's leg, and I'm going to return the favor." With this said, Miss. Lemons tore into the guy with everything she had, putting into practice every maneuver she'd ever learned in class, and while he was down, she jumped down hard on his leg, causing it to snap. As if that wasn't enough, she managed to break his nose, and slap the shit out of him. Bill finished off the last one even though that wasn't in the bargain.

"Jesus, that bastard bloodied up my dress—it's ruined," Miss Lemon yelled. "Think I'll kick him in the balls once for that."

"Come on guys, the fun is over. Time to leave," Art said, as they all climbed into the car.

No sooner had they prepared to leave when two of the bastards who could still walk started pulling their buddies into their car, before Miss Lemons decided to take them all on.

"They won't be back, I bet you that. Now how about a cigarette, it's like dessert after a good fight—what you think, guys? And wasn't that a super show? We gotta all go back again, sometime soon," Art said as he lit up and took a deep puff on the bent cigarette he was holding.

On the way back, they all joked and laughed and bragged a bit. "Yeah, it sure was a swell night," David said, as he put his arm around John and pulled him as close to him as he could. "You deserve this, John," and without hesitation, David kissed John squarely on the lips. "Now that's your dessert, John. It's better than a cigarette, isn't it?"

"Yeah, David, it sure is. You can do that anytime—almost anytime, that is." There were no longer any doubts, John loved David and David loved John, although never once would they claim to be anything more than the very best of friends. The trip back to Art's house couldn't have been more pleasant, and it was something that neither one could ever forget.

"OK, guys, this is your room. Bill is sleeping with me. We're kissing cousins, you know. Bill goes either way, so I guess I'm in luck."

That night as David came out of the shower, he looked more handsome than he had ever looked while back at the base. "I sleep in the raw. How 'bout you, John?"

"Yeah, me too, David—that is, because you do, now let's go to bed. Don't turn out the lights, I want to look at you."

The following morning, David and John were just getting dressed when Art came into the room. "Come on, guys, up and at 'em, I'm taking you all out for breakfast. I was going to cook, but my cousin Bill wore me out. He's more of a hunk than I ever guessed. How'd your night go, guys?"

"Great—couldn't be better, but we got to keep this a secret between ourselves, OK?" David said, with a sheepish smile. "Let's pretend it never happened. We're soldiers, you know, no different from any other soldier, and we're going to keep it that way."

"Now where do you guys want to go next? Anywhere you want to go, just say the word, and I'll take you," Art said, as he tried to change the subject.

"Hell, if it's anywhere, how about Santa Cruz? Maria, back at the base, said the beach was great and the view was fantastic. We could pick up bathing suits on the way," John remarked, as he reached into his pocket to pull out a cigarette.

"It's a little distance, but we got all day, so why not? We'll stop for gas after breakfast, and then we're on our way. By the way, no need to buy trunks—I got about twenty of them. All styles and colors. Take your pick. We're all the same size. Oh, I'm sure some of us are a little bigger in front, but that shouldn't make a difference," Art said, as he started to laugh at his own joke.

"Hey, David, I'll take this blue one," Bill jokingly said, knowing quite well he would never wear it. Not one with a big red heart across the crotch and a small purposeful tear, strategically placed on the rear. "Maybe I'll wear this one instead. It's more my speed, a plain blue one—boxer style. In case I get a boner, it won't be as noticeable. This one would look good on you, David," as he pulled out a bright red one, sort of like a pair of Jockey shorts, without the fly. "And here's a matching pair for John. It's beige, and I think he'll look good in it. What do you say, guys, how's that for a good choice?"

"Couldn't have done better," John answered. "Now let's get on the way."

After a quick breakfast, they made their way up the mountains, and finally into Santa Cruz where they'd spend the day swimming and bathing in the sun.

"Jesus, John, are you getting red! You better get out of the sun right now, before you burn up," David said, as he covered John with a towel they had brought along.

It was true, John got burned pretty bad, and this more or less ended what remained of a pleasant weekend pass. That night as David and John went to bed, David rubbed John gently with some lotion that Art had given him for burns. "Why'd this have to happen to you, John? I can't stand seeing you suffer this way. Next time we go to the beach we'll know enough to take a good supply of body oil along with us." With that he once again gave John a gentle kiss upon his lips, then took his place on the opposite side of the bed, so as not to cause pain by his touching.

Art and Bill sat up for several hours before finally turning in for the night.

"Hey, Bill, what you make of those two? I think they care more for each other than they lead you to believe. Whatta you think? I been noticing how close they stick together; and I think I saw a little jealous streak in both of them, back at the club. One thing's for certain, they sure in the hell can fight when they want to. I'd hate to be the one that comes between them. They're good sports though, and I like them. Yeah, I like them a lot. Bring them back anytime, will you, cousin? By the way, remember when we were kids and we used to fool around? Generally, when you grow up, there's never a second chance at it, but, Jesus, it sure was worth waiting for. If you weren't my cousin I'd marry you. Now, cousin or not, let's go to bed and take care of business."

The following morning, Art volunteered to drive them back to the base, as John was too uncomfortable to travel by bus.

"Remember the time that I got stung by that bee?" David said, in an effort to be reassuring. "Now, just like me, you'll be better in no time."

Chapter 3

"Hello, what's your name, young man, and whatever happened to John?" Maria asked, as David started to sweep the floors.

"My name's David. I'm John's friend. We went on a trip to San Jose, and then to Santa Cruz, where John got a terrible sunburn while at the beach. I'm sort of covering for him until he gets better. After I finished my assignment, I dashed over here to get his work done."

"Why, I think that's most commendable, David, but I feel partly responsible for whatever happened to John. You see, it was I who suggested the beach in Santa Cruz in the first place. I do hope it's not too bad, and he recovers soon. And by the way, my name is Maria. Tell him I asked of him."

"I sure will, Maria, but I've got to hurry and finish as I still have a lot to do before I knock off for dinner. Do me a favor, Maria, and don't tell anyone that I am doing this for John. They might not like me covering for him."

"You can count on me, David. If there is any other way I can be of help, please, don't hesitate to call on me."

David quickly finished his work and hurried back to the barracks, where he found John taking a cold shower to reduce the pain. "I got you something from the infirmary. The doctor said it should help with the healing and cut down on the pain. I don't think that shower is good for you, John. The pressure of that water might make it worse. When you get out of the shower, I'll pat your back dry. OK?"

"Thanks, David, I really appreciate what you're doing for me. You know I'd do the same for you, don't you?"

That evening, Harold, Bruce, and Green stopped by to tell of their adventures in Frisco.

"Hi, John, I hear you got careless and ended up with a burn. I thought you knew better, but looks like you learned the hard way," Harold said, as he almost instinctively started to pat his brother on the back. Then he continued, "Boy, did we have a great time. We did the Fisherman's Wharf, the cable cars, Chinatown, a burlesque, and even a place where they had female impersonators who used their own voices. You wouldn't believe this, but they actually looked like and sounded like real women. The burlesque was a little disappointing though. We expected them to take it all off—but they didn't. Just teasers, you know, and a couple of jokers who put on a comedy show. After that we checked into a hotel and they sent some girls up. Too expensive, so we ended up hot and horny, with nothing the whole time. Oh, well, better luck next time. How'd your weekend go, John? Better than ours, I hope."

"Yeah, except for this damned sunburn, we did a lot better. Met three girls that Bill's cousin had lined up for us. They screwed like minks. Went out for dinner a few times, but actually didn't see much. Bill's cousin sure had a big enough house—we each had a room of our own. Of course, once I got this sunburn, that ended it for me. I was forced to sleep by myself, and the girl went home."

"Hey, maybe we'll look up that cousin when we get around to San Jose—yeah, maybe in a couple weeks," Green said. "I could use a little pussy, other than the four-legged kind."

"Now don't get yourself all worked up, Green. First off, his cousin is busy as hell, and before he dropped us off back at the base, he let us know he couldn't do it again as his wife and kids would be returning home early next week. Too bad, guys, you would have liked him," John said, as he pulled back his shoulders in an attempt to pull the shirt away from his skin.

After about an hour or so, Harold and the others made their excuses, and took off to town.

"Boy, did we handle that right! Didn't we, David? I wonder if they actually believed that line of shit we handed them, but then again, why not? They didn't have any reason not to believe us. If they ever found out the truth, I think they'd shit."

"You did the right thing, John. What they don't know won't hurt them. Besides, what we did doesn't make us less of a man. Bet they couldn't have handled themselves as well as we did, when we took on those four punks at Madam's Place."

"By the way, John, Maria sends her regards and said that if you needed anything to let her know. She really seems to like you. Who wouldn't, you've got the perfect personality, you're good looking, good at conversation, and hardworking—when you're not laid up, that is."

"Thanks, David. Maria's really a nice lady. Guess I'm lucky to have met her, and by the way, you're everything you said I was, and then some."

By the end of the week, John was feeling a lot better, but not well enough to go too far.

"Hey, John, how's 'bout you and me looking up that church you talked about? After that, we could visit those guys again at the ship. That'll give us something to do."

"Sure, David, why not. I was beginning to get a little bored just sitting around like this. I just gotta change uniform, and we'll head out.

"Oh yeah, before I forget, Standish, I mean Bill, called his cousin in San Jose, who said he had a lot of friends in Frisco, if we wanted to go there. He said to just let him know and he'd fix us up." This time, as David, and John made their way down the hill and into town, they walked with a distance between them as there were two other guys behind. When they arrived at the church and knocked at the door, they were greeted by a man probably in his late fifties or early sixties, short and squat, with thinning gray hair.

"Welcome, I'm Reverend Gambino. You can call me Mario, if you like—actually, I prefer it. Have you come to see the church? We're always happy to have young visitors like you. By the way, are you from Fort Ord, or the Presidio?"

"The Presidio," John answered, "and we're glad to meet you. We've been planning to stop by for some time now. I'm John and this is my buddy, David. Boy, does this place look old."

"It is old, over a hundred years, I'm told. See this baptismal font? It once belonged to Queen Elizabeth. It was a gift to this church by a nobleman when the church was built. Would you care to join me for a glass of wine? I always have one around this time of day."

"Gee, thanks, Mario. We sure would," John answered, without hesitation."

"I have a small apartment attached to the church. Actually, I don't live there, but I stay over now and then, when I have work to do. We'll have our drinks back there," Mario said, as he started to lead the way to the rear of the church.

"We can't stay long," David remarked, as he and John made their way to the apartment. "We got friends on that Navy ship, and we're going to visit them."

"Now isn't that a coincidence," Mario said, as he poured three large glasses of wine. "I also know someone on that ship. Do you know Steve? He's a member of this church. He has a friend named Paul, from your base. They stay overnight here once in a while, when they help out at the church or just don't want to go back that night."

"Sure, we know 'em. They're both nice guys. Hey, we'd better finish off this drink and head down to the ship, before it gets too late. Thanks a lot for everything, Mario, and we'll see you again soon," John said. After shaking hands, David and John made their way from the church, and started walking toward the ship.

"What did you make of him, John—Mario, that is? Did you notice how he kept staring down at my crotch the whole time we were talking? I have an idea what he likes, don't you?"

"Yeah, it sort of looks that way to me too, David. At any rate, we know where we can get a drink when we want one. I wonder what Steve and Paul do at the church, when they stay over?"

"Who knows, maybe one day we'll find out—not that I'm looking for a foursome, that is. Just like us, what they do is their business, and what we do is ours," David said, as they soon approached the ship.

As David and John went aboard, they were greeted by Gary, who was just coming out on deck. "Hey, guys, how you doing? Haven't seen you in a while, where you been?" Gary asked, as he offered his hand in a friendly greeting.

"San Jose and Santa Cruz, where I got one hell of a sunburn, see this, I'm still peeling," John said, as he showed Gary his right arm. "Hey, by the way, where's the other guys?"

"Dale went out somewhere. Probably a restaurant, you know how he likes to eat. Steve got himself a car, so he went to pick up his friend Paul at the Presidio. Guess they're going out somewhere. Larson's taking a nap. You haven't met him yet. He usually goes on liberty the moment he finishes for the day."

"What do ya mean by liberty?" David asked.

"Oh that's just Navy talk. You call it a pass, we call it liberty. While I'm at it, the walls are bulkheads, the floor is the deck, the ceiling is the overhead, the bathroom is the head—you guys call it the latrine, the hatch is the door, the portholes are the windows. The gangplank is the ramp leading from the ship, you can call it the ramp if you want. I guess that's enough to remember for now. You guys want a beer? We're not supposed to drink on ship, so don't ever mention it to anyone. The bottles might taste a little salty—we keep them in a net, over the side of the ship and in the water—the best refrigeration you can find."

"Sure, why not, we'll help you pay for it. The last beer we had was over at the fort, when we were visiting my brother," John remarked.

"Sorry we ate already, or I'd offer you something. How about some chips with the beer?" Gary offered.

"Sure, Gary, we both like chips," David answered, as he took a seat next to John and opened a beer.

Gary stood braced against a post, as he kept pulling his uniform away from his crotch.

"Boy, Gary, you look a little uncomfortable down there. How'd you ever get that uniform to fit so tight?" John remarked with a smile, as he noticed that Gary's pants were so tight they left little to the imagination. "I bet that really turns on the women."

"Yeah, they're not the only ones that get turned on, if you know what I mean. Whenever I need relief, I can always find someone to take care of me. You guys want another beer? And by the way, I got the duty this weekend. That means that I have to work, and can't go on liberty."

"Sure, Gary, why not. Another beer sounds great," John said, as he finished drinking the first one. "We only work Monday through Friday. How'd you like to go with us to Frisco a week from this Friday? Bill's also going along. You've never met Bill, have you? He's stationed with us. Well, one thing's for sure, you'll like him. He's a really nice guy, so how about it?"

"Sounds good to me, If I'm not doing anything else, and I'm off that weekend. You guys can meet me here at the ship. I got a car. Not much to look at, but it's a car, and it runs."

"Gee, that's great, Gary. We'll pay for the gas. It sure beats hitching a ride," David said, as he opened another beer.

"Hey, I gotta wake up Larson pretty soon, he's got the next watch. Not that either of us are going anywhere. He put in on the beer, so got to make sure he gets his share. After he drags his ass up, I might get in a little sack time myself—if you guys don't mind?" Gary said.

"No, we don't mind. We gotta be getting back pretty soon anyway." No sooner had John said this than Steve came into the room.

"Hi, guys, I see you already met my friend Paul at the Presidio. How'd you like him? We just went out for a movie and a hamburger. Oh, yeah, I heard you guys also met Mario, at the church. What'd you think of him?"

"He seemed OK to me," David answered, not wanting to go into detail. "Yeah, we had a glass of wine with him. He sure is friendly. He mentioned that you and Paul stay over once in a while. Hey, it's starting to get a little late. John and I had better be taking off now. We'll stop by again—soon, if you guys don't mind."

"Sure, anytime." Steve said, "Maybe you guys, Paul, and me can all go out together some night. How about it?"

"Sure, Steve, why not," David remarked, as both he and John started out the hatch, toward the ramp.

As both John and David left the ship and were starting up the hill on their return to the Presidio, John grabbed hold of David's hand, then placed his arm around his waist.

"What you make of Gary?" John asked. "Like what he said about how he could always get taken care of, one way or another, and how he kept pulling at his crotch? I think he either is, or goes both ways. Most likely he goes both ways, as he's sure one horny son of a gun, isn't he?"

"I think it's both ways, John; but as for Steve, there's no doubt about it, he's one way only, and that's straight for Paul. And while I'm at it, I don't want to see you spending too much time looking at either one of those two guys, or any other guys for that matter. That is, except for me. Got it?"

"Sure, David, you don't have to worry about that," John answered, as he let his hand gently slide down David's hip. "What do you say we have something to eat at the Fisherman's Wharf tomorrow? We haven't been there yet, and it looks like fun."

"Sounds like a great idea to me, John. Should we ask Bill if he wants to go? You know, we owe him something for putting us up in San Jose."

"Sure, why not, the more the merrier. Hold on a minute while I light up a cigarette. Here's one for you," John said, as he lit a cigarette from his lips and gave it to David. John was beginning to look forward to these walks with David, and secretly, he would much rather have spent tomorrow alone with him.

The following morning John had breakfast and then reported to work as usual.

"Good morning, John Earl English," Maria said. "I'm really pleased to see that you're finally up and about, and I missed you. Oh, by the way, you certainly have a wonderful friend, and I might add quite a handsome young man. You're lucky to have someone as thoughtful as David. Incidentally, Thursday is my Names Day celebration, and I would very much like to have you as my special guest. Would you come?"

"Sure, Maria, I'd love to, but what's a Names Day? Would you mind if David came along?"

"Certainly, by all means bring David along. In answer to your other question, in the Russian Orthodox Church we celebrate the day of the saint that we are named after—just like you celebrate your birthday. Don't eat, as we will have plenty of food. I didn't mention this before, but my husband and I are very good friends of the commandant, and I'll arrange for you and David to be off-duty Thursday through Sunday, as there will be something to do each day. I'll tell him I need you both to help me out."

"Wow! Maria, you can do that—getting us off-duty, I mean?"

"Sure, John, I guarantee it. My husband and I will pick you both up at noon on Thursday. We can meet right here. You won't forget now, will you?"

"Are you kidding, Maria? No way will we forget," John answered.

"After Thursday's celebrations both you and David can stay in our guest room. We'll get up early and after breakfast, we'll all drive to San Francisco for another, and bigger, celebration at the cathedral. We'll stay there that night with an old friend, and leave early the next morning for our return home. I think you'll both enjoy your visit, and my husband will teach you how to say 'It is a pleasure to meet you, hello, good evening, yes and no' in Russian. We have never been blessed with children, so we would be honored if you and David would consider yourselves our sons for this special time in my life."

"Sure, Maria, I'd be honored, and so would David. I know it. By the way, David and I are going to have dinner at the Fisherman's Wharf in town tonight. We're treating our friend Bill, so I'd better hurry up and finish so we can get ready. Don't worry, Maria, we'll be here Thursday at noon, for sure. See you tomorrow." With this said, John made his way back to the barracks to get ready, and to tell David the good news.

The Fisherman's Wharf was really great. One of the shops was actually made out of empty bottles. "I'm going to have lobster, I've never had it before. I don't think The Home could afford it," John said, as he scanned over the menu.

"If it's good enough for you, it's good enough for me," David remarked, as he started eating the bread that was brought to the table.

"Hey, this looks good. Think I'll have this abalone steak. That sure sounds different. Wonder why they call it a steak? Do you think it's beef?" Bill said as he sipped at a glass of water.

"No, it's some sort of shellfish. Like some kind of huge clam—only with just one shell. Someone told me they pounded them flat to make them tender. I'll let you taste my lobster if you let me taste that abalone. What you say we start off with clam chowder; the waiter said they make it with fresh clams. Then we can have a crab salad. John and I had some not long ago, and it was really great," David suggested, as he helped himself to another piece of bread.

"You sure you got enough money, David? This sounds like it's going to be a little expensive," Bill asked.

"Don't worry about it. Like I said, John and I are treating you. If we didn't have it, we wouldn't be here. Besides, you're our best friend, and we've known you for one hell of a long time. Who better to share with than friends?"

"What do ya think, isn't this like in the movies? Like those rich people eating out in one of those real fancy places," Bill remarked, as he also helped himself to the bread.

After they had each placed their orders, the waiter asked if they wanted to order wine with their meal. "Sure, why not, we'll have a bottle of white wine. Not too expensive though," David quickly answered, aware that the waiter had not asked to check for proof of age.

After taking the orders, the waiter left briefly then returned with the wine, which he opened and placed on the table. "Hey, this is really great," John said, as he poured each of his friends a glass of wine. "Maybe we'll order another bottle when this one is gone. The price was right."

By the time the three of them had each finished a glass of wine, the food arrived and was placed on the table.

First the clam chowder was served, followed by a side order of mussels to be shared among the three.

"Can you beat that? This is the first time I ever had clam chowder, that they left the shells in the soup. I hope they washed them good before they cooked 'em," John said with a laugh.

"Wow! Look at this," David remarked, pointing to the lobster on his plate. How would you like to have this one grab hold of your ass. I bet those pincers really hurt. I wonder how you eat these suckers. Maybe that's what these nutcrackers are for—to break 'em open, that is."

"I don't know 'bout you guys, but this abalone thing sure has one hell of a beautiful shell. I wonder if they let you keep it. One thing's for sure, it won't be on the table when they clean up. I'm taking it back with me. I bet it would make a nice ashtray if it weren't for all these holes. Hey, this thing actually tastes good," Bill said, as he cut off a small portion of meat and tasted it.

After the meal, John paid the bill, gave the waiter a tip, and the three of them left the restaurant and walked to the end of the pier. The smell of sea plants, salt, and fish combined to make that special odor that comes with the sea made them want to linger longer. A gentle warm breeze and seagulls swooping down to find a meal or a spot to land only added to the beauty of this special place.

"Hey, look at that—down there in the water, on that post. It's a starfish. First time I ever saw one—alive, that is. How 'bout you guys?" Bill said in an excited voice.

"I think that goes for both of us. Naw, don't think we ever saw one either, and look at those," David added, pointing to clumps of small black shellfish clinging to ropes of what looked like seaweed and attached to several piles nearby. Aren't those some of the things we had as a side dish? I think they called them mussels. Maybe they got 'em from here. Oh, well, what's say we head on into town. John's brother said he was going to meet us near the pawnshop in about an hour."

With this said, the three of them made their way into town, stopping briefly at Yorky's, a small donut shop, which also served soup and sandwiches. Sergeant Yorky and his wife Rose, opened the business shortly after he was transferred to Fort Ord.

Yorky's had become quite popular with a number of men from both Fort Ord and the Presidio because of the wide variety of freshly made donuts and the friendly atmosphere.

Just as they were leaving, Harold and his friends were passing by.

"Where you three whores off to?" Green said jokingly, as he slapped John across the butt.

"Come on, Green, keep your hands off my ass or I'll have to start charging you," John quipped, as he started to laugh at the thought of it.

"Hey, the three of us just had dinner at the Wharf. It was really great. You guys should try it sometime," David remarked, as he accepted a lit cigarette from John's mouth.

"Bunch of rich bitches, aren't ya?—too rich for our blood. We're more into hamburgers and fries. How 'bout something to drink? I'll go in and get it, all you have to do is chip in—OK?"

"Sure, why not. How's wine sound? It's about the cheapest buzz we can get for the money," Bill remarked.

"Wine it is. If it was anything stronger, you pussies couldn't take it. But that's OK, I can drink anything," Green bragged, as he started into the store. "And by the way, we met this corporal from our company who has a place here in town. We'll drink there tonight."

Green returned shortly with three bottles of wine, two large bags of chips and some pretzels. "Come on, the place is only a few blocks from here, so we'll walk."

It was less than ten minutes before they arrived at the door, and were greeted by a rather muscular guy with blond hair and blue eyes, wearing tight, slightly worn Levi's and a T-shirt, probably in his early twenties.

"Come on in, guys, my name's Rick—Rick Taylor. I already know Harold, Bruce, and Green. What's your names?"

"I'm David, and these are my buddies, John and Bill."

"How'd you ever manage to get a place of your own, Rick?" David asked, noticing that it was a small ranch-style house, big enough for two, but plenty of room for one.

"My parents have money—oh, not a lot of money but they pay for this place and my meals. I have to pay for anything else. Not bad, huh?"

"Remember that broad I was seeing at the EM club?" Green interrupted. "Well, one night I saw her husband. He was big as a gorilla, and nasty as a wild bull. Heard him say that he'd break every bone in her body if he caught her with another man, and that was only the start of what he'd do to the guy if he caught him. Needless to say, I'm staying away from that place for a while—a long while."

As the evening progressed everyone told jokes and laughed a lot; and as they got drunker, they bragged about their female conquests (real or imagined), which served only to make them horny with no possibility for relief.

"Hey guys, it was really great. About the only thing that was missing was a woman. See you guys again soon," Rick remarked, as he said good-bye, and closed the door.

"See you later, guys," Harold said. "We're heading back to the fort."

It was already getting rather late when David, John, and Bill started making their way up the hill toward the Presidio. As before, John put his arm around David's waist, feeling a little too high to care if anyone noticed, and actually comfortable doing this in Bill's presence.

"Come on, you guys, you're making me horny, and by the way, if you guys ever need company—you know what I mean—just let me know." With this said, Bill pushed his way between David and John, and the three of them made their way back, walking close to one another, with their arms around each other's waists.

"Jesus, Bill, you shouldn't have any trouble finding someone for yourself, you're one of the best-looking guys—other than us—that we know of. Why don't you take Paul and Steve, they might like it?" David said, as he started to smile. "One thing's for sure, if we ever wanted someone else, you'd be the first in line."

At noon on Thursday, David, and John walked the short distance from the barracks to Maria's office, in anticipation of a long weekend away from the base.

"Well, John and David, I see you have arrived promptly as agreed," Maria said, as she offered her hand in a friendly greeting. "This is my husband, Niki. I have told him so much about you that it is as though he already knows you. Don't worry now, as I have arranged for you to be off-duty the rest of the week, as I said I would. Incidentally, the commandant will be a guest tonight, and if you have not yet done so, you shall have the honor of meeting him. Come now, we must be going, so as to get ready—so much to do. By the way, you both look so handsome in your uniforms, and I'm glad you brought a change of clothes and an overnight bag."

Niki now extended his welcome by accepting both John's and David's hands at the same time. "Like my wife, Maria, I too feel that I have known you both for a very long time, and we are honored that you have consented to be with us, as family, during these celebrations. I'll be driving, so perhaps we should all leave now and get on our way."

John and David followed Maria and Niki to their car, and after they were well on the way, Niki said, "It won't be long, as we don't live far away. Our home is rather small, but it's sufficient for the two of us. You and David will be sleeping tonight in our guestroom, although it might be rather late before you get to bed. As Maria has already told you, I shall teach you a few words in Russian that might prove useful to you. But don't worry, most of our guests speak English as well as Russian. You're going to have a wonderful time, if we have anything to say about it, and we do."

After a brief ride, the car pulled up in front of a small white bungalow with green shutters and lots of geraniums planted between two large yucca plants.

"This is our home," Maria said. "Come in and we'll have lunch, but we mustn't eat too much, as there will be so much food later tonight. If you're tired you can rest in your room, as there will be plenty of time before the guests arrive." With this said, Maria escorted John and David to a small room, which was occupied by a dresser, a vanity, and a standard-sized bed. Two pairs of pajamas were laid out on the bed. No doubt they belonged to Niki as they were a little large.

"Thanks, Maria, this should be just fine," David said. "There's more than enough room for the both of us," as he lay back on the bed as though he were testing it for comfort. Actually, we're not really tired right now, so if there is anything we can do to help, we'd be glad to give you a hand."

"Well, we are going to do a little last minute shopping, so if you want to come along, we'd be happy to have your company," Maria answered, as she started toward the door.

John and David helped carry the packages that Maria and Niki purchased at several stores, and after a little more than two hours they were back at the house again. Shortly after returning, several women arrived to deliver some of the many trays of food which they had prepared. As more and more food arrived, John wondered how many people were coming to this event, and how this small house could ever accommodate so many.

An Orthodox priest arrived at six PM and started incensing every room in the house, as he chanted prayers in his native Russian language. No sooner had he finished than a steady flow of guests started to arrive. Among the early arrivals were the commandant and his wife.

John and David greeted the guests as they arrived, with the few Russian words that they had learned earlier from Niki.

"Well, so you're the lucky men I gave several days off to. I'm Colonel Hendricks, and this is my wife, Joanne."

"It's a pleasure to meet you, sir, and you, Mrs. Hendricks. This is my friend David, and my name is John."

"Well, you're sure two fortunate young men to have such good friends as Maria and Niki," Col. Hendricks said, as he and his wife started into the front room to greet the other guests.

Throughout the evening, more and more people arrived with gifts, while others left, after first eating, drinking, and offering their very best wishes to Maria. Many said they would join the festivities at the cathedral the following day.

"Come, John and David, and help yourselves to all this wonderful food, and here is a special drink for each of you: it's tea with strawberry preserves and vodka. There's also lots of other drinks, but be careful not to drink too much," Maria cautioned, "as we have a long drive to San Francisco in the morning, and lots of festivities once we get there."

"Have you ever seen so many different things to eat, David? I never tasted half the things they fixed before now, but you know I actually liked 'em. I didn't think I would at first, but after I tried 'em, I went back for more."

"You're right about that, John," David remarked, as he helped himself to a cherry tart. "I could eat this kind of food every day. Didn't know what a lot of it was, but it tasted great, except for that stuff they called caviar. Some sort of salty fish eggs, someone said."

As the evening progressed, Maria and Niki introduced many of their guests to David and John, who by now were enjoying themselves far more than they ever thought they would. Around ten most of the guests had left and, thanks to a number of the women who remained behind, the house was placed in order and everything was put away. It was time to retire for the evening, and John and David could hardly wait to go to bed.

"Hey, David, you'd better watch over me tonight. I think I had too much to drink."

"Who's going to watch over me, John? I drank as much as you, so what's say we try to get some sleep, before we both pass out for the night." With this said, David ran his fingers through John's hair, and pulling John's head close to his, he said, "I'll watch over you, John, I always will." After this he kissed him and let his head fall back on his pillow, with John's head resting upon his arm. Both of them quickly fell asleep.

The following morning both John and David were awakened to the sound of knocking on the door. It was Niki. "Time to be up, gentlemen. Maria will be making breakfast shortly. If you would like to use the bathroom, both of us are finished with it. Feel free to use the shower if you care to."

"Thanks, Niki, we'll be up soon," David said, as he pulled himself up in the bed. "It might take us a while. I think we had too much to drink last night. Maybe after a shower we'll be good as new."

"Take your time, boys, and here's a couple robes to use while you're getting ready," Niki said, as he opened the door wide enough to hand them to David.

"Thanks, Niki, I'll go first. This will give John a few more minutes to sleep. I think he had a little more to drink than I did." With this said, David put on a robe and headed for the bathroom with a small bag containing a toothbrush, toothpaste, razor, and other toiletries necessary for grooming. A short time later, David returned.

"OK, John, you're next. I feel a lot better since I showered, and so should you."

By the time the two had returned to their room and finished dressing, they became aware of the pleasant odor of just-fried bacon, and the smell of freshly brewed coffee, which would no doubt aid in their recovery.

"Good morning, John Earl English, and likewise to you, David, and don't you both look wonderful—so fresh and clean. If you don't mind, right after breakfast, we'll be on our way, as we have some distance to travel," Maria suggested, as she poured each of them a most welcome cup of coffee.

Following breakfast, the four of them took their places in the car, and proceeded on their journey. About one-third of the way there, they entered into a rather dense fog which cut visibility in half. "We're lucky," Niki said. "Frequently, the fog is so dense that you can't travel at all. At least we can keep going, and it won't be long and the fog will clear. It sure is some beautiful scenery on the way to San Francisco. Perhaps about halfway, we can stop for coffee and rest a while."

"Sounds good to me, and I don't think it will matter one way or the other to John. It looks like he's sound asleep. Would you mind if I had a cigarette?" David said, unsure if it was permissible to smoke in the car.

"No, not at all," Maria answered. "Niki also smokes, and I'm surprised he hasn't had one as yet."

"Where are we?" John asked as he suddenly awakened when the car came to a stop a little over halfway on their journey."

"Not too far from San Jose. It won't be long now, as the fog has completely cleared. How about some coffee? And the rest rooms are inside if you need them," Niki explained, as the four of them made their way into the small restaurant, not far from the gas pump. "When we arrive in San Francisco, we shall have lunch in a very nice Russian restaurant that is owned by a good friend that we knew back in Russia."

After refueling, using the rest rooms, and drinking their coffee, the four of them proceeded on their way. This time both John and David slept the remainder of the trip.

At last they arrived in San Franciso. Both John and David suddenly awakened as though in anticipation of an exciting day.

"Wow! San Francisco, and I can see the Golden Gate Bridge. Boy, this is really something to write home about," John remarked as he looked about—too excited to sit still.

At this time, the car pulled in front of the restaurant, and the four of them made their way in.

"Welcome, Princess Maria, and Niki. Come, I shall prepare a wonderful lunch for you, and these two handsome gentlemen." And turning to John and David, he said, "My name is Misha, which means in English, Michael."

At this point John and David introduced themselves and followed Misha to a table, which had already been prepared.

"Wow, isn't this something," David remarked, pointing to the fresh-cut flowers and the beautiful silver candleholders set upon a fine lace tablecloth.

"It sure is, David. I've never seen anything quite like it," John answered, as he also noted the large amount of silverware that surrounded the beautiful porcelain plates. "And look at these glasses, they have to be the best crystal I've ever seen. "

"My dear Princess Maria, this shall be the most beautiful Names Day that I have ever catered. I have been preparing for days," Misha said, as he summoned waiters to the table. "Immediately after the service at the cathedral, I will be ready to serve the meal in the church hall. As I said before, Princess, this is my gift to you, and I am honored to be able to do it. Please enjoy your lunch, and feel safe to leave your car with us. I have arranged to have you chauffeured for the remainder of your stay, and you shall be staying overnight as guests of the Count. After lunch, you will be driven to his home, so that you might freshen up for such a busy day."

"Thank you so very much, Misha, you have always been one of our dearest friends. And we would be honored if you should say the grace," Maria said, as she bowed her head.

The meal was excellent and John and David were as excited as children, having never experienced anything this grand before.

Following lunch the four of them were driven to the home of the Count. It was a large and stately old house something like those beautiful old homes of the movie stars.

"Welcome, my dear Princess," the Count said, as he directed his guests into the house. "I have more than enough room. You, Princess, and your husband, Niki, shall have this room here. Your two gentlemen guests shall share this room. Both rooms have a private bath, and I shall do everything I can to make you comfortable. My wife shall help you select one of her gowns, as well as jewelry, that you might honor us by wearing this evening. Once again, we're delighted to have you as our guests."

After a short nap, John and David were more than ready for the festivities ahead.

They arrived at the church at six and as they entered, David noted that the church was already filled to near capacity. Immediately the bishop took both Maria and Niki by the hand and led them to the front of the church where they were seated on two very ornate chairs. John and David were escorted to their seats at the rear of the church. At this point Maria turned to the bishop and said, "My dear bishop, where are my two sons, with whom I arrived?"

"Do you mean those two gentlemen in uniform? Forgive me, Princess, and turning to one of the priests he ordered two additional chairs to be placed at the front of the church close by Maria and Niki. "Again, please accept my apologies. I didn't know they were your sons. We are honored to have them here with us."

Quickly, John and David were ushered to their new seats, causing John to blush, embarrassed at the thought of being given such an honored place.

"We are gathered here," the bishop said in English, "to honor Princess Maria, on the occasion of her Names Day. We are further honored by the presence of her husband, Niki, and their two handsome young sons." After these brief remarks, the service began.

Following the service, which lasted well over an hour, Maria, Niki, John, and David, were escorted to the head of a table, which was located to the front of the church hall. Like the restaurant where they had their lunch, every table was beautifully set with the finest tableware to be found. A waiter was stationed at every table and soon the feast would begin.

As they did the night before, John and David drank and ate far more than they had planned. It seemed everyone wanted to toast their health, and this, of course, did not add up to a sober night. Following the meal there was live entertainment, dancing, and much laughter accompanied by the flow of vodka and other alcoholic drinks. It wasn't until shortly before twelve that the final guest had left, the chauffeur arrived, and John and David finally found themselves back in their room for the night. Both fell back upon the bed, never bothering to undress, as they shortly fell asleep.

Late the following morning, John and David awakened to no more than a headache and wrinkled clothes. They both had brushed their teeth, shaved and showered and slowly left the room. Then they were greeted by the Count.

"Good morning, gentlemen. Please join us for breakfast," the Count said, as he led them to a small dining room downstairs.

Shortly before noon, Maria, Niki, John, and David were chauffeured back to the restaurant, where they picked up their car and began their journey back to Monterey.

It was an event unlike anything John or David had ever seen before, and something they thought they would never see again.

Chapter 4

"Boy, what a week this has turned out to be. Who would ever have believed we could have such a good time staying with Maria and Niki; and no one, and I do mean no one, would believe what we did. I guess the best thing to do is just say we were off a few days to help her out with something, and let it go at that. You got a cigarette, John? I ran out," David asked.

"Sure, David, let me light it for you," John said as he removed a cigarette from his pack, placed it between his lips and lit it. "I think you're right. We're best off to say as little as possible. I'm sure they're already jealous that we got the time off. They'd go nuts if they knew any more. How about you and me taking in a movie tonight?" John asked. "After that long drive back from Frisco, I think I'm a little too tired for anything else. It's a good thing we didn't tell Gary we'd go to Frisco this weekend or it would have turned out to be a double trip in the same day. By next weekend I'll be ready to go again. By the way, can you believe, we slept together for two nights and nothing happened—at least I don't think anything happened."

"About the only thing that happened is we both got drunk, and we both passed out. Yeah, a movie sounds good, if I don't fall asleep in the middle of it. Let's stop by that store first, so I can pick up a pack of

Luckies," David said, as he finished his cigarette and tossed the butt to the curb.

John and David stopped in a nearby store and made their purchase. On the way out they ran into Steve and Paul, who were just walking by.

"Hi, guys," Steve said. "Haven't seen you in a few days. How you doing?" Not waiting for an answer, Steve continued, "Paul and me just came from the church. We were going to stay over there tonight, but changed our minds. Right now we're planning to take in a movie. Want to join us?"

"Sure, Steve, we were planning to see a movie anyway. It's an old Bette Davis flick, but we haven't seen it, so why not? We can stop at Yorky's, have a coffee and donut, and kill a little time until the movie starts," David suggested.

About a half-hour later, all four took their places in the theater. John and David sat next to Steve and Paul, who were busy talking and sharing a large bag of popcorn as the theater darkened and the movie appeared on the screen.

After about a half-hour, David noted that Steve's hand was resting next to Paul's leg, with his fingers gently touching him. Paul had his arm to the rear of Steve's seat while casually placing his hand near his shoulder. At one point, Steve actually moved his hand across Paul's leg, and rested it momentarily on his lap. He quickly removed his hand when he thought that David might be watching. It was no longer a matter of guesswork, Steve and Paul had something going—as more than just friends.

"Hey, how do you like the movie, Steve?" David asked, as he purposely leaned over and placed his hand near John's lap so that Steve would see. "Maybe we should do this together more often. What do ya think, Steve?"

"Yeah, I think you're right, David," Steve said, as he followed David's example, and leaned closer to Paul.

Following the movie, Steve suggested the four of them meet again tomorrow and visit nearby Carmel. "Paul, and I are invited to a party, and they said to bring along some friends. Sounds like fun. How 'bout it, guys?"

"Sure, tomorrow's Saturday, why not. We're not doing anything else. It's OK with you, isn't it, John?"

"Sure, David, I've never been there. Yeah, it sounds great. What time you guys want to meet us?" John asked.

"How bout around six?" Steve said. "That way we'll all have time to eat before we go. Anyway, the fun don't really start until later in the evening. Hope you guys like parties. By the way, be sure to wear uniform. You'll find out why when you get there. Do you mind if Paul walks back with you? I didn't drive tonight."

"No, not at all, Steve. We'll walk you back first, then we'll head back ourselves."

After leaving Steve and making their way back to the Presidio, Paul finally said, "I think you guys know about Steve and me. I mean, like, it doesn't bother you, does it?"

"Hell no, Paul, it's the same story between David and me, so relax now and enjoy the walk."

"Jesus, David, I'd never have guessed it. No, never. Really, there's nothing feminine about either one of you. You're both as masculine as they come. I hope we don't look feminine."

"Come on, Paul. Hell no. I'd never have guessed except by the way Steve talked about you. Like how good-looking you are, and all of that. Also at the movie, I'm not exactly blind, you know. By the way, next time be more careful, the wrong guy could be watching you, and I'm sure you know what that could mean."

"You're right, David. We do have to be more careful. A lot more careful, I guess, and thanks for everything. Steve and I really like you guys, and we could really use a couple good friends. You're someone we could talk to, other than Mario at the church. All he really wants is to put the make on us. He never gives up trying. The thought of it almost makes me sick," Paul remarked.

"We're going to Frisco next weekend," David said, as he placed his arm over Paul's shoulder. "We'll leave Friday night. Gary's driving, so why don't you and Steve join us. I'm sure Gary won't mind. It'll be a little tight as Bill's also going. That makes six of us. Nice and cozy, don't you think? From what I gather, Gary will go either way, so I don't think we have to worry about him."

As they arrived at the barracks, David turned to Paul and said, "Just a word of warning, anything you saw or heard tonight is strictly between us, and no one else, just so we all understand each other, OK?"

"Sure, David, you got my word on it. I'm not exactly stupid, you know. Oh yeah, about tomorrow—Steve said he'd pick us up here at six, so that gives us plenty of time to eat and be ready."

The following day, John and David spent most of the day just lounging around and resting up for what promised to be quite an exciting night. Around four, they showered, shaved, put on clean uniforms and headed to the mess hall, where they ran into Paul. After laughing and joking around with some of the other guys who were sitting nearby, it wasn't long before all of them had finished eating and were ready to go.

"Steve should get here any time now, so what do ya say we head out to meet him, OK, guys?" Paul said as he prepared to leave the table.

"Yeah, Paul, we're done too, so let's get on our way," John answered, as he and David got up and headed toward the door.

Just as they approached the street, Steve pulled up and they all climbed in, and headed out into town.

"Boy, you sure believe in being on time, don't you, Steve? And by the way, you going to tell us where we're going, or is it some sort of a secret?" David asked, as he flicked the ash from his cigarette into the ashtray.

"Naw, not really," Steve replied, "we're going to Ken Hallard's house. You know, the movie star. Paul and I met him a couple weeks ago through Mario. Seems he goes to our church. I think Mario fixes him up once in a while. At any rate, according to Mario, he sure can give one hell of a party. I guess the party is more or less the surprise part of it. All I know is, he said if we wanted to be popular—wear our uniforms. Other than that, I really don't know anything more than you, so your guess is as good as mine."

"You sure about this Ken Hallard guy?" John asked. "Everything I ever heard or read about him has been women, and more women. He always plays rough, he-man roles in the movies."

"Don't know, John, but we'll find out real soon. This is the place," Steve said, as he drove up to the gate that surrounded a rather large Spanish-style house.

The guard at the gate made a call, and shortly after he directed Steve to the far end of the house, where there were a number of other cars already parked.

"What's say we head on in, guys. They must be expecting us, or they wouldn't have let us in," Paul said as they got out of the car and headed toward the house.

Steve rang the doorbell, which was soon answered by a rather muscular-looking guy wearing only a pair of tight Levi's, a super dark tan, and nothing else. He probably spent most of his time on the beach or lifting weights, John thought, as they were admitted into a very large room. About fifty or so other men were slowly moving about the room. Most of them had drinks in their hands, and some were snacking on hors d'oeuvres from several silver trays which were located on a table near the door. At the other end of the room was a rather large bar, which was tended by another muscular guy wearing very tight shorts, a tan, and a smile.

As Steve and the others headed for the bar, it became apparent why they had been asked to wear uniform. Every eye in the place was glued on them, and you could almost cut the lust with a knife.

"I think these guys are expecting a lot more than they're going to get. One thing's for sure, that beyond a look, they're not getting anything from me or David," John commented, as he looked at Steve.

"That makes four of us then," Steve said. "You know how I feel about Paul, and I'm not sharing him with anyone. I guess as long as they think they have a chance, we can stay. Oh, I might let them pat my ass, or something like that, but nothing more—but I don't want 'em touching Paul."

"Boy, you're a jealous one, but I got a feeling you're going to be the most popular guy here, Steve. I think they like that tight Navy uniform more than they like ours. Not only that, you got that innocent-looking baby face. One thing's for sure, they get to see lots of us soldiers but not many of you. Besides, it's you sailors that got that kind of reputation—you know what I mean," David said, as he smiled and gave Steve a quick pat on the ass.

"My name's Joseph," the bartender said as he extended his hand to Steve. "Boy, Ken sure knew what he was doing when he invited four good-looking studs like you, but out of the four, I think I like you the best. I always was fond of seafood. What'll you have—to drink, that is?"

"I like him best myself," Paul cut in, "and he's 'my' seafood for the night. You might think I'm the greedy type, but I'm keeping him for myself. How 'bout a screwdriver for me and one for Steve."

John and David were getting ready to order from Joseph, who had now redirected his attention to them. "Jesus, when God made you two, he really threw out the mold. I'm getting horny just looking at you even though you're covered with clothes. Look at me, I'm hardly wearing anything, and it's you that turns them on. Is it true that a man in uniform looks as good with it on as he does with it off? What can I get for you handsome guys?"

"We'll have the same thing as Steve and Paul," David said, a little embarrassed by all the attention they just received.

"Hey, look at that," David said, pointing in the direction of two women who had just entered the room. "Maybe all that stuff about Ken Hallard and women is true."

Both women headed straight for the bar, ordered drinks and made their way to David, who was talking to John at the far end of the bar.

"Hi, you guys from Fort Ord? The reason I ask is we're stationed there ourselves. I'm Mary, and this is my friend Joan."

Mary was really good-looking, auburn hair, big blue eyes, slender hips, and a well-endowed bust. She wore a crystal necklace, a bracelet, and long matching earrings that complemented her dress. Joan on the other hand was a little on the plump side, with sandy hair, brown eyes, little makeup, and no jewelry at all. She was, nonetheless, still an attractive woman.

"Do you mind if we join you until our friends arrive?" Mary asked as she sipped at her drink, while holding Joan's hand.

"Sure, why not, it might be good for our reputation to be seen with two good-lookers like you," David answered as he looked to John for approval.

About twenty minutes later, two more women entered the room, one dressed in men's slacks and looking more like a man than many of the men present. Her friend wore jeans and a blouse, which did not detract at all from her femininity.

After a brief introduction all the way around, the women excused themselves and made their way to another part of the room.

"Boy, for a moment I was worried that those four dykes were going to take up all your time," the bartender said, as he reached over and took hold of David's hand.

"You don't have to worry about that," David remarked. "We had planned to move around and have a little fun. How 'bout another round before we do?"

"Sure, handsome," Joseph replied, "and here's a little special one for my sailor friend." He poured two shots into Steve's drink.

"Hey, Paul, if that one didn't look so much like a man, I'd never have guessed they were like us. What do you think?" Steve said, as he put his hand around Paul's waist.

"What do I think? I think you're about the best-looking, the sexiest, and the hottest guy here. I don't want to think about anything else." With this said, Paul pulled Steve close to him, and kissed him on the lips, oblivious to anyone around him.

"Come on, Paul, cut it out," David said, as he pulled him away from Steve. "Remember what we talked about last night on the way back to the base? You can't take chances like that. You don't really know these people here. You're not the only one that's horny, but if you want him that bad, wait until you're in private. Why don't you two guys separate for a while, meet some of the other guests and just try to forget about it for now, OK?"

"Yeah, you're right, David. I'm so hot, I could shoot off right now. Maybe I'll talk to that old man over there, that should cool me off, but I'll have another drink before I go."

Four hours had passed, and the room was now so crowded that the guests overflowed into other parts of the house. Finally, Ken Hallard made his grand appearance.

"Hello, darlings," Ken yelled out as loud as he could. "I could really use something to eat right now—or is it, someone to eat, and I think I see something over there," as he headed straight toward Steve.

"Hi, sailor, my name's Ken. Ken Hallard, your host. I can see right now that you're exactly what Mario said you'd be. By that I mean sexy and cute. You have to be the one he's talking about, you're the only sailor around. And where's that sweet little soldier of yours?" After saying this, Ken, placed his hand on Steve's behind. "I hope he's not around … and look at all those buttons," he remarked, as he quickly moved his hand to Steve's front.

"Come on, Ken, you're embarrassing me," Steve said, as he pushed Ken's hand away.

"Touchy, touchy," Ken remarked, "but I don't give up that easy. I'll be back. Besides, from what I could feel, it's no wonder that soldier friend of yours is so jealous. Mario told me all about him. Oh well, got lots of other people to see—so don't go anywhere, OK?"

About this time, Mary came up to Steve.

"Boy, that Ken is something else, isn't he? He really seems to be after you. Do me a favor, will you? I would like to keep contact with you guys. Here's our name, and phone number. Give us a call. Maybe we can get together tomorrow. Around two."

"Sure, why not," Steve answered as he glanced down on the small piece of paper with the two names Mary Gates and Joan Braden along with a phone number where they could be reached.

"We could meet at Yorky's on Del Monte Ave., not far from the Presidio, and a couple blocks from Pacific. How's that sound to you, Mary? I know Paul will go, and I'll ask John and David. What do you say around six?" Steve asked.

"Sure, that's fine with us. We'll be there right on time, but don't you forget now," Mary answered. "Mentioning John and David, boy, are they having fun," Steve commented. They sure do mix well. And look at that. Ken has his hands on both their butts."

"Yeah, Steve, but he's looking over at you while he's doing it." With this said, Mary excused herself and left to pick up another drink, and rejoin her friends.

"Hey, David, quick, look over there by that big palm. Would you believe it, that guy is actually taking a leak on it. Hell, I've seen everything now."

"Yeah, he ain't looking like anything, but he's got a big dick. Maybe he's trying to attract attention."

"Maybe you're right, but that's not the way to do it. They'll be throwing his ass out," John said, as he started to laugh.

"I think we better go over and rescue Paul from that fat little queen he keeps trying to dodge. Besides, I can tell he's getting a little too edgy about all those guys who keep going over to Steve. Oh, shit. There goes that Ken again, and he's heading straight for Steve. I better try to get Paul's attention away from them," David said, as he started to make his way to Paul.

"OK, sailor boy," Ken said as he placed his hand directly on Steve's crotch. "Let's quit playing games. You know why you were invited, and it won't take much of your time."

"Come on, Ken, take your hand away. People are looking," Steve said, as he grabbed hold of Ken's hand. But as he did, Ken got a tighter grip on Steve, in an effort not to let go.

"Suddenly, Paul almost ran to where Steve was standing, and in one quick punch, he knocked Ken straight to the floor. "We're getting out of this goddamned place. That son of a bitch isn't going to touch you again."

At that moment, John and David arrived at the scene. "You're right about that, Paul," David said. "We're getting the hell out of here now, before they throw us out."

The four of them were out the door, into the car, and well on their way before they even realized the consequences of what had just happened.

"Well, it looks like we won't be back there again for a while—ever again, that is," David remarked as he continued to calm Paul down. "Did you have to punch him like that—I mean right in the face?"

"Yeah, I had to. He had hold of what belongs to me," Paul said, as he burst out laughing.

"Oh, before I forget. Remember Mary and Joan, the two women we met at the party? Well, Mary wants all of us to meet her tomorrow at Yorky's at six. Is that OK with you guys?"

"Sure, it's fine with us, but what are we supposed to do, bump pussies?" David joked, as he started to laugh.

"We could have coffee and donuts, if nothing else," Steve answered. "Maybe we could have pizza later on. Anyway, we'll find something to do."

"If you guys don't mind, we'll drop you off near the base. Paul and I are staying over at the church tonight. We both need relief, and I got the keys," Steve said, as he pulled into town.

"Hey, Steve, they got another bed in that place? If they do, we'll stay over with you," David quickly added.

"Sure, David, you and John can sleep on the couch. It makes into a bed."

A short time later, Steve pulled the car onto the church lot, and the four of them soon found themselves in the apartment and into their beds.

"Close your door, Steve, you're already getting a little noisy," John said with a smile as he moved a lot closer to David. "They're not the only horny ones, you know. And we're not too drunk tonight. So what's say we do something about it?"

"Fine with me," David said, as he rolled over on John, ran his fingers through his hair, and kissed him gently on the neck.

The following day, John and David arrived at Yorky's about fifteen minutes early. Steve and Paul were already there, sitting at a table having coffee.

"Hey, Steve and Paul—been here long?" John asked.

"No, not really," Steve answered. "We got here about five minutes before you. Do you think Mary and Joan will remember? After all, it was their idea—getting together, that is."

"Sure, why not." John answered. "Matter of fact, here they are now."

"Hi, guys. Looks like everyone remembered, which isn't bad, considering how much we had to drink last night. Anyone got a car? We know a really nice bar not far from here, in Pacific Grove. No problem about being served, the place is owned by a cop who's a friend of ours. They've also got really great food. Sound good to you guys?" Joan asked."

"Sure, Joan, let's go. We can all go in my car," Steve replied as he got up from the table.

The drive to Pacific Grove didn't take long, and soon they arrived at the bar. Over the door was a sign which read "The Golden Goose."

"Boy, this is really nice. Sure has a great view of the ocean," Paul remarked, as they went inside and sat down at one of the tables near the piano.

"If it isn't Mary and Joan. What brings you here so early—friends of yours?" the bartender asked, as he prepared to take their orders.

"Sure, Larry. They're really nice guys. Everyone drink beer? If so, I'll order a pitcher."

"Beer's fine," Paul answered. Yeah, we all drink beer. How 'bout us getting the first round."

"Don't worry about it, Paul—today it's on us."

"Come on, Joan, how about giving us a few tunes on the piano?" Larry requested, as he brought the beer to the table.

"Sure, Larry, anything special?" Joan asked as she took a seat at the piano. "By the way, these are our friends," as she introduced each of them by name. "If they stop by again, you'll know they're OK."

"Glad to meet you guys, come on back anytime. How about Bye, Bye, Blackbird?" Larry asked, as he made his way behind the bar.

"You always did like that song, didn't you, Larry?" Joan said as she started to play, with Mary singing along.

"What do you like, John, I mean, like what's your favorite?" David asked, as he reached under the table and took John's hand.

"I think my favorite would be As Time Goes By, followed by Blue Skies."

"How 'bout playing As Time Goes By, for John?" David asked. "I'll sing it, if you don't mind."

"Sure, David, it's one of my favorites also. Come on up to the piano," Joan said, as she played a short introduction.

David looked straight into John's eyes as he started to sing in a strong and rich baritone voice. As he continued to sing, tears fell from John's eyes, as he knew this would always be "their song" from now on.

After David finished, John could hardly contain himself, "Jesus, David, I never knew you could sing like that. You got the most beautiful voice I ever heard. I think you surprised me as much as you did the rest of us. God, it was beautiful. How 'bout one more, OK? Can you do Blue Sky?"

"Come on, Mary. Let's do this one together, you have a beautiful voice yourself—Whatcha say?"

"Sure, David. It's also a favorite of Joan's. I'll be singing to her, while you're singing to John. Now how's that for romance?"

After they finished singing, Steve and Paul requested David sing Mona Lisa especially for them. While Larry wasn't looking, Paul gently rubbed Steve's leg then gave him a hug, as they listened while David sang the song especially for them.

For the next couple hours, Joan continued to play many of the old favorites while David and Mary sang a few more songs together.

"Anyone hungry?" Joan asked, as she took her place back at the table.

"Sure, I think we all are," Paul answered as he poured another beer.

"How about hamburgers for everyone? They make really great ones here."

"Sure, Joan, sounds good to us," Paul added.

Joan called Larry to the table, and after placing the order they continued to talk about their relationships with one another and some of the many things they had in common.

"Hey, guys, it's getting a little late. We're supposed to meet a couple of women from the base at six thirty by the Fisherman's Wharf. Do you mind if we head back? It's really been great, and we'll have to do it again soon," Mary said, as she got up to leave.

After they arrived back in town, Steve let the women off by the Wharf, and headed for the Presidio to drop off John and David before heading back to town with Paul.

The following morning John and David arrived at the maintenance office to check in.

"OK, English, I need you to help out Standish this morning, refinishing those desks. He'll show you what to do. You can get back to your regular job this afternoon. And by the way, this is for everyone. Wednesday, half of you will be spending the day at Fort Ord for rifle practice; the other half will go the next day. Check the list to find out when you go. Now everyone—back to work."

"Hey, John, I see they sent you, like I asked 'em to do. Here, take this piece of sandpaper, and start sanding on that spot. I'll show you what to do from there."

As John bent over the table and started sanding, he suddenly jumped forward, as though struck by a lightening bolt.

"Jesus, Bill, what the hell was that? It felt like some kind of super vibrator."

"Oh, you mean this?" Bill answered, as he burst out laughing. "It's only my sander, John."

"Sander! What the hell you putting it on my ass for?"

"If you think that was something, here, feel this," as Bill quickly placed the sander on John's crotch and turned it on.

"Oh, shit! Take it away, I almost came in my pants."

"That's one way of getting off with the least effort," Bill said. "What do you think, John?"

"I think you better keep that damned thing to yourself. That's what I think. Now show me what to do, and no more fooling around, got it?"

"OK, I'll do the sanding, and you can do the staining. Now what's been happening lately? Haven't seen you around all week. Where you been?" Bill asked as he started sanding a nearby table."

"Believe it or not, we went to a party with Steve, you know, that sailor from the ship, and Paul from our base. I guess you heard of Ken Hallard, the movie star? Well, it was at his place. A real asshole, and gay as a goose. It's a long story, I'll tell you all about it on our way to Frisco this weekend. Oh, by the way, Steve and Paul are going along. That'll make six of us. Cozy, isn't it? We'll all chip in on the gas. Do you think someone can put us all up while we're there?"

"Sure, why not, like I told you, my cousin knows lots of guys there. Most of them are looking for something a little more than just guests, but I think they'll settle for good looks, if nothing more. By the way, you and David ready for Wednesday, for rifle practice, that is? I saw your names on the board. I go the same day. That's one way to be shooting off and not enjoying it. Sounds like fun, doesn't it?"

"Yeah, if you like snakes and scorpions out there in the boonies. Oh, another thing, We went to a Names Day party—something else to tell you about later, and yesterday we met two girls from Fort Ord. You're not going to believe this, but we actually went out together, to a bar in Pacific Grove. We really had a good time. They had the same thing going between them that we had between us."

"You mean they actually served you at this place?"

"Sure, both of them know the owner. We'll take you there sometime, if they say it's OK."

"Hey, we've been at this all morning. It's time for lunch, and if you don't need me anymore today, I still got my work to do."

"Fine with me. Guess we're about caught up anyway, so let's head out to eat. Wonder what's on the menu for today?"

"Ham, baked potatoes, peas, salad, and pie. Not bad," John answered.

After lunch, John hurried with his assignment saving Maria for last.

"Well now, John Earl English, I see you haven't forgotten me. Did you and David enjoy yourselves at my Names Day?"

"Sure, Maria. God, it was great! I never thought it would be so much fun, but it was. David said he'd drop by and tell you himself, how nice it really was. Boy, you sure made us feel like royalty, and you can consider us your sons anytime. I won't be by on Wednesday. David and I have rifle practice at Fort Ord. Friday, we're back to San Francisco with some of our buddies for the weekend, but it couldn't be as nice as it was with you and Niki, that's for sure."

"Perhaps you and David would like to come for dinner one day next week. You could both stay over if you'd like, and leave for work with us the next morning. We just got a television, so you might enjoy watching it."

"Sure, Maria, we'd love to come. Maybe you could fix some of that good Russian food, like we had at your party."

John finished sweeping the floor, and after emptying the baskets he bowed down low with a smile on his face, said "goodbye Princess," and headed back to the barracks, where he waited for David to arrive.

"I see you beat me here. Tomorrow's some sort of Awards Day, so we only have to work half-day. How 'bout you and me taking in a flick after we eat tonight?"

"Sure, David, a movie sounds fine. By the way, where'd you find out about this Awards Day thing?"

"It was posted on the board, and also the first sergeant reminded me to be there. Maybe we'll get an award for making out," David said with a big broad smile.

"Yeah, more than likely I'll get an award for cleaning latrines. This is one job I wouldn't tell people that I did," John said, as he returned the smile.

"By the way, I stopped by to thank Maria for everything, but you had already left for the day. She mentioned about staying over, and that's fine with me," David said, as the two of them prepared to leave for dinner.

"What's the movie tonight?" John asked.

"Would you believe Bataan? I remember seeing it during the war when I was a kid. I don't think they ever get anything new here. Well, better than nothing, I guess."

The following day John and David got an early start and managed to finish most of their work before noon. "They want us in dress uniform, so we better hurry and get ready. I gotta shave and shower before I get dressed, and you better do the same," David told John as they hurried off to lunch.

The ceremony started with the arrival of Col. Hendricks and his staff. After a brief speech a variety of awards were handed out. Niki got an award for organizing the Russian Department, while Maria got an award for the best secretary of the year. Finally, the Colonel remarked that it was a great honor to name the man who was chosen as "soldier of the year."

"As you know, the man who is chosen for this prestigious honor must be a man who is not only well liked by all, but also a man who is a willing and hard worker. He is a man who brings credit not only to himself, but to the US Army, and the nation as a whole. It is therefore my privilege to present this very special award to David Marconie, our 'soldier of the year.' Along with this award, he will also receive a four-day pass."

"God, David, you won. I can't think of anyone I'd rather see get it, and I think that goes for all of us," John said, as he congratulated David on winning.

The following day John and David had breakfast, then boarded the truck that took them to Fort Ord for rifle practice.

"David, I was right about this place. It looks like a desert, and it smells like gun smoke already," John remarked as they got off the truck and formed up in single file where they were greeted by a rather burly looking old sergeant.

"All right, men, get your ass in gear, and get yourself a rifle. I want you ready on the firing line in fifteen minutes. We don't have all day to waste, so get moving. Do I make myself clear?"

"Yes, sergeant," almost everyone answered, as they formed up on the line.

"Hey, David, remember that rifle pledge we learned back in Basic? 'This is my rifle, this is my gun. This is for killing (pointing to his rifle), and this is for fun (pointing to his fly).' Well, if we haven't learned how to use them both by now, we're in trouble," Bill, said as he burst out laughing.

"All right, men. It looks like everyone is ready. Now I don't want to see anyone pointing their weapon at anyone else. When you're not actually firing, I want those weapons pointing upwards, and toward the range. If I see anyone doing otherwise, I start kicking ass. Once again, do I make myself clear?"

"Yes, Sergeant," they all answered again.

"OK—up targets. Ready on the right? Ready on the left? Ready on the firing line? Get ready. Ready, aim, fire at will."

After everyone had finally finished taking their turn on the line, they were all reassembled to the rear of the range.

"All right, men, after we finish with this next task, we'll be finished for the day. I want everyone to fix bayonets. Each of you will be issued two clips of blanks. As you may or may not know, this range has more than its share of snakes, so that's why you're here now—to get rid of them. Now remember, they bite, so don't get too close. When you see one, stop a few feet away, place the muzzle of your rifle toward its head, and fire. If you need it, that's what the bayonet's for. Now I don't want to see or hear of anyone pointing his rifle at another soldier, or at his foot. The last time I was out here, some asshole blew off part of his boot, and a toe with it. He claimed he was shooting at a spider. Blanks aren't to be screwed with, they can maim, and they can kill. Just like you're going to kill those god-damned snakes. Do I make myself absolutely clear?"

"Yes, Sergeant," everyone yelled, actually anticipating the hunt.

"OK, spread out and good hunting."

As David proceeded a short distance he noticed a snake bathing itself on a sandy dune nearby. Carefully, he approached it, and as he heard the first rattle he took aim, and fired, blowing its head from its body. Here he was, "soldier of the year," killing snakes. What next, he thought.

Chapter 5

John and David arrived at the ship, just as Steve and Gary pulled up in the car.

"I guess Steve told you that there would be six of us, didn't he? Paul and Bill are coming along. It'll be a little crowded. Hope you don't mind. We'll all chip in on the gas."

"It'll be a little crowded up front, but hell no—no problem as far as I'm concerned. We'll be OK, just as long as everyone is ready to go when it's time to come back. We can't be waiting around for anyone, you know," Gary said just as Paul and Bill arrived. "Oh, yeah, hope everyone brought along civvies and an overnight bag. I think we can get everything in the trunk."

"Sounds fair to us," David replied. "How 'bout Steve and Paul up front with you. Bill can sit in the back with us, if that's OK with everyone else?"

"Sure, David, sounds fine with us. Now let's get started," Bill said, as he took his place in the car. "Oh, yeah, my cousin is going to meet us in Frisco when we get there. He gave me this number to call him when we arrive. He said it's no problem, he's got friends who will put us all up."

As Gary made his way to San Francisco, everyone laughed and told the latest jokes. John went into detail about the party in Carmel, meeting

Mary and Joan, and going to the bar. Steve wanted to know about rifle practice, so Paul told him all about it.

"Hey, Christmas is coming up next month. Where you guys planning to go?" Gary asked, as he continued on the way.

"Paul and I are going to LA," Steve answered, as he lit up a cigarette and handed it to Paul.

"David isn't sure yet, but he might be going to Detroit with me," John, added. "I had a good friend while I was in The Home. He got out about a month before I did. I wrote him a couple weeks ago and he said we could stay with him at his apartment. Harold says he's going to stay with one of his friends."

"Where you going, Gary?"

"I don't know, Bill. I'm not going back home, that's for sure. I was an orphan, you know. They treated me like shit in that place. My mother and father were killed in a crash when I was about five. Naw, no way, am I going back there again."

"How 'bout coming home with me, Gary. It would really be great having you along. I'd have someone to talk to and go out with. I don't have any brothers or sisters, and I know my ma and dad would be happy to have you stay over. We got lots of room. What do you say?" Bill asked, feeling a little embarrassed for asking.

"Gee, thanks, Bill. Sure—I'd be glad to take you up on your offer. It sure beats being here by myself."

About midway through the trip, Gary pulled over for a piss-stop and the six of them took turns in the latrine. It felt good to be able to stretch and move around.

"How about coffee and donuts, guys? And I'll get a dozen to go. I'm buying," Bill, said, as he took out his wallet and pulled out a five.

"Gee, thanks, Bill. I think this will help keep us awake, just so we don't have to piss again between now and the time we arrive. Coffee is almost as bad as beer when it comes to pissing. Anyway, I sure needed that donut. I was starving," Paul remarked.

After eating, Gary pulled over to the pump to refuel. Everyone helped pay for the gas, and they got on their way.

As Gary proceeded down the road, a fairly heavy rain appeared, making it impossible to continue any farther. A small clearing to the right made it safe to pull off the road.

"Shit, how long do you think we'll be holed up here?" Gary asked, as he brought the car to a stop. "Nothing much else we can do, so if you want to take a snooze, go right ahead. I think that's what I'm going to do. If anyone's still awake when this stuff clears, wake me up, OK?"

"Sure, Gary," Steve said, as he placed his head on Paul's shoulder and closed his eyes. The sound of the rain pouring on the roof felt comfortable and reassuring, as Steve enjoyed the security of the car, and that of Paul and his friends close by.

In about an hour the rain suddenly stopped, and after Gary was awakened, they were once again on their way.

"Looks like we'll be about an hour late," Bill said. "I guess Art will be wondering what happened to us. On the other hand, if I know my cousin, he's probably having so much fun he'll hardly know what time it is."

At last they pulled into Frisco. It was already dark, but the lights of the city looked as welcome as daylight, with their magnetic attraction to everything going on.

"What's say we park the car near the Greyhound.

We can all wait there until my cousin comes to get us. I better tell him we'll follow, as there's no way seven of us can fit in this car."

Gary found a spot not far from the station, and they all made their way to the restaurant inside. Bill headed for the phone after everyone placed their orders.

"Looks like we're living off these friggin' things," John commented as he bit into a jelly-filled donut and washed it down with a cup of coffee.

"Hey, guys. Guess what. One of Art's friends is having us all over for dinner tonight. Boy, that's great, isn't it. I'm so hungry, I could eat the ass out of a elephant right now," Bill said, as he scoffed down the roll he had ordered.

"If you want to bite into some ass, how 'bout trying this," Paul said jokingly as he patted himself on the butt.

"Naw, can't take you up on that, I'd be getting into Steve's territory, I think," Bill answered, giving a friendly slap to Paul's arm.

In less than a half-hour, Art arrived with one of his friends. "This is Cliff, I've known him forever. My other friend Brad is waiting outside in the car. You can introduce yourselves, guys."

"My God, where did you ever find so many gorgeous men, all at one time," Cliff exclaimed, as his eyes darted to each of the men in turn.

"You know my motto, don't you?" Art asked, as he put his arm around Bill's waist.

"Yeah, as I remember, it's 'fighting, flowers, and men.' We could sure do without the fighting this time," Bill said with a laugh.

"No, you're wrong, when I'm here in Frisco, it's 'find 'em, feel 'em, fuck 'em, and never forget 'em—especially when they're good.' Bill can ride with Brad, and I'll ride back with you guys, 'cause I know the way. Boy, will Brad be excited to have Bill sitting next to him on the way back. By the way, Bill, where'd you run into that good-looking soldier and these two cute sailors you brought along? I haven't seen them before."

"Oh, Steve and Gary are from the ship in Monterey, and Paul is stationed with us. He's Steve's friend. I think you know what I mean."

"Yeah, I know what you mean. Too bad though, as John and David are a pair, that doesn't leave much to go around. What about that Gary over there?"

"I don't know, I heard he went both ways. At least we think he does."

"Good. One thing's for sure, he won't be a cherry by the time he goes back. Now what's say we all shove off. Brad will be wondering what ever happened to us," Art, said, as he motioned the others to follow.

After leaving the station, Art introduced Bill to Brad, as he and Cliff got into the car.

"My God, Art, did you save this one just for me? I hope we don't get into an accident on the way. I can't keep my eyes off him," Brad remarked.

"Don't get your tits in an uproar. I might need that sweet little thing myself. We're kissing cousins, you know; besides, Brad's supposed to be sleeping with me," Art, said, as he left to get into the other car.

About twenty minutes later both cars pulled up to a house, which was located on a rather steep hill. Everyone got out and proceeded to enter. Inside were six other men, all in their early twenties, and all sitting around and drinking, as soft music played in the background. It was evident that everyone smoked.

"Come on in. Get yourselves a drink, and introduce yourselves. We've got plenty of food. It's buffet style, so whenever you're hungry, just help yourself. Everything's on the table. You'll find plenty of cigarettes in boxes on the coffee table. We'll talk about who's staying with whom, later on, after we all get acquainted," Brad said, as he poured himself a bourbon on the rocks.

"Boy, I'm staying here this weekend. Just look at all this food," Bill said, as he started to help himself to the ham. "How about you, Gary? You could share the room with me. Brad asked me to stay on the way over here, and he said he had enough room. My cousin said he'd share with Brad, and Cliff is staying somewhere else with one of those guys in the other room. One thing's for sure, we won't have to worry about cigarettes, booze, or food. This place has just about everything you could possibly need. What do you say, Gary? Do you want to stay here with me?"

"Sure, Bill, I wanted to stay with you the first time I saw you. Guess that settles that, so let's join the others. We got the whole night ahead of us once the party is over."

After they had eaten, Bill and Gary joined the others in the front room. By now two of the men were dancing to a record that Cliff had put on.

"I never danced with a guy before, but would you mind dancing with me, Gary? I wouldn't mind dancing with you, OK?"

"Sure, Bill, why not. I think I'm going to like this as much as you. Wait until we get to bed though, that's when we'll really be close. Come on now, let's give it a try. All you have to do is stay close to me, we don't have to move around much. Let's keep it slow and easy."

As the evening progressed, Steve and Paul found a place to stay, while John and David were invited to stay next door, with two of Brad's best friends.

"Hey, Steve, don't do anything we wouldn't do," David said, as Steve and Paul left out the door.

"Yeah, like there's something you haven't done already?" Steve answered back as he gave a wink and a smile, then headed down the street.

"See you in the morning, Bill and Gary. We'll be next door," John said. "So give us a call when you're up. We can all have breakfast together. By the way, this is Jim and Cal. We'll be staying with them."

"It's nice meeting you guys. I hear Steve and Paul are only a block away, so that should make it easy on everyone," Gary said, as he started to close the door and finish his drink.

"Come here, Bill. Let's start getting close right now. How about it?" Gary asked, as he pulled Bill's head to his, and gave him a long and passionate kiss on the lips.

"Goddamn, Gary, if it's going to be anything like this, I can hardly wait to get started."

"No, I want it to last all night. Let's start by having a drink together, in the living room—alone."

"Sure, Gary, but I'm so hot right now I think I'll explode."

"Let's try this once more" Gary, said, again kissing Bill, with even more passion than before. "Now we can go to bed."

As they started toward their room, Bill was already removing his shirt, and Gary was preparing to follow suit. His neckerchief came off first, then his jumper, and his shoes.

"Now you can help me with these buttons," Gary said, as he lay back on the bed, waiting for Bill to remove his pants.

"Get closer, Bill, that was only a warmup, in the other room."

"Jesus, Gary, you're about the hottest man I've ever met. It was worth the trip just to be with you," Bill remarked, as Gary held Bill's hands down next to his head, kissing him on the lips, the neck, and his chest.

The following morning Bill and Gary were still up when Art appeared at their door.

"OK, you lovebirds, up and at 'em. Let's get up and get dressed."

"Already? We haven't been to sleep yet," Gary said, as he rolled back over onto Bill.

"Well, if you're not up in five minutes, I'm climbing in between you."

"Oh, shit, Art, we're getting up, but make sure you have the coffee ready." After saying this, Gary got up, grabbed a towel, and made his way to the shower.

After returning to the room, Gary looked at Bill, and said, "If it weren't for your cousin, we'd start all over again. You better take your shower now while I'm cooling off."

After Gary and Bill finally arrived downstairs, John and David were already at the table having coffee with Art. Brad had just got off the phone.

"Paul and Steve should be over in about an hour. They just got out of bed. After they get here, we're off to 'The Big Banana' for brunch."

"Why did they name it 'The big Banana?'" David asked, as he poured another coffee.

"If you ever saw the owner, you'd know why, and I don't mean with his clothes on," Art said, as he started to smile.

"Hey, Bill, how'd you and Gary get along last night? You both look like hell this morning," David asked, as he switched his attention to them.

"I don't know. All right, I guess," Bill answered. We slept all night. Too much booze, I think."

"Yeah, too much of something, and I bet I know what it was. Your cousin said you were at it all night. Sounds like you're having a good time."

"You got that right, David, but I don't think you and John been wasting any time either—when it comes to fooling around, that is. Excuse me while I go in the front room a minute, I ran out of cigarettes last night. If

I remember right, they had a couple boxes of them on the coffee table," Bill said, as he started out of the room.

About twenty minutes passed before Steve and Paul finally arrived with the guys they were staying with, as well as Jim and Cal from next door.

"OK—everybody ready? We can walk there from here. It's a little chilly this morning but it's not that far, and it would take three cars if we were to ride. Anyway, the fresh air and exercise might do us good. So let's get started," Brad said as he motioned everyone outside.

"What you got planned for today, Brad?" Gary asked as they continued their walk down the street.

"After brunch, we'll take the bus to Market Street where we'll catch a streetcar to China Town. After we finish there, we catch another bus to the cable cars, and then to Fisherman's Wharf. We'll have something to eat there. When we get back home, we'll freshen up a little, and you guys can change into civvies. We're going to a great little bar, where they won't check your age, or steal your man, for that matter. Since there are twelve of us going, we'll take three cars. We'll finish off at my place for cocktails. Should be a busy day, but a lot of fun. By the time we finish for the day, you guys should be too pooped to do anything else—on the other hand, maybe you won't be."

"Boy, you sure got this planned out good. We're sure glad you're a friend of Art's," John said, as they finally arrived at 'The Big Banana' for brunch.

"My god, Brad, what did you do, raid a ship and the army camp? Looks like you took the cream of the crop. Hi, guys, I'm Amo, the owner. Enjoy the brunch and if there's anything you need, just let me know. I'd be happy to be of service—or service you. Take your choice."

"Now you've seen him. That's the one with the big banana. Nothing to look at, but he sure has something to compensate for looks," Brad said, as he helped himself to the coffee.

"Brunch is on me, so whenever you're ready just head on out to the tables and help yourself," Art said as he got up to get a plate.

"Wow, I've never seen so many different things to eat in my life, at least not for breakfast," Bill said, as he started to pile up his plate. I bet you could fill up on salad alone. What I really need is the roast beef and ham to build up my energy for tonight. I might try eating a little of everything they got."

"If it's anything like last night, you'll need all the energy you can get," Art said, with a laugh. After everyone had eaten as much as they could, he paid the bill, and they were on their way.

"Oh, man, I think I ate too much," Steve complained, as he climbed aboard the bus. "Maybe when we get to China Town we can walk around a bit to wear off all this food. I think we'd be better off with something lighter tomorrow. What do you think, Paul?"

"Yeah, I go along with you, Steve. I'm really not one for heavy meals, but I guess it don't hurt now and then."

"What do you make of those two guys in the back row, David? They've been staring at us since we got aboard. Don't know why, but somehow I just don't trust them. Wonder what they're up to," John, said, as he tried to avoid their eyes."

"From the look of the haircuts, the clothes and their shoes, I'd bet they're Marines, looking to cause some shit. Wait a minute, I thought they looked familiar. That's two of the guys we kicked the hell out of back at 'Madam's Place,' in San Jose. That's why they've been watching us so close. They sure don't want to tangle with us again. You can bet your ass on that."

"You're right, David, it's them alright. Bet they can't wait until we get off the bus," John said, as he began to laugh. "And I doubt if they've been back to that club since then. I wonder what ever happened to the one Miss Lemons tore apart. I thought she'd never stop kicking him in the balls. Maybe he's still in the hospital."

"OK, guys, this is where we get off," Brad said, as the bus came to a stop.

There was no doubt about it, this had to be China Town. It was almost like another world. All around were big bright signs with Chinese characters, painted dragons, colorful lanterns, pagodas, and pointed roofs to ward off evil spirits.

"OK, guys, there's too many of us to stick together, so it's everyone for themselves. There's so much to see and do. Now let's all meet back here by three," Brad, said, as he checked his watch for the time.

As they broke up into pairs, John and David headed for a nearby shop that specialized in oriental gifts. Bamboo fans, chopsticks, painted umbrellas, paper flowers, and a thousand other things intrigued and entertained them. After spending ten to fifteen minutes there, they went next door, where all sorts of foods were sold that are not found in Western stores. Hanging from ropes in the front window were smoked chickens, sausages, and other meats. Large barrels were stocked with cookies, dried mushrooms, seaweed, and many other things uncommon to Western eyes.

"Look, David,—almond cookies. Think I'll get a bag to give to Maria when we get back to the base. And these are for you," John said, as he purchased another bag for David.

As they proceeded down the street, they entered what looked like some sort of temple. To the far end was a statue of Buddha, the largest statue they had ever seen. Several people were lighting sticks of incense and sticking them into large pots of sand; perhaps as prayers, or just good luck. Nearby was a man, said to be a monk, who for a small donation read your fortune, which was spoken in a few short words.

"You go first," David said, "and see what he has to say for you."

John sat down on a small seat in front of the man and, as requested, he held out his hands.

The monk looked troubled as he said, "Together, you are closely bound, but soon you shall mourn the other."

"What'd he tell you, John?" David asked, as he too took a seat in front of the monk.

"Nothing, David, except that we're close to each other, and I don't know what he meant by the rest."

As he held out his hands, the monk now looked deep into David's eyes and said, "As love now binds you both together, so shall you always be remembered."

"The guy is strange to say the least," David commented, as he and John left the shop. "I wonder if he guessed about us. You'd think he would say something like 'you're coming into money' or something like that. Not 'As love now binds you both together, so shall you always be remembered.' Sounds like I'm getting transferred, or something worse."

"Don't worry about it, David. It can't be bad. After all, we lit one of those incense sticks for luck—remember?"

"Hey, let's stop over there, John. I bet you never seen so much brass in all your life."

This was one of the largest shops around. Row upon row of candlestick holders of every size and shape. Huge temple dogs set upon large brass stands and they seemed to watch your every move. Chimes and bells, spirit houses, teacups and pots, cricket boxes, Buddhas, and other gods were but a few of the many brass things to be seen.

On a shelf nearby stood a statue of Hoy Tin, small enough to carry in your pocket for good luck.

As they were leaving the store, John stopped briefly at the counter to pay for something he had planned to buy.

"Here, David, I want you to keep this with you, all the time. They say if you rub his belly, he'll bring you good luck. It's that Hoy Tin statue we saw on the shelf."

"Gee, thanks, John, I could always use good luck.

One thing's for sure, I was lucky when I ran into you. Let's hope our luck holds out—forever. How 'bout me treating you this time," David said, as he put his arm over John's shoulders and pointed to a teahouse nearby.

"Sure, David, I'm not really hungry, but that sounds good to me. Let's go."

In the hallway was a bamboo curtain that you passed through to enter. Paper lanterns, phoenix birds, and dragons added warmth and color to the room, and on every wall hung lacquered plaques with scenes in mother of pearl.

"We'll have won ton soup, a fortune cookie, and tea. We just ate not long ago, and we're not too hungry," David said, after placing his order with the waiter. "Maybe I'll have a better fortune with this cookie than I got with that monk."

"We better start watching the time. Remember, we have to be back where we started by three. This must be a pretty big place. I haven't seen the other guys since we left 'em back there by that store with all the dragons. Wonder if the Fisherman's Wharf is anything like the one in Monterey? I heard it's a lot bigger," John said, as the waiter brought the soup, the tea, and fortune cookies.

"Here's to us, David. Let's hope nothing ever happens to either of us, and that we stay together forever."

After this toast, John added, "That's the only bad thing about this army life. You can never really plan together, and you never really know where they'll send you next. Wherever it is, I hope they send me with you. I'd be lost without you, David, and if you went somewhere without me I think it would tear me apart."

"I know I'm not really good at words, John, but I feel the same about you as you do about me. Come on now, we're getting too sentimental. How about breaking open the fortune cookies and see what we got?"

"Sure, David. Listen to this," John said, as he removed the fortune and began to read it. "'A sudden move is in your future.' That's bound to happen, but let's hope it's not soon. What's yours say, David?"

"'You shall soon be going on a long journey from whence you won't return.' Jesus, that sounds as bad as the fortune I got from that monk. I better start rubbing that Hoy Tin's belly right now."

After a few more cups of tea, John and David made their way back to meet the others.

"Well, how'd you like it?" Art asked. "Lots to see, wasn't there? Hope you guys didn't buy all kinds of stuff you didn't need. I usually do when

I'm down here. I bought a really nice bowl that I'll use as a planter. If I get tired of it, I can always sell it at the thrift shop for a profit. We're all here, so let's get started on our way."

A short time later, they were there. There was no doubt about it, the Fisherman's Wharf here was much larger than in Monterey. On either side of the entrance, huge barrels of water were boiling, and men with long dippers hauled out lobsters and crabs freshly cooked and ready to eat. Many restaurants, bars, and clubs offered tables for those who chose to drink and eat outside.

"Boy, this place is great, and a lot bigger than I thought," Steve commented, as he and Paul made their way along with the others. "I think we went in about every shop in China Town. How'd you guys like it there, Gary?"

"Yeah, we liked it. We liked it a lot. Think we'll come back, next time we're here."

"OK, guys," Art said. "Since the sun is out and its warmed up quite a bit, here's some tables over here, and everyone should be hungry by now. My friends and I chipped in, and we're treating you guys. If it's all right with everyone, the Super Combination is really great. I've had it before. You get just about something of everything. All you'll have to order is your drinks. Anyway, it'll make ordering a lot easier."

"Sure, why not," everyone agreed. Shortly after, a waiter arrived, took the orders, and returned to the kitchen for the salads and drinks.

"Hey, tell 'em about those screwy fortunes you guys got, David," Paul asked.

"Other than I'm supposed to be going on a long trip and I won't be back, there's not much to say. Actually, I don't want to think about it anymore. Anyone want to rub my belly," David asked with a smile, as he pulled out his statue of Hoy Tin.

"Sure, I'll go first," Brad said, as he placed his hand on David's abdomen, pushed his fingers under his shirt, and started massaging his belly.

"You got the wrong belly," David said as he pulled Brad's hand away and began to tuck in his shirt. "What are you trying to do, turn me on?"

"What are we doing tomorrow?" Steve asked, as he lit up a cigarette and leaned back in his chair.

"First off, it's breakfast at Bert's—a small cafe nearby; then the wax museum, and later a picnic at Golden Gate Park. After that we'll head back home. When we get back, we'll rest up a bit, and spend the rest of the evening at Jim and Cal's. That should make for a nice full day. By the way, don't forget, no uniform when we head out for the bar, OK?"

"Man, would you believe this?" David, said, as he pointed out the various things on the plate the waiter had just brought him. "Look, John, it's got shrimp, scallops, mussels, clams, crab, lobster, fries, and slaw. It's more than I can eat, that's for sure."

"I told you you'd like it, now eat up everyone and we'll head back after this. You'll have plenty of time to rest before we hit the bar tonight."

"You're right about that, Art. This combination thing is great. Now we'll need all the rest we can get after eating so much food," Steve said, as he moved his left hand under the table and placed it on Paul's leg.

For the next half-hour, everyone laughed a lot, told jokes, and talked about everything they could think of.

"OK, guys, time to head back," Brad said, as he paid the bill and got up to leave the table.

Later that evening, everyone headed for the bar as planned. "Hey, Gary, those Levi's are about as tight as that uniform that you wear. You must really be trying to turn 'em on tonight. Wish it were for me, but I guess that would be getting into my cousin's territory. Hell, I'm even losing out on him since you came along." Art said, as he put his hand around Gary's waist.

"Here it is, the place I been telling you about," Brad said as they all went inside. "We can grab those tables over there before they're all gone."

After they all sat down, a waiter arrived and asked what they wanted to drink. After placing their orders, everyone sat back and looked around.

"Boy, I don't see many men here, do you, Steve?" Paul, said, as he waited to be served.

"Now you know what I meant when I said, 'They won't steal your man.' Guess you can figure out why by now. But if you can't—this is a woman's bar. Want you to meet Big Red, she's a good friend of ours," Brad said, as he picked up the drink the waiter had just brought him. "She's coming in right now."

"Hi, baby," Big Red said, as she went around giving everyone a hug. "Too bad I'm not straight, you've got some good-looking men here tonight. What you trying to do, change this into a man's bar? Have you met Kitty before? She's my latest, since I left Monique."

"My God, Red, you've had more women than any straight guy I ever knew. Sit down and have a drink with us. What's on the agenda for tonight?" Cliff, asked as he made room for Red to sit down.

"Have you ever seen drag in reverse? You know, women as men, instead of men as women. They're just the opposite from the men. They tape down their chests and stuff their pants. Now how's that for a good kick in the ass?" Red, said, as she ordered whiskey straight and beer as a chaser.

As the evening progressed, Red introduced woman after woman to the group. They all seemed friendly, and were a lot of fun. Finally it was time for the show.

"Ladies, if there are any present, and I think I see what looks like men— you never know these days—our first guest is Mr. Percy Pecker. Let's all give her a big hand," the announcer said as she finished her introduction.

This act was followed by Tennessee Twat, Mr. Harry Bush, Sylvester Snatch, Timothy Tits, and finally Christopher Cunts, the comedian.

John was laughing so hard that tears streamed down his face as he took in the show. "What do you think, David? This show was just as good as the one at Madam's Place. I'm glad they brought us here. Didn't think I'd like it when we first came in, but it sure is great, isn't it?"

After the show, they said goodbye to Red and all her friends, and made their way to Jim and Cal's, to finish off the evening. Steve and Paul went to their room for something they said they needed to do, and that was the last anyone saw of them for the night. Gary and Bill left early, probably for the same reason the others had left. John and David soon followed suit.

The following morning they met at Brad's, and leaving in three cars, they headed to the cafe for breakfast.

"Where are we going from here?" Steve, asked.

"First, we're doing the wax museum. Next, coming back home to pick up our lunch, and then heading for Golden Gate Park. We'll spend the rest of the evening at my place, like we did on Friday night. After breakfast tomorrow, I guess you'll be heading back to the base. Hope you guys are enjoying yourselves as much as we enjoy having you here."

"Sure, Brad, you've been really great, and we're enjoying every minute of it, especially the time I'm getting to spend with Steve," Paul said, as he winked at Steve, and smiled.

Following breakfast, it was off to the wax museum to spend an hour or so.

"Boy, it looks like she could jump right out at you," John said, as he pointed to the figure of Saint Joan. "And I sure in hell wouldn't like to run into him on a foggy night," referring to Jack the Ripper, with his victim lying dead at his feet.

"Yeah, I've never seen anything quite like this before. It'd scare the hell out of you, if you ever got locked in here at night," David commented, as he continued to work his way from one wax figure to the other.

"This place would be one hell of a lot more interesting if they had figures of you guys in the nude, but since they don't I guess that's about all there is to see. Let's head back to the cars," Art said, as he started toward the door.

After returning home, picking up the lunch and driving to the park, everyone made themselves comfortable at a couple tables that they pulled together. It was an unusually warm day for late November.

"Don't look for anything homemade, you guys. It's going to be one of those deli specials and wine. I think that's the best way to picnic. No work, and you throw away everything when you leave," Brad said, as he started pulling things out of a bag and placing them on the table.

"Boy, was this a great idea. I haven't been on a picnic since I was a kid," Bill, said. "How 'bout you Gary?"

"You're not going to believe this, but this is my first one. It's sort of nice eating out here in the park. Wait a minute, I take that back. A bird just shit on my plate," he said, as he burst out laughing.

The next hour or so was taken up with good conversation, six bottles of wine, and all of the food. After everyone finished eating, they broke up in pairs, and went for a stroll through the park.

Later that evening, everyone gathered for the final fling. Brad prepared hors d'oeuvres and lots of drinks. By the time the evening was over, everyone was more than ready to turn in for the night.

David was almost asleep by the time he climbed into bed, and John soon followed him in. It was the end of a perfect weekend, with perfect hosts, perfect lovers, and perfect friends. They definitely would be back.

Chapter 6

Time seemed to pass by so quickly and it was now early December.

David and John had just finished dinner and were heading into town. The streetlights were draped with garlands and the store windows were decorated for the season.

"Isn't that great, David. They approved our furloughs. Hard to believe that it's just three more weeks to Christmas. I guess without the cold and snow it doesn't quite seem like it, does it?"

"No, not like Detroit. Think I like it a lot better here. But I still want to go with you. You sure your friend can still put us up?"

"Sure, David—why not? He said he would. Anyway, we'll get by one way or the other. You know, I haven't been back since I joined up. I bet Mr. Alan will be glad to see me. He's the one that sends me something once in a while. And of course Miss Tingsley writes every so often."

"All I got is an aunt and I sure in the hell don't want to stay with her. She's the reason I ended up in The Home. And that's why I joined the Army. I'm glad I did, or I wouldn't have met you. If we weren't going on furlough together, I guess I just wouldn't be going," John said, as he put his arm around David's shoulders, gently rubbing the back of David's neck.

"You know you're my best and closest friend. Don't you, David? It's hard to even imagine going on furlough without you. Anyway, I can hardly wait. Wait until Mr. Alan, the counselors and all those kids see me—both of us, that is, in uniform. I bet that'll be something," John said. "By the way, my friend's name is Barry Drexel. He's really a great guy. He was one of my best friends in The Home. From what he writes me, I'm sure he's gay. He's got a roommate, you know. His name is Bob. You're going to like Barry. I know you will. And from what Barry tells me about Bob, I think we'll both like him just as well. I told Barry all about you in a letter I wrote not long ago. He said he can't wait to meet you. Hey, how 'bout you and I stopping at the church tonight. Haven't seen Mario in quite some time now."

"Sounds good to me, John. Bet the church is really decorated to the hilt—sure, why not? I'd like to see it."

John and David made their way to the church and were greeted by Mario at the front entrance.

"Haven't seen you young men for a while. How you been? Come on in. How about a glass of wine with me to celebrate the season?"

"Sure, Mario. We'd love to. I bet you been working hard getting ready for Christmas," John said, as he and David entered the church.

"Boy, is it beautiful. If you did all this by yourself you sure been working hard," David commented as he looked around.

"Steve and Paul have helped a lot. They did all the climbing and high-up work. I sure hope they don't get transferred anywhere soon. I'd be lost without them," Mario said as he led the way to the apartment at the rear of the church.

"Yeah, I know what you mean. We'd be lost without them too. They're our buddies, you know," John said, as he accepted a glass of wine that Mario had just poured.

"What are you two boys doing for Christmas? You're welcome to share it with me if you want. We should have plenty to share."

"Thanks, Mario, but David and I are going to Detroit for the holidays. We got two weeks furlough coming. We'll be leaving December forth."

"Detroit, is it? Which one of you lives in Detroit? You don't both live there, do you, and where will you be staying when you get there?" Mario asked.

"I'm from Detroit and David moved there before he joined up. Neither one of us has family so we'll be staying with a friend," John answered.

"Why, I think that's just great and I'm sure you'll both have a really good time together. Guess there's lots to see in Detroit since it's so much bigger than Monterey."

"Thanks, Mario," David said. "One thing's for sure, if there's a good time to be had, we plan on finding it."

After a couple more drinks and an hour or so of conversation, John said, "Well, guess we'll be heading out. Got a few more stops to make before the night's over. If we don't get back before we leave, Merry Christmas and have a really great New Year," as John and David started for the door.

"Merry Christmas, John, and to you too, David. And may the New Year, and all the years ahead be good to both of you. Thanks for stopping by. You know you're always welcome here."

David and John made their way out of the church and over to the ship to visit Steve and the others.

"Hey, Gary, is Steve still here, or is he out with Paul?" John asked, as both he and David came aboard the ship.

"It must be your lucky day," Gary answered. "Steve is still on board. He's waiting for Paul to arrive before he takes off on liberty. That's another Navy word you just learned. Liberty is the same thing as an Army pass. Hey, take a look at this. Dale found this really wild bush and we decorated it for Christmas. Quite a Christmas tree, isn't it?"

"Yeah, I can't say I've ever seen anything quite like that before. If I were you I wouldn't be lighting up a cigarette too close to it. Looks pretty dried out to me," David said, as he stood a good distance away and removed two cigarettes from his pack, lighting one for himself and one for John.

"What you guys doing for the holidays, Gary? I'm gonna be staying with John at his friend's place in Detroit. Sure wish you guys could join us, but I don't think John's friend would have room for all of us."

"Steve and Paul plan to spend the holidays with Mario," Gary answered. "Sure sounds boring to me, but who am I to say? One good thing will come of it, they get to stay at the apartment in the church alone at night, as Mario has to be with his family except for the church services on Christmas Eve and Christmas Day. As for me, I plan to head up to Frisco and just make out where I can."

After spending an hour or so talking with Gary and Steve, Paul arrived and the five of them headed into town just to walk around and take in the sights.

"How 'bout coffee and donuts? It's on me," Gary said, as they neared Yorky's.

"Sure, why not. We don't get paid until we go on furlough, and that's a week away. You sailors sure are lucky, you get paid every two weeks and we have to wait a whole month between paydays," David said, as he started into Yorky's, which was empty except for a soldier from Fort Ord.

"We're sure going to miss you two when you take off for Detroit," Steve said. "It's gonna seem a little lonely without you guys around. Paul couldn't get a furlough—that's why I'm staying behind to be with him. I hear Bill Standish is going to stay with his cousin in San Jose. From what he says, he plans on really having a great time. By the way, there was about ten guys from Fort Ord last night singing 'Deck your balls with bowls of honey,' 'I came upon a midnight lay,' 'Oh horny night' and a few other Christmas carols that they made up new words to. They all seemed drunk to me, and as they got louder and louder, it wasn't too long before the MP's loaded them up on a truck and took them back to the fort. I gotta admit that they sure livened things up a bit."

"Pick out a couple donuts and coffee, guys. We'll sit back there in the booth so we can talk. By the way, I think I'll ask that soldier over there to join us. He's not bad looking and he looks a little lonely. I think I got just what it takes to cheer him up," Gary said, as he motioned the corporal over to join them.

The soldier got up from his table and came over to their booth. "Where do you want me to sit? Looks like it might be a little crowded with six of us."

"You can sit next to me," Gary answered. "These booths are big enough to seat three on each side so long as they aren't fat like someone we know. Sit down and join us."

After everyone moved over a bit and the corporal took his place next to Gary, Gary could feel a slight nervous movement in the soldier's leg as it was pressed close to Gary's.

"What's your name, soldier?" Gary asked as he pressed his leg a little closer to see what kind of reaction he would get from him.

"My name's Don. How about you guys?"

"That's Steve, that's Paul, this is John and David, and I'm Gary."

Don had a slightly rounded face, sandy brown hair, blue eyes, and medium build, was about five foot ten inches tall and all in all was quite handsome and appeared a little shy.

"Where you from, Don?" Gary asked.

"Believe it or not, I live not far from here. My father owns a motel just outside of town. If you want to stay overnight free of charge, we got lots of vacancies and it would be no problem for me to get two extra rooms if you all wanna stay," Don said, as he pressed his leg even closer to Gary's.

"Hell, yes, I'm game, and I'm sure I can speak for the rest of us. Got anything to drink?" Gary asked.

"Sure have. That is if you guys like wine. I also got a fifth of whiskey for anyone not into wine. Whatcha say we finish up here and head out to the motel, as it's already getting a little late?" Don suggested.

"No problem, I'm ready and the others are ready too. If you don't mind, Steve and Paul can share one room, John and David the other, and if you want I'll share with you. Of course, we could all start out in your room as you got the drinks. OK with you, Don?"

"Fine with me," Don answered. "If it's OK with you guys. By the way, I got a car, so we can drive there."

When they arrived at the motel, Don went into the office and came back with keys to two rooms. He already had a key to his own room. "Come on in, guys. This is as close to home as I can get for the time being."

Don's room had a couple chairs and two twin beds, along with a sofa bed.

"Have a seat, guys. A couple of you can use the chairs and the rest of us can sit on the bed. I'll start us out on wine and when that runs out we can open the whiskey, if that's OK with everyone?" With this said, Don opened the first of three bottles of a German white wine, which he poured into six glasses and then handed everyone a drink. "How about a toast to our good health and to everything that we want?"

"I'll drink to that, especially that part about getting everything we want," Gary said, as he took his first drink and sort of propped himself up on the bed next to Don.

After the wine was gone along with a couple shots of whiskey, Steve and Paul as well as John and David decided to leave for their rooms. It was Friday evening so they wouldn't have to be up early in the morning.

After everyone had left, Gary removed his uniform, stripped off his underwear, and lay back on the bed. Don quickly followed and it was quite obvious that Gary wouldn't be disappointed this night.

"Mind if we have a couple shots of whiskey just to loosen us up a bit?" Don asked, as he appeared a little nervous seeing the both of them naked on the bed.

"No, I don't mind, but for my part I don't want anything more to drink," Gary said. "I wanna know what I'm doing. OK?"

"Sure Gary. I feel the same. That is about knowing what I'm doing. I only need just enough to relax me a bit.

"After Don finished drinking a shot of whiskey," Gary turned toward Don and asked, "You good at wrestling? I hear the Greeks did it in the nude. Wanna give it a try?"

"Sure, why not, but somehow I get the feeling you'll win. You look a hell of a lot stronger than me. Sure, why not. I'll try anything once, and I never tried that before."

"OK Don, we'll do it like the Greeks did, now let's give it a try." With this said, Gary grabbed both of Don's arms and rolling over on top of him quickly pinned him to the bed. Gary was right—he wouldn't be disappointed and neither would Don.

Early the next morning everyone was up around eight, and after getting dressed they walked next door to the small restaurant attached to the motel to have breakfast.

"My treat," Don said. "That is, if everyone orders the breakfast special. Saturday and Sunday are our busy nights so I doubt that I can get the two extra rooms again, but if you wanna stay over with me for the next two days, you're welcome, Gary. If you other guys don't mind being a little cramped, my room has twin beds and the sofa makes into a bed."

"Thanks Don," Gary answered, "think I'll take you up on that. If it's anything like last night you're damned right I'll stay over. Whatcha say, guys. You wanna join us?"

"Sure, why not," Steve answered. "it beats staying on the ship and sleeping by myself. How about you, John and David, you game for staying over?"

"Sounds a little too crowded for us, and John and I are more into privacy. Guess we'll stay the night on the base, but thanks for the offer," David answered. "How 'bout John and me getting together with you guys in the morning after we have breakfast on the base? We'll meet you at Yorky's—say around nine, if it's OK with you?"

"Sure, David, we'll meet you at nine then and we'll make our plans from there, OK? I'll drive the both of you back to the Presidio. You other guys make yourself comfortable while I'm gone. I'll be back shortly and I'll stop and get a couple bottles of wine on the way back," Don said as he prepared to leave.

It wasn't long before Don arrived back at the motel with two more bottles of that good German wine.

"It's far too early to start drinking now so what's say we just bum around a bit and return back here later tonight, OK?"

"Sounds good to us. Maybe we'll have lunch and dinner at the Presidio. That way it won't cost us anything," Paul said as they prepared to leave Don's room.

"My father owns the restaurant here and he's away until Monday so all four of us can eat here free. If that's OK with you, we can do the Presidio tomorrow," Don said as they headed toward the car.

"Sure, sounds really great," Steve remarked, "and I'm sure that goes for the rest of us."

The remainder of the day involved riding around and visiting some of the sights that Don thought might be of interest to everyone.

By the time they returned to the motel it was around eight p.m. and everyone was getting into the party mood.

After pouring four glasses of wine Don proposed a toast by saying, "OK, guys, let's drink to good friends and good times."

"I'll drink to that," Gary said as he raised his glass along with the others.

After they finished the wine, they polished off what remained of the whiskey from the day before. By this time everyone was quite drunk and ready for bed.

"Hey guys, I got an idea, how 'bout us changing partners for the night?' Gary suggested. "I'll sleep with Paul, and Steve can sleep with Don. So whatcha say we give it a try? One thing's for sure, it's nothing serious and only for tonight."

"I'll give it a try if it's OK with Paul," Steve answered.

"If it's OK with you Steve, it's OK with me just as long as we don't make a habit of it," Paul said as he started to undress. "I guess these twin beds are big enough for the two of us."

"It was big enough for Don and me last night," Gary remarked as he got undressed along with the others.

"One thing's for sure, John and David are a little too close to go along with anything like this. Maybe it's a good thing they went back to the base. By the way, let's keep this to ourselves, OK?" Paul said, as he got into bed with Gary, whom he always secretly wanted to be with just once. He was glad things turned out the way they did.

The following morning couldn't have been better. The sun was out and it was really great weather. "After we have breakfast we better go into town and pick up John and David, then we can just drive around for a while," Don suggested. "Paul said we could have lunch at the Presidio then we could decide where to go from there."

"Great, it's settled then, let's drive around Carmel and see what's going on. Anyone have some other ideas?" Don asked.

"Sounds OK to me," Steve answered. "What about you guys, can you think of anything else?"

"No, not at the moment, so what's say we order breakfast and take it from there?" Paul answered.

After breakfast everyone headed to Yorky's where John and David were already waiting.

"Hey, guys, how'd things go last night. One thing's for sure, we sure had one hell of a hangover this morning," John added, as he and David sat drinking their coffee and each eating a donut.

"Not bad. We ran around for a while, saw a few places and when we got back to the motel, we polished off two bottles of wine and the rest of the whiskey," Steve answered. "We were too drunk for anything but sleep, and I think we all fell asleep the moment we hit the sack. How we ever managed to get up by eight, I'll never know."

"How about a drive to Carmel, guys, and by the time we get back it will be time for lunch. You did say we could all eat at the Presidio, didn't you?" Gary asked.

"Sure, no problem. This won't be the first time someone brought a guest, and you are in the service," Paul answered.

After driving around Carmel for an hour or so, everyone got out of the car and just watched the seagulls as they flew around the ocean below them.

"Boy, wouldn't it be great having a place right about here overlooking the ocean," Steve asked, as he put his arm around Paul's waist.

As John and David walked a little distance away from the others, Steve and Paul walked in the opposite direction. After a while Steve whispered to Paul that he had something to say.

"OK, Steve, what's on your mind?" Paul asked.

"Let's never do that again," Steve answered. "I mean what we did last night. You know how I feel about you, and I don't want you with anyone else."

"I feel the same about you, Steve, and I promise it won't happen again. It's you and me and no one else. Now let's just forget about it and have a good time for the rest of the weekend, OK?"

"Sure, Paul, I just wanted you to know how I felt about it, and now that you've answered my question I won't bring it up again. Here come John and David, so let's talk about something else."

"Hey, John, what you and David got going for today? Are you two planning on staying on the base again tonight?" Paul asked.

"Guess so. David and I planned on going to church this morning but didn't make it, and we're supposed to meet Harold and the others for coffee about two. After that I guess we just plan on walking around town to see what Harold and the others are doing for the holidays, then we'll probably head back to the Presidio for dinner. Maybe we'll rest up a bit and talk over our plans for vacation. We'll be leaving on Friday, you know."

"Well, Don invited us to stay another night," Paul said, "but we both have to be up early in the morning for duty, so we'll have to cancel out. Guess we'll spend the rest of the day together before we head back to the base. After all that drinking last night we need time to pull ourselves together and get a few things straightened out. After lunch we'll probably stop by the church, visit Mario a while, and stay in the church apartment to get rested up. Anyway, Mario leaves the church to spend the rest of the day with his family around two. We have a key, so we can lock up when we leave."

"We're getting hungry, how about you guys? So what's say we head up to the Presidio for lunch," Paul suggested, as he made his way toward the car.

"You guys staying over again tonight?" Don asked.

"Thanks anyway, Don, but I think we'll be staying at the base and Steve's staying aboard ship. We got to rest up after the last two nights and we also have things to do tomorrow—like getting up early for duty. Thanks again, but in the meantime let's head for the Presidio. It's time for lunch. You don't mind if us guys call it quits for the rest of the day after eating, do you?"

"Hell, no, in fact I think I could use a rest myself," Don said, as they made their way to the Presidio.

After lunch Don drove Steve and Paul to the church and dropped Gary off at the ship, while the others remained on base.

"Well, now, John Earl English, where have you been this weekend?" Maria asked the moment John came into the office to clean the room.

"Oh, David and I just ran around with some of our buddies. Actually, we didn't really do much. Walked around town a lot and made it to Carmel for a while. Can't do too much when you can't afford it, you know. Guess I told you that David and I are going to Detroit on December 4th and coming back on the 14th, so we can be here with our friends for Christmas."

"How are you going to Detroit? Do you plan on the bus or the train?" Maria asked. "I'm sure you don't plan on hitchhiking there."

"Nope, neither one of those. David and I plan to go to the Air Force base and hitch a ride on any plane going in our direction. I was talking with some of the guys on base and they told me it's really fairly easy to hitch a ride if they have the space—that is unless someone of higher rank bumps you. The Air Force base isn't really that far away from here, anyway. We're going to give it a try. It will sure save us quite a bit of money and give us more time to spend in Detroit."

"One thing you can count on, John Earl English, and that is that Niki and myself will be praying every day for your safe journey, a wonderful vacation, and your safe return. By the way, Niki has a friend stationed at that Air Force base in San Francisco who I'm sure can arrange the flight for you. His name's General Martin Cannon. He might even be able to arrange a flight back to California as the general has a friend at Selfridge Air Force base near Detroit. Just promise me that you'll never tell anyone else about this except your friend David."

"Wow! Thanks a million, Maria, and I promise you we'll never breathe a word to anyone else—ever, and that's a promise on my honor as a man and a soldier."

"Thank you, John, I knew I could trust in you the first day I met you and I'm sure your friend David is just as nice as you."

At last it was time to begin the furlough. Both David and John had packed the day before. They planned to take the bus to Fort Ord and from there to hitchhike to San Francisco, where they would apply for the first flight heading to Detroit.

It wasn't long before they were picked up by a guy wearing an Air Force uniform, and as luck would have it he was going directly to their destination. They couldn't have asked for better luck. John couldn't help but believe that Maria's prayers were the reason for their good fortune.

"Hey, my name's Larson, what's yours?"

"I'm John and this is my best buddy David."

"By the way, do any of you guys smoke?" Larson asked. "If you do, I could sure use one right now."

"Sure, and keep the pack—that's the least we can do for the ride," David answered.

Larson was one of those guys who just kept on talking, which helped to pass the time. Probably a good thing, as John and David really didn't have too much to say.

On arriving at the air base, John gave Larson five bucks to go toward the gas. From the main gate they were given directions by an MP as where to go. The base bus came by about 15 minutes later and it wasn't long before they entered the building and signed the logbook for persons wanting flights to specific destinations.

After a short wait an airman called off their names: "David Marconi and John Earl English. Hey it seems like the two of you got friends in high places. We got orders to place you on flight priority. By the way, if you don't mind waiting a couple hours we do have a flight going to Selfridge Air Base and that's as close as we can get you to your destination. It's going to be a little crowded as we're carrying cargo, but there's room for about six passengers. You'll be wearing parachutes, by the way, but someone will help you with them. You'll also be getting box lunches, which really aren't so bad. In the meantime there's coffee over there and you can walk around if you want. Just stay clear of the runways and be sure to be back here on time. Oh, yeah, if you have to use the latrine you better do so before you board the plane."

Finally, John and David were safely aboard without being bumped from the flight. One of the airmen instructed them on how to wear the parachute and what to do in case it became necessary to bail out. Not long after this the plane taxied to the runway, and after a brief wait they were on their way.

"Wow! Can you believe this, David? This is the first time I have ever been on a plane and I'm not even scared. How about you, David?"

"Yeah, it's the first time for me too and I really like it. You know that stuff about bailing out? That doesn't even scare me. They said we'd be landing somewhere to refuel but we shouldn't be delayed too long. Boy, this sure beats all the other ways of traveling, doesn't it?"

"Sure does, David, and we have to thank Maria and Niki for arranging it for us."

Two of the passengers were officers and the other two enlisted men, but it wasn't long before everyone started talking in a more or less relaxed and friendly manner. This sure helped to pass the time and made the trip seem a lot shorter than it actually was.

"OK, men, we're going in. Fasten your seat belts, no smoking, and we hope you enjoyed the trip."

After the plane landed and came to a stop, John and David made their way from the plane into the terminal where they hitched a ride into Mount Clemens to catch a bus bound for Detroit.

"Boy, you sure can't beat this, can you, David? We were in Monterey this morning and here we are in Mount Clemens the same day. Guess we had better check into a hotel for the night and take a bus into Detroit in the morning. How's that sound to you, David?"

"Fine with me. I sure could use some sleep right about now."

After checking into the Barley Hotel, John and David each took a shower and went to bed. It wasn't long before both were sound asleep.

Early the next morning John was up first, and after brushing his teeth, shaving and getting dressed, he awoke David, who was next to use the bathroom.

"What's say we have breakfast and head on to Detroit?" John suggested. "Maybe we could even hitchhike there, and save bus fare."

"OK with me. Two good-looking guys in uniform shouldn't have any trouble hitching a ride. What do you think, John?"

"I think you're right about that, David. Someone's bound to pick us up even if it's just for the company."

John and David made their way to the main highway where they caught a ride in less than a half-hour.

"You wouldn't be going to Detroit, would you?" David asked the man and his wife.

"Yes, matter of fact we are. My name's Arnie, and this is my wife, Bess. Do the both of you live in Detroit?"

"Well, sort of," John answered. I lived in a children's home, and this is my friend David. He was also an orphan but lived in a different home. By the way, my name's John. Anyway, we're going to visit some of the people back at The Home I was in and we're staying with one of my best friends from The Home, but he has an apartment now." We're stationed in Monterey, California."

"You plan on staying over for Christmas?" Bess asked.

"No, actually we plan on being back by the fourteenth, so Christmas we'll be back in California with our buddies there."

"You boys hungry?" Arnie asked. We plan to stop shortly for lunch and we'd like to have you as our guests."

"Gee, thanks, Arnie. That would really be great," David answered.

After lunch John and David continued on their way to Detroit, and after finally arriving Arnie dropped them off directly in front of The Home.

"You two are really some swell people, and before we leave we want to thank you and wish you both a really merry Christmas and a very happy New Year."

"The same to both of you, and have a great vacation and a wonderful Christmas and New Year when you return back to California," Arnie said before driving off.

As they left the car it had already begun to snow and the snow itself reminded both John and David of part of the reason that they had returned there.

"Well, David, this is the place I lived in since I was seven and up until I joined the Army," John said as they entered the door and made their way into the lobby.

No sooner had they entered the lobby than Mr. Alan came out of his office to greet them, as he had seen them coming up the stairs from his office window.

"Well, well, well, didn't you turn out to be a handsome young man and you certainly look splendid in that uniform. And this must be your best friend David whom you have written about so many times. Why he's as handsome as you are, John, and I think the Army should be proud to have you wearing their uniform. Miss Tingsley has been on pins and needles waiting for your arrival. As you can see, the children are in the dining room having lunch, so let's go in. I want all of them to see the both of you."

On entering the dining room Miss Tingsley immediately got up from the table and gave John a big hug and a kiss.

"How about me?" David asked. "Don't I get a hug and a kiss too? After all, I'm John's very best friend. By the way, my name's David."

"Sure, David. It's almost like I know you from John's letters. Sure, let me give you a hug and a kiss also just for being such a wonderful friend to John."

"Now children, and also you young men and women sitting over there, I want you to meet John, who many of you already know, and also his best friend, David. If you've never seen a real soldier before, you're looking at two of the Army's very best and we're really proud to have them pay us a visit."

After touring the home and meeting almost everyone, John and David made a call from the lobby to Barry and Bob. "Hi, Barry, it's me, John, and I got my friend David with me, we're at The Home right now. Do you think you could pick us up?"

"Hell, yes, we can," Barry answered. "It's only Saturday. How in the hell did you two get here so soon?"

"We were lucky. We hopped a military flight to Selfridge air base and hitched a ride to The Home," John answered.

"We'll be there in twenty minutes, so how about you guys standing outside as there's nowhere to park in front of the building."

It wasn't long before Barry and Bob pulled up in the Ford that they had recently purchased.

"Come on, guys, hop in. It's not the newest car you've ever seen but it runs like a top. By the way, that friend of yours is even better looking than you described in your letters. He looks more like a movie star. By the way, I'm Barry and this is Bob. We bought a small pine and it's all decorated so that we can celebrate Christmas together. I hope it's OK with the two of you, but we only have two bedrooms with single beds, so you two won't mind sleeping together, will you?"

"Hell, no, in fact we prefer it. That is, David and I are pretty close if you haven't already guessed from my letters," John answered.

"And I guess you already know that Bob and I are also real close. I won't beat around the bush. We're gay."

"So are we," John said with some hesitation, as the word "gay" seemed to somehow reflect upon his masculinity.

"Anyway, now that that's settled, it sure in the hell should make things a lot more comfortable for all of us," David said, as he moved closer to John and put his arm around John's shoulders.

"Are you two lovers?" Bob asked.

"I don't know if I'd use those words," David answered. "But let's say we're as close as any two men could ever get with each other. I'd put my life on the line for John, and I know he'd do the same for me. I feel that I'm part of him and that he's part of me. Does that answer your question? If you don't mind, I think that we would rather you not use the word 'lovers' but instead refer to us as 'very best friends' when you introduce us to your friends and others. Is that OK with you?"

"Sure, David, that's not a problem for us. We call each other best friends lots of times, especially when we're not among other gays and even sometimes when we are."

After a short ride they arrived at the apartment.

"Well, what do you think?" Barry asked.

"I think it's really beautiful. If I didn't know better I'd think it was already Christmas," John said as he looked at the tree and all the decorations.

"Well, anyway, this is our home, now let me show you around," Bob said as he started with the kitchen and the dining room. "Now, of course, here are the most important rooms in the place—the bedrooms. We weren't planning on the two of you arriving so soon, so we won't be celebrating our early Christmas until Friday night. We invited a lot of our friends over, and will they be surprised when they see what really great-looking guys you really are. Don't be surprised if everyone in the place doesn't try to put the make on you. I promise I won't say you're 'lovers, but I will let them know that you are together and not available. That'll at least be enough said for them to keep their hands off the two of you. If one or two should slip up, just be polite and say no because the two of you are together, OK?"

"To make things easier on everyone, you don't need to say anything," David answered. "Actually we'd be flattered by the attention. They can touch all they want so long as it's not on the one area that belongs to us alone, and you know where that is. You don't have to worry—when the party's over it's going to be John and me and no one else. We're here for a good time with good friends and that's the way we want it to be. We're both grown, and we know how to say no when we need to. Now whatcha got planned for tonight?"

"How about me calling Ben and Joe for dinner?" Barry asked. "They live just down the hall. You'll really like them, I know you will. They're older guys in their late fifties but they got more life in them than men half their age. They'll be coming to the party on Friday but this way they get a sneak preview. I know they're home because they said they didn't plan on going out tonight because they were expecting a friend later on that they just recently met. They already agreed that while we were at work they would be happy to take you around the city and show you the sights. They're both retired and they can't wait to meet you."

Barry defrosted some pork chops he had in the freezer, made stuffing, green beans, baked potatoes and a salad. Rice pudding with rose oil left over from yesterday would be dessert. Ben and Joe were delighted with the invitation and arrived promptly on time.

"Holy mother of God, you never told us that these friends of yours were so beautiful—I mean handsome. Looking at them is dessert enough even without the meal," Ben said, as he walked over and gave both John and David a big hug and a kiss on the cheek, which was immediately followed by Joe doing the same.

After dinner Ben and Joe returned to their apartment so as not to miss their new friend who was to arrive by seven. The remainder of the evening was spent listening to radio as Barry and Bob had not yet purchased a TV. Soon it was time for bed, and after John and David showered they said good night, closed their bedroom door, and spent their first night together at the apartment.

The following morning was Sunday and both John and David were awakened to the smell of fresh-brewed coffee.

"Get up, wash up, and get dressed, you sleepy heads. After we have coffee and a cigarette we're taking the two of you out for breakfast," Barry said, as he started pulling the sheets away from John and David.

"OK, OK. We're getting up. Give us about twenty minutes and we'll join you for coffee, and going out for breakfast sounds great," John said as he got out of bed and headed into the bathroom. David was also up and getting dressed while he waited for John to wash up and shave.

A little over twenty minutes passed and finally John and David entered the kitchen, poured themselves a cup of coffee, and joined Bob and Barry for a cigarette.

"Boy, it didn't take the two of you very long to get ready. You must get a lot of practice in the Army," Barry commented, as he lit up his second cigarette and poured another cup of coffee. "We know a really great little restaurant not far from here called the 'Oven.' They have a breakfast special that can't be beat. What's say we head out as soon as you two finish with your coffee. It's close enough to walk and the exercise should do us good. Ben and Joe are going to join us so I'd better let them know we're ready to leave. I'll go down the hall and let them know we're ready."

Just as Barry, said, the breakfast was really something special. After they finished eating they all headed back to the apartment for an hour or so before heading out to Belle Isle, then from there they'd go to visit a long time friend of Ben and Joe.

"Hi, I'm Jess and this is Drew. We've heard a lot about the two of you and from what we can see, it's all true. Anyway, you're going to stay for lunch and later on we plan on about six more of our friends to join us for dinner. Hope you don't have other plans."

"Thanks, Jess," John answered, "No, we have no plans at all that we're aware of, and thanks for the invitation. Boy, this is sure one big house, and you sure know how to decorate."

Around six PM the guests started to arrive. Much to the amazement of John and David, most of the guests were in their early twenties or thirties while Jess and Drew were well into their sixties. As the evening wore on both John and David drank far more wine than they had planned to and although they had a really good time, they had to leave around ten to get back to the apartment and get some sleep.

It was certainly true, Ben and Joe had more energy than you could possibly imagine. John and David were taken from one place to another, met many more of Ben and Joe's friends, were constantly being treated to lunch and sometimes dinner. By the time Bob and Barry returned home from work, John and David were happy to spend the evenings just resting up before going to bed.

Finally the day of the big event arrived. It was now Friday, and as the guests entered the apartment they brought with them a dish to share. By the time everyone had placed their dish on the table, there was so much food that no matter how much you ate, there would be plenty left over. John and David couldn't get over the number of guests who arrived. There must have been about fifty or so—mostly young but there were ten to fifteen in Ben and Joe's age bracket.

John and David had made a special effort to look their best, dressed in their Army uniform. Needless to say, they received far more attention than their hosts, or anyone else for that matter. The party went on until shortly after one, at which time the last guest left and John and David almost collapsed on their bed to sleep off the overindulgence in food and drink. It was a really wonderful party with wonderful friends and guests.

Finally, it was time to leave and Bob and Barry drove John and David to the air base where they planned to hop a ride back to San Francisco. This time they waited almost four hours before they were able to board a plane back to Frisco. Once again the plane was carrying cargo, but this time it was some sort of huge machine which was fastened to the center of the plane. It sure looked heavy and John and David wondered if the plane would even get off the ground. As before, each of the passengers was issued a parachute and instructed in its use.

As the propellers spun faster and faster, the plane started to shake as it readied for takeoff. Finally the plane was racing down the runway and nearing the end, it pulled up and into the air with not a moment to spare.

About four hours into the flight the plane encountered heavy turbulence as it entered into a terrific storm. Lightning was striking everywhere and as John looked out the window he noted a large hole in the wing.

"What's that?" John asked one of the men sitting next to him.

"Probably an air vent," the man answered.

"An air vent, hell, it's so damned cold right now my feet are freezing," John said, as he lit a cigarette in an effort to relax

After a couple more hours of continued bad weather, someone appeared from the cockpit and handed a written message to be passed on to all the passengers. The message read: "We have had our left landing light torn from the wing. Conditions are such that you are advised to prepare to bail out when given the order."

Actually the thought of parachuting sounded a little exciting to both John and David, but the uncertainty of just where you would land along with the possibility of being struck by lightening was enough for everyone on board to pray for a safe landing.

At last the storm seemed to subside and the plane landed on an airfield in Texas. On debarking the plane, there was a gentle warm rain as they headed to the terminal to arrange another flight. After a short stay in Texas, they would hop a flight into San Francisco and from there they would take a bus back to Monterey. This vacation certainly provided plenty of interesting things to talk about with their friends after returning to the Presidio.

Chapter 7

"Hey, John, you got a call from some girl named Mary. She gave me this number and wants you to call her if you get a chance. Said it was important."

"Gee thanks, Sarg. She's a friend of mine. I'll call her right away." John then made his way to the day room where there was a public phone.

"Hi, Mary. What's happening? It sounded important."

"I can't talk about it right now. Can you meet Joan and me for coffee—say around six-thirty tonight?"

"Sure Mary. You mean at Yorky's, don't you?"

"Yes, I just couldn't say it over the phone."

"No problem. Mind if David comes along?"

"No, not at all. Sure, bring David. In fact, I think it's a good idea. I really can't say any more right now. We'll meet you there."

"Don't worry, we'll be there right on time." Finishing the conversation, John hung up, wondering all the while what was happening, and why this call was so important. I'll tell David at dinner tonight, he thought, as he made his way back to work.

"Hi, David, I got the strangest call today—from Mary, hope she's OK. Sounded important. Hope she wasn't in some sort of accident or something. At any rate she wants to meet us at Yorky's at six-thirty tonight. Wonder what it's all about."

"Guess you'll find out when we get there. Now how'd your day go, John?"

"Not bad. I spent about a half-hour with Maria. I save her office for last. Don't forget we're supposed to spend the night at her place this week. She suggested Friday. That way we wouldn't have to get up early for work the next day. Sound OK with you, David?"

"Sure, John. Now, when you're finished eating, let's head on down to town. We don't want to be late."

"Hi, Mary. We just ate on base, but I suppose we have room for a donut and coffee. By the way, where's Joan. She sick or something?"

"I really don't want to talk about it here; so after coffee we'll go for a walk and I'll tell you all about it, OK? By the way, how was your trip to San Francisco?"

"Great. We can hardly wait to go back. By the way, we went to a women's bar where they had women dressed up like men. They called the place The Club. Ever been there?" David said, in an effort to make conversation.

"No, can't say I have. Joan and I have been in Frisco two or three times, and it seems you guys know more about these places than we do," Mary said, as she finished sipping from her cup.

"Well, it looks like we're all finished with our coffee, so how about us heading out toward the wharf," Mary said, as she got up from her chair.

After everyone had left Yorky's and were headed on their way, Mary seemed rather nervous as she fumbled for words.

"We just had a visit from the CID. They kept us for questioning for about four hours, saying they had proof that we were lesbians. You haven't heard anything, have you?"

"Jesus, Mary. I've heard about this sort of thing, but this is the first time I ever knew it to be true. No, we've not heard a thing. Maybe because we're on another base is why we never heard about it."

"Well, all I can say is, it was hell. Joan got so upset she almost got sick. We thought it best not to be seen out together. That's why she's not here tonight. You know, I really can't understand how they would have gotten our names. We really don't know any women on base—lesbians, that is. Maybe it's because we hang out together. Hell, I really don't know. Joan thinks it's because she doesn't look feminine enough."

John looked shocked and a little puzzled as he commented on what Mary had to say.

"Jesus, Mary. Neither one of you really looks the part they're trying to lay on you. I still can't believe it's happening. Do you think some guy turned you in because he couldn't get any?"

"Oh, it's happening all right, but I doubt a man turned us in. Sure, we turned down enough of them. It was just after we had breakfast when we were told to go to Building 249 and report to Sgt. Spotley. For the life of me, I never in my wildest dreams would have thought it would be something like this. Anyway, when we got there we were told that these were the offices of the CID. It still didn't ring a bell. I heard the CID mentioned once or twice, but mostly I associated it with those old war movies."

"Yeah, I know what you mean," David said. "Just like you, I thought all that CID stuff was something in the movies. Sort of like that spy stuff, you know."

"When I first found out it was the CID, I thought they had picked us to be assigned there. You know, like maybe we were recommended. At any rate, they had Joan go into one room, while I went into another.

"After a while this woman comes in, dressed in civilian clothes. She seemed really pleasant enough. Trim and rather nice-looking. I noticed she had a wedding band on. Strange how I would notice that. Anyway, the best I can describe it is that it went something like this:

"My name's Jennifer. Jennifer Spotley. You can call me Jennifer if you want. How you doing? I guess you're wondering why you were called here. I don't want you to be nervous, but why do you think we called you and your friend down here?"

"I couldn't begin to know why. Were we recommended for a transfer or something?"

"No, Mary. You don't mind if I call you Mary, do you?"

"No—if you want. But if it's not for a transfer, what is it?"

"To be quite frank, and putting everything on the table—you and your friend Joan have been accused of having lesbian relationships."

"Lesbian relationships? Who in the hell would make such an accusation. Where's the proof? Jesus, I can't believe you're saying this. It's like a bad dream."

"No, Mary, it's not a bad dream. It's the truth. I can't tell you how we obtained our information. The fact is, we did and we're going to find out everything. Everything, do you hear? We want names, names, names. And if you have any names of homosexual men, we want them also."

Sgt. Spotley suddenly changed from pleasant to a more hostile behavior. The look on her face became hard and intense as she continued.

"You know, Mary, when you joined the Army you understood perfectly well that there was no place here for homosexual men or women. You might recall that part of your physical that asked you if you had homosexual tendencies? I'm sure you checked that you didn't. Most homosexuals don't admit it—or do you prefer to be called a lesbian?"

"No. I don't admit to anything. I still want to know who brought this charge against me. I have a right to know. Isn't there something in the Constitution that says I have a right to face my accuser?"

"Come on now, Mary. This is the Army. You're not a civilian now. Once you get that straight we can get back to where we started. We know you're a lesbian. We know your friend's a lesbian and we know that you and your friend have a lot that you will eventually tell us."

"Like I said, this went on for about four hours. Joan was too upset to tell me everything but she did say that she told them nothing. I still can't believe this is happening. We both have only two months to go, and were planning to re-enlist. Now, if we get through this somehow, there's no way in hell that either of us would even think of another term," Mary said, as she wiped a tear from her eye.

John put his arm around Mary's shoulders and David took one of her hands in an effort to comfort her. Somehow they both felt a closeness to her that they had not felt before.

"Everything's going to be all right now, Mary. You'll see," John said, as he tried to reassure her. "We'll think of something. There has to be a way to help—to get you out of this mess. One thing's for certain, you and Joan have to keep cool. Say absolutely nothing that can incriminate either of you, or anyone else for that matter. Promise me?"

"Sure, John. I promise. That is, we promise."

"OK. Now let's stop by and have something at the Wharf. We're almost there. Somehow you got to get your mind off this, even for a little while. Tomorrow you and Joan meet us at Martin's on the Wharf at six-thirty. It's best we don't meet at the same place every time. On the other hand, it might look like we're going together, and that can't be too bad. After we meet tomorrow, we'll head out to Pacific Grove. You know, The Golden Goose, that really great bar you took us to awhile back."

"Sure, John, that's a great idea. I think Joan and I both need to go somewhere where we feel relaxed. I guess comfortable is a better word."

"Do you mind if we bring Steve and Paul along?" David asked. "Steve's got the car, you know. You can be sure they wouldn't say anything. In fact, with all of us putting our heads together, we've got to come up with something, or some way, to get you out of this mess. Let's see now, tomorrow's Tuesday. We could meet any day except Friday. David and I are staying overnight at Maria and Niki's place on Friday. They're civilian friends from the Presidio. I'll tell you all about 'em later."

"Let's make it tomorrow then. I don't think I could stand waiting any longer, and Joan needs to get away really bad. We'll probably take off somewhere Friday ourselves—maybe Frisco. Let's see now, just to be certain, we're meeting at Martin's on the Wharf, right?"

"Sure, Mary," John answered, as he gave her a big hug and a gentle kiss on the cheek. "You can count on us, we'll be there—all of us."

The remainder of the evening involved idle conversation in an effort to avoid any further discussion of the matter. After having coffee, Mary headed back to Fort Ord, and John and David back to the Presidio.

As they walked up the hill John put his arm around David's shoulder.

"Do you think this is going to turn out for the better, David? I mean, I don't see how we can help, although I know we have to."

"I don't want you to start worrying now, John. It'll work out OK in the end—it always does. You'll see," David said, in an effort to reassure John that everything would be all right.

"As soon as we get back to the base we had better put in a call to Steve just to be sure he doesn't have the duty tomorrow. If he does, we might have to take a taxi to Pacific Grove."

"Hi, Steve, this is John. You free tomorrow evening?"

"Sure, John, I don't have the duty until Thursday night and the weekend. What's on your mind—you got something planned?"

"Yeah, Steve. Remember that really super bar we went to with those two gals, Mary and Joan? You know, The Golden Goose in Pacific Grove. How'd you like to go back there again? You can bring Paul. That'll make six of us—like before."

"Tell me where and when and I'll meet you there," Steve answered.

"Meet us at Martin's on the Wharf at six-thirty, Steve."

"No problem, I'll be there. How about you guys getting hold of Paul for me."

As planned, everyone arrived at Martin's on time, and after having iced tea together they proceeded to Pacific Grove. On the way John briefly went over the reason for this meeting. Joan seemed rather nervous and it was quite obvious that she was embarrassed at having this rather intimate secret unfolded in front of everyone.

"Here we are, back again," Mary remarked after they arrived at the Golden Goose. "How you doing, Larry? You mind if we sit over there? It's the same spot we had before."

"Go ahead, and what can I bring you? To drink, that is."

"If beer is OK with everyone, how about starting out with a couple pitchers," Mary said, as she looked around for approval.

"Sure, Mary, beer is fine. Guess I can speak for the rest of us," John remarked.

After everyone was poured a beer, John offered a toast.

"Here's to Mary and Joan in hopes that everything turns out all right."

Everyone lifted their glasses and after also toasting to everyone's health and well-being, Mary started going into the events of that day as it related to Joan and her:

"It was 5 a.m. when we were awakened by one of the office staff and told to report to Building 249. I sure could have used a cup of coffee but we were told we had 20 minutes to be dressed and get over there. Once we got there, we were again placed in separate rooms. This time it was a man and a woman who interviewed me. Both wore civilian clothes. I never saw either one of them before. The woman was very quiet and somewhat comforting. The man, on the other hand was loud and hostile.

"I see you finally made it over here. What took you so long." And without waiting for an answer, he continued: "You know this isn't a social visit. I don't have time to waste on a couple goddamned dykes, so you better start talking."

"I have nothing more to say that I haven't already said," I answered.

"What the hell do you mean by, what you said before. You haven't said a goddammed thing before. You know what I'm going to do for you, Dyke? I'm going to send a letter to both your parents and let them know the kind of disgusting shit you been up to. When I get done with that I'm going to recommend a court-martial for both of you. I bet you end up with 10 to 15 years at least. Now start talking, goddamn it, and we might go easy on you. How many other Homos do you know? I want the names of every one of your dyke friends along with the men queers you know."

"I want a lawyer," I remarked. "I have a right to legal representation and I want it not only for myself, but for my friend Joan as well."

At this point the woman interceded.

"Certainly, you do have a right to legal counsel and I'll arrange it. I guess my partner here has been a little rough on you, hasn't he? Let me get you a cup of coffee and I'll arrange for both of you to go have breakfast. I bet you're getting hungry. I am too, for that matter."

At this point the woman escorted me to another room where Joan had been going through much the same treatment as me. These people were something else. They could turn on the charm and just as quickly turn on you—like a snake," Mary said, as she cautiously looked around to see if anyone was listening. Fortunately, the only other people in the room were two guys sitting at the bar well out of hearing range.

"After we had breakfast we casually walked back to continue with interrogation I think all those insults and threats somehow made us stronger. By the time we arrived back we had made up our minds that no matter what they did to us we'd never admit to anything. Like before, I was taken to a room separate from that of Joan. This time there was a fat little man who introduced himself as Mr. Supple."

"I'm contracted by this agency to do lie detector tests. I'm sure you have nothing to hide so you shouldn't mind taking the test. It doesn't hurt at all. I just connect a few wires to you, and you'll be asked some questions. Your answers will be monitored and interpreted. I just want you to sign this consent form and we'll get started."

"I'm sorry to disappoint you, sir, but I have to refuse. I'm not doing anything without legal advice from an attorney."

"With this said, the man took his equipment and left the room, presumably to try and get Joan to consent. I knew she wouldn't, as we had discussed this possibility beforehand.

"Do you mind if we don't talk about this anymore for the next hour or so. I gotta relax and get my mind off it?" Joan asked.

"I can sure understand why you don't want to think about it, Joan. I think it would drive me nuts going through something like that," Steve said, as he refilled everyone's glass. "How about you playing a few songs, Mary? Like the last time. Remember what a good time we had? Go on over there with David, and sing us a couple songs, OK?"

"Sure, Steve, I'd like that. Come on, David, we'll sing the first couple songs together. Guess the first song will have to be for Larry. You know, 'Bye, Bye, Black Bird,'" Mary said, as she took David's hand and started to lead him over to the piano.

"Thanks, Mary, I'm sending over a pitcher on me. You sure know how to get to a man's heart by playing that song," Larry said, as he made his way from the bar to the piano. "Why don't you kids stop by tomorrow? It's the boss's birthday. We're having a band, plenty of food, beer, and wine on the house. You won't beat the price anywhere else, you can be sure of that."

"Gee, thanks, Larry. I wouldn't miss it for anything. How about you guys?" Mary said as she continued playing.

"Sure, Mary," Steve answered. "You can count on us. Not every day we get an offer like that. Now how about you playing that song that David sang for John the last time we were here?"

As Mary continued to play, Larry headed back to the bar to wait on a couple more customers who had just taken their place at the bar. One guy put some money in the jukebox, so Mary finished playing and returned to the table.

"Well, that was a nice break. It sure got my mind off my troubles for a while," Joan said, as she started filling everyone's glasses. "You know, I was thinking. As much as we like you guys—you're like brothers to us—I wonder if it's a good idea if we continue seeing each other after tomorrow. I mean, if somehow you guys were to get involved because of us I don't know what I'd do, and I know that goes for Joan as well."

"Look Mary, let's get one thing straight here and now. We're not deserting you, and I think you'd do the same for us if we were in that situation. Now what we gotta do is start thinking of how we can help you get out of this mess," John said, as he put his arm around her shoulder and gave her a hug. "Anyone with an idea?"

"Yeah, I got an idea," David said. "Now don't anyone laugh. I've been thinking about it for a while now, so here goes. Mary and Joan rent two motel rooms down at the Prairie Motel. Either John or me will make a call to one of those CID people and tell them we heard the two of you would be checking in with two other lesbians and if they wanted to catch you in the act, all they had to do is show up. When they get there, what they'll really find is Mary in bed with John, and me in bed with Joan. Now what do you think of that?"

Everyone burst out laughing, after which Mary remarked, "I think that's the wildest thing I ever heard of. I love you for it, but I think it's too dangerous for you guys."

"I think it's a great idea," John said, as he fought to keep from laughing again. "One thing's for sure, if they think you're doing it with a man it would be hard to prove something else—you know, that lesbian charge. That settles it, if we all agree to this plan, raise your glass."

After a brief hesitation, Joan and Mary lifted their glasses in agreement and the plan was sealed.

"Anyone else with an idea?" John asked, as he continued to chuckle.

"Yeah, I got an idea," Steve offered. You know my shipmate Gary is bi—that is, he goes either way. Well, if I can get him to go along with it, I could have him put the make on one of those officer broads at the CID. Yeah, you got it, blackmail—to get her to have the charges dropped. Don't laugh now. Stop and think about it. You know how cute Gary is, and how tight he wears his uniform. If she's straight, he can make her. You can count on that. By the way, mind if we bring Gary along tomorrow? He's a really great guy and lots of fun."

"Sure, Steve. Bring him along. You guys are really great, but I think we had better leave that plan involving Gary as a last resort," Mary said, as she went over and gave Steve a really big hug. "You know, Joan and I were so damned nervous and upset we almost didn't want to go out tonight, but thank God we did. Between good company, great ideas, and good beer I think I feel almost as good as I did the last time we were here. Look, that guy is leaving that kept feeding the jukebox. Now maybe I can play a few more songs, David can sing a few, and we'll just live it up for the rest of the night. Another toast: Here's to four of the greatest guys any girl could possibly have as friends."

"Jesus, Steve, that had to be you that just pinched me on the ass. I know damned well it wasn't Mary. But what the hell, I liked it," Paul said, as he reached over to Steve and returned the favor.

John couldn't help but laugh, as Steve looked so innocent. But innocent he wasn't, for he sure knew what he wanted and didn't stop until he got it.

The jukebox started playing again. "Good music for dancing, you want to dance?" John said, as he took Mary by the hand.

"Sure, John, I'd love to, although I think if we were in the right surroundings, David would have made a better partner than me. In the meantime, how about dancing with Joan, David? If we're going to go to bed with you guys, we might as well start by dancing together. Get ready, Steve, you and Paul are next. Dancing with us, that is."

The next couple hours passed quickly as everyone continued to drink, laugh, dance, and just enjoy each other's company. Tomorrow would be another torturous day for Mary and Joan, although both of them would be better prepared than they had been before. The relaxation of the evening had been a blessing.

It was pouring rain the following morning and, like the day before, Mary and Joan were awakened early and told to report to Building 249. On the way over, both Mary and Joan seemed much more relaxed and far less fearful of what lay ahead of them.

"Remember, Joan," Mary reminded her, "admit to absolutely nothing. They can threaten all they want, but they have no proof whatsoever. They'll even resort to lies but remember, no matter what, admit to nothing."

"You can count on me, Mary, that much I promise. I think the harder they come down on me, the stronger I get."

After they arrived, Mary and Joan were separated once again and the interrogation was renewed.

"Well, Mary, I see you managed to make it through the rain all right, but I guess you dykes were always stronger than the average woman. Now you know who I am," the man said, as he continued without waiting for an answer.

A chill ran down Mary's spine when she realized she was alone with this man. Where was the woman? At least she'd felt more comfortable when she was present.

"You fuckin' dykes make me sick. What you really need is a good man to lay you down and put a fuck to you. You know, I wouldn't mind watching two women making out sometime. I bet you really know how to eat pussy good. Don't you?"

"How'd you ever get this job? And what makes you think you can talk to me this way? I want a lawyer. Get that woman in here or I'll scream," Mary yelled.

"Listen, you queer, lesbian, dyke bitch; you can scream your fuckin' head off and I'll deny everything. We all know how you queer mother-fuckers lie. You lie about everything. Now you open your fat fuckin' mouth and I'll make sure you don't see the light of day for one hell of a long time.

"Do you know a broad by the name of Angie Jacobson? Sure you do. She's another one of your lesbo buddies, isn't she?"

"Yes, I know her. She's in my outfit but I never knew anything about her personal life. We know each other only through work."

"Come on now, she claims you been eating her pussy for a long time now. Do you know Sandra Savor? She's another one of your dyke friends.

Isn't she goddamn it? Don't just sit there acting like you don't know what the fuck I'm talking about. You know goddamned well what I'm talking about. It's about you fuckin' dykes.

Both of these broads gave me your name and also your lover's name. You wonder how we find out? Well, this is one way. We get names. Now all you have to do is admit what you are; and if you give us a few names, we'll let you off easy. How's a General Discharge sound to you? That sure in hell beats a dishonorable—now doesn't it?"

"I can only tell you again. I don't know these people and they don't know me, except that we're stationed together. That's it now, I'm not answering another question until I see my legal representative. Is that clear?"

"Here's a piece of paper and a pen. You don't need to say another word, just write down everything you know about your gay and lesbian relationships along with names and outfits. Now that shouldn't be too hard, should it?"

With this said the man who never introduced himself left the room and didn't return. It was about a half-hour later that the woman from yesterday came into the room.

"Hi, Mary. Can I get you a cup of coffee? You look a little wet. It sure is nasty out, isn't it?"

"Please, ma'am, don't let that man back here again. You'll never believe how bad he talked to me. Can you give me his name?"

"I'm sorry, dear. I can't. I can't give you his name, that is. The only thing I can tell you is that I didn't hear anything out of place, and I'll have to say that I've been in this room all the time. I'm coming up for promotion soon and I can't jeopardize that now, can I?"

"If you can't tell me his name, maybe you can tell me when I'll be seeing a lawyer. Now, when will I see one?"

"Well, Mary, we were hoping that you might consider signing some papers waiving your right to an attorney."

"What do you mean by waive my right to an attorney? I'm not going to do that."

"Well, Mary, it's like this. You sign the paper and make your confession and it means no court-martial. No prison term. A General Discharge and you're out. I don't know why you don't just make it easy on yourself."

"I told you once, and I'll tell you again. You have no proof of your accusations and that's the only confession you'll be getting out of me today, tomorrow, and any other day."

"OK, Mary, have it your way, but I've got something to tell you that I really didn't want to say. I was rather hoping that you'd come clean with me and it wouldn't be necessary, but what your friend Joan told her interviewer doesn't match what you're telling me."

"What do you mean, doesn't match? Tell me what you mean by that."

"I guess what I mean, Mary, is that your friend says the two of you are lesbians and have been having a lesbian affair for some time now."

"You're lying. Joan would never say that. If you think I could fall for a lie like that, you're crazy."

"OK, Mary, I think that about wraps it up for now.

So how about you and your friend knocking off for breakfast. We might be seeing you later, so be available. Is that clear?"

Mary was escorted down the hall and into a room where Joan sat with one hand covering her eyes.

"Let's go, Joan," Mary said, as she patted her friend on the back in an effort to comfort her.

As they headed to the mess hall, each told the other what had transpired.

"Jesus, Mary, just like you, they told me you had made a confession about me. I can see now, they'll go to any length to get what they want. They're almost as bad as the Nazis. You can believe one thing though, I never said a word. If they said I did, they're full of shit."

"I knew you didn't say anything. If nothing else comes out of all this, it sure in the hell has made us stronger. If they call us back this afternoon, I think I'm about ready for anything, and I guess that goes for the both of us. What do you say, Joan?"

"Sure, Mary. I don't think they could do or say anything more that could hurt either one of us. Anyway, if they don't call us back today, we still have tonight to look forward to. You haven't forgotten the party at The Golden Goose, have you?"

"No way Joan. After this, I can hardly wait."

It was now six-thirty and Joan and Mary had already been waiting for almost a half-hour. They were a little early, but it didn't matter as they enjoyed the freedom of just being away from their base.

"Hi, kids," John said. "Looks like you made it here before us, but we're all here, including Gary, so let's get going. I got a feeling we're going to really have some fun tonight. What do you think?"

"I think you're right," Mary answered as she got into the car. "In fact, I know you're right. Anything has to be more fun than what happened with us today."

On the ride to the club, Mary went into the details of their meeting with the CID. Everyone agreed that they had handled everything the right way.

Gary was sitting between Joan and Mary. "Boy, you two sure have been going through hell, haven't you?" With this said, Gary gave each of them a big hug and a kiss square on their lips. "Don't worry, somehow we'll get this thing all straightened out."

When they arrived at the club, Mary said, "It's a good thing we left when we did. Looks like the place is beginning to fill up already. Come on, let's go in, I want you to meet Scott. He's the owner of this place. You're going to like him. By the way, he's one of us, if you know what I mean."

As they entered the door they were greeted by a rather tall, good-looking guy who looked like he could have been a muscle builder, or even a movie star.

"Hi, Mary and Joan. Sure glad you could make it. And who's your friends?" Scott said with a friendly smile.

"First, this is Scott, everyone. And, Scott, these are my friends," Mary said, after which she introduced everyone.

"Hey, Mary, look over there. No one got our table yet. I'll run over and grab it for us," John said, as he made his way over to the same spot they'd had the last two times they had been here.

"The reason no one got that table is because of the reserved sign I put on it," Scott said as he walked over to the table with them.

After they got seated, Scott made his way just behind Gary. "You taken?" he said, as he placed his hands on Gary's shoulders. "I could understand if you were. It's not just that tight uniform but also what's in it that turns me on. I sure would like to have you stay with me tonight."

"No, I'm not taken, and sure, I'd like staying with you. Yeah, I'd like it a lot," Gary answered, as he raised his arms up and placed his hands over Scott's.

"Drink all the beer you want. It's on the house. So is the food. Just don't get drunk. And as for you, sailor boy, I got a special reason to want you sober tonight."

By this point the band had taken its place and started playing. People had started helping themselves to the wide variety of hors d'oeuvres and snacks covering two eight-foot tables, and several couples had taken to the dance floor.

"Well, before the fun begins, let's get down to business. David and I got everything planned for our motel project. You haven't forgotten, have you?" John said, as he looked to Mary for approval.

"No, John, we haven't forgotten, but we still can't believe that you would really go through with this."

"Hell, yes, we're going through with it. What are friends for if they can't be there when you need them? Anyway, Steve is going to drive us there. After you and Joan register for two separate rooms, we sneak in, and Steve calls the CID from a public phone. He tells them that two lesbians have checked in with two other women. The rest is up to us."

At this point Steve lifted his glass. "A toast to the motel caper and four naked bodies. You will be naked, won't you?"

Mary couldn't help laughing as loud as she could. Once Mary started, everyone joined in. The thought of it, two lesbians and two gay men lying there together, naked as jaybirds, and nowhere to go but to go on with it.

Gradually the bar began to fill up as more and more of Scott's customers and friends began to arrive.

"Anyone seen Steve?" John asked.

"Sure, he's in the john getting rid of some of that beer," Paul answered. "And I think I'm next. Once you start going, the beer just runs through you. Here he comes now. That sure took a while."

"I'm back. Boy, is that place crowded. See that old guy over there with that woman? I think he tried to put the make on me. He made me so nervous, I could hardly pee. You never know, do you?" Steve said as he sat back down at the table.

"What do you expect, Steve? Those sailor uniforms will do it every time," Paul said, as he casually put his arm around the back of Steve's chair so as not to be conspicuous.

"Oh, God," Mary suddenly yelled out. "See that man sitting over there at the end of the bar? That's the CID son of a bitch who interrogated me and refused to give me his name. Jesus, I hope he didn't see me."

"You mean he's the one? Shit, you won't believe this, but I've been to bed with him a couple times. What an asshole, I can't believe it. I'm going to ask your friend Scott if he knows his name," Gary said, as he got up from his chair and started toward the front door where Scott was talking to a couple of guests.

"Hey, Scott, come here a minute. Do you know that guy with the blue striped shirt sitting at the end of the bar?"

"Sure Gary. See, I remembered your name. Yeah, I know him. His name's Major Jeffreys—Daryl Jeffreys, with the CID at Fort Ord. He's the head man there. Why you asking—you're not interested, are you? I hope not."

"No way, no—no way in hell. Mary needs to know. Do me a favor and don't mention it to him for any reason. I don't want him to know that I asked."

"Sure, Gary, if you say so. Now don't forget about tonight. I'm counting on you."

"You don't have to worry about that. I want to be with you as much as you want to be with me. I have the duty this weekend so I'm off today and tomorrow. See you later, OK?"

After leaving Scott, Gary walked slowly over to Daryl at the end of the bar and sat down on the empty seat next to him. "Hi, Daryl, remember me? You told me your name was Ron, but that's OK—I told you mine was Jeff."

"How'd you find out my real name?"

"I find out things the same way you do, I ask. Man, you are one rotten son of a bitch, aren't you? You see those two ladies over there? Well, it seems you been putting them through a living hell. Let's put it this way, an officer who has sex with an enlisted man has just opened the door to prison. Let's face it, you had sex with me, and now you're going to make good on it. Tomorrow morning you're going to your office and say that because there is no evidence to support a case against either Joan or Mary, you find them not guilty of the charges. And then you'll close the case for good. Oh, yes, if you don't drop the charges, I'll have to say that you got me drunk and forced me into sex with you. The guy at the motel will recognize the two of us as having got a room twice. For myself, I don't have a lot to lose. But for you, Jesus, they'll lock you up so long your ass won't see the light of day for years. Oh, yeah, one more thing. Who was it that gave Joan and Mary's names to your office in the first place?"

"All I can say is tell them to be careful around Janis Larson. Does that answer your question? OK, you got a deal, but promise you won't say anything to anyone beyond your friends over there. I'm married and have a couple kids. If this ever got out, I'd be ruined."

"A deal, but if I don't hear that it's over by tomorrow, I'm spilling every-thing. Got that, asshole?"

"Yeah, I got it. You got my word. It's over, now I got to go. I wish I had-n't come here in the first place."

Gary got up and headed over to the table where he joined his friends. After picking up a pitcher of beer and filling everyone's glass, he said:

"A toast to Joan and Mary and to the end of all the shit they just went through. As it turns out, I didn't sleep with that asshole for nothing. He just dropped all the charges. How's that for the price of whoring? Now, here's to John and David, who won't have to show their bare asses to any-one but themselves."

"We'll drink to that," John added. "Now come on everyone, let's eat, drink, dance and spend the rest of the night celebrating the biggest victory this Army has ever seen—thanks to Gary."

Chapter 8

"Wow! Talk about a beautiful day. Just look at that sun!" John said, as he pushed away the sheet and sat up on the edge of his bunk. And turning to the guy in the next bed he added, "What you doing today, Mel?"

"Same old shit, I guess. Once I get done with my assignment, think I'll rest up a bit and head into town. You can join me if you want. And if you didn't already know, that sun out there is the reason why they call this place sunny California. By the way, you got a really big package in the first sergeant's office. I never get packages. Why are you so lucky?" Mel remarked as he stood up at the side of his bed, scratched his ass, raised his arms up behind his head, stretched his muscles, then started running in place for about thirty seconds. "Guess that's enough exercise for today. I better head to the latrine to shit, shave, shower, and shampoo before breakfast."

"Thanks, Mel. I got something planned for tonight but I'll take you up on going out together another night. OK?"

John grabbed his shaving kit and followed Mel into the latrine. After showering, shaving, and brushing his teeth he got dressed and headed for the mess hall to join his buddies for breakfast.

"Hi, David. Boy, did I need this cup of coffee. That was sure one hell of an evening last night, wasn't it? Think I'll ask Joan and Mary to join us when we head out to San Francisco. What you think, David?"

"Sounds great. I bet they're sure having one hell of a celebration this weekend—thanks to Gary. I got here a little early so I'm going to shove off now. See you later, OK?"

After breakfast, John left the barracks to pick up his package before reporting to work.

"Holy shit, where in the hell did he get all these samples?" John said. "I could kiss Mr. Alan for sending them. I never seen so many cigarettes in all my life. There's not even enough room in my footlocker to store all this. Guess I'll take a big bagful to the guys I work with. They sure in the hell won't be smoking butts today." John then headed out to work.

"You're sure one swell guy, John. Not many guys would share those cigs with his buddies like you just did. We'll love you for life. By the way, they've formed a volleyball team on the base. How about you joining our team? We're going to play one or two days a week. No weekends—that's our time for getting some, if we're lucky."

"Hell, yes, I'll join. Haven't played in a while, but I'll catch on, like everything else, I guess," John said, as he lit up a cigarette and waited for any additional assignments before going to work.

"Good morning, Maria, how you feeling today, and how is Niki?"

"Why, good morning, John Earl English. We feel just fine, and you couldn't look better. You haven't forgotten that you and your friend David are staying over with Niki and me this weekend, have you?"

"No way, Maria, actually we've been looking forward to it. We can't stay Sunday though, because my half brother, Harold, wants us to spend the day with him."

"No problem, John. We're happy just to have the two of you staying over Friday and Saturday. Is there anything special you might want me to cook for you?"

"No, nothing special. We both like anything you cook. You know, Maria, you're the best cook anywhere, and I really mean that. I'd better hurry up and finish cleaning this office. I've got a lot of work to get done before I get off-duty. Oh, by the way, David and I are planning to go to San Francisco in a couple weeks. If you know any good places to visit, be sure to let us know. We had planned to go to San Diego or L.A. but they turned out to be too far for a weekend off."

"Sure, John, we'll check around with our friends. We'll also get you some maps and Niki has a package he got from the chamber of commerce a while back. Oh, yes, meet us here at the office tomorrow at five-thirty, and the two of you can ride with Niki and me."

"Thanks, Maria, you two should have been our parents for real."

After finishing up with his cleaning, John made his way down the road to visit briefly with Bill Standish and let him know all about the happenings at the Golden Goose.

"Too bad you couldn't have been there. You'd never believe it. Gary was the hit of the evening. It's almost unbelievable." With this said, John went into all the details of the evening.

"You know, John, I only wish you hadn't mentioned about Gary staying over with that guy from the bar. I know I shouldn't feel this way, but I think I'm getting a little too close to that guy. Actually, you haven't told me anything that I didn't already know. I guess it's no secret that Gary sleeps around so I suppose I'll just have to settle for being with him when I can."

"Damn, Bill, I didn't know you felt that way about Gary. Now you're making me feel guilty that I even told you about some of the things that happened last night. Tomorrow's Friday, and David and I are staying at our friend Maria's place for a couple nights. We're not doing anything tonight. Why not join us after work? It might help you get your mind off Gary."

"Sounds good to me, John. How about meeting me after chow. Got anything in mind?"

"Yeah, thought we might check in with Rick Taylor. You know, that corporal who lives off base. Haven't seen him in a while. Can't quite figure him out, though. He talks about women a lot, but I really have my doubts. What do you think, Bill?"

"Yeah, I had my doubts the first time I saw him in those tight jeans and T-shirt. He's too good-looking not to have a woman living with him—full time, that is. By the way, he said any time we wanted to stop by for a drink we were welcome. Hey, that was a great idea about stopping at his place tonight."

It was a little past six, and Bill, John, and David made their way into town. They were in luck—Rick was home.

"Hi, Rick, remember us? You said to stop by sometime. You don't mind, do you?"

"Hell, no. Come on in. I just got off-duty myself. Nothing else planned tonight. You guys want a drink? Just name it, and I probably got it."

"How about beer?" Bill asked. "I drink about any kind except that real dark stuff."

"John and I'll have a screwdriver, if it's not too much trouble?" David said, as he lit up a cigarette and handed it to John.

"No trouble at all. I got lots of orange juice and more vodka than the liquor store. By the way, John, aren't you Harold's brother? I see Harold almost every day. He told me he'd be seeing you this Sunday. He said he'd be sure to stop by."

After about four hours of drinking, telling jokes, feeling horny, and going along with stories of nonexistent female conquests, everyone seemed about ready to crash.

"How about you guys staying over tonight? That couch makes into a bed and one of you can share my bed for the night."

"Man, that really sounds great. I'm about ready to fall out," Bill said, as he made his way to the bedroom.

"Well, Rick, looks like you and Bill will be sharing, so David and I will take the pull-out. Thanks for letting us stay over. I don't think any one of us is in any shape to make it back to the base tonight. By the way, can you set the alarm so we're not late in the morning?"

"Sure, guys, I have to set it anyway. You're not the only ones who don't want to be late."

Bill had just started to get to sleep when he became aware of Rick's leg resting on top of his. Rick's closeness felt good, and there was no longer any doubt of what was going to happen next.

John and David hadn't been in bed long before the sounds of labored breathing seemed to mark the fulfillment of what had been a perfect evening.

Morning came early, and after coffee and toast, Rick drove Bill, John, and David back to the Presidio and then proceeded to Fort Ord.

It was now Friday and both John and David headed toward Maria's office.

Five-thirty and at last it was time to meet Maria and Niki.

"Why, John, I see you and David are right on time. Niki will be here any minute and we'll be on our way. I'm fixing you boys something real special today. I hope you like it."

"Like I said, everything you fix is real special, Maria. I know David agrees with me. Don't you, David?" And without waiting for an answer John added, "Here comes Niki now, so I guess we'll be heading out."

"Boy, was that great, Maria. What was it?" David asked as he finished a second helping.

"Stroganoff. Maria makes the best I've ever eaten," Niki answered as he filled everyone's cup with more tea.

"Even the tea's fantastic," John added. "What kind is it?"

"Oh, it's not so much what kind it is, as what I put in it," Niki said with a smile. "Blueberry preserves and vodka give it the real taste."

Dessert consisted of vanilla ice cream and, of course, more liquor poured over it for added flavor.

"I hope you don't mind having us stay over like this. You know, David and I have never really had a home to go to before. Both David's and my parents died when we were little."

"Certainly we don't mind, and you want to remember, it was we who invited you here. I think I mentioned before that Niki and I never had children, but if we had, they couldn't have turned out nicer than the two of you boys. We would have felt blessed had you been our sons."

"Remember how you told that priest we were your sons at the Russian cathedral—on your Names Day?" John asked "You may not know it, but David and I really felt like we had a family, for the first time. If you and Niki don't mind, how about us adopting you as our parents?"

"Why, John," Maria said as she fought to control her excitement. "We'd be honored—and we've prayed for something like this. Now, for the first time, we feel like we have a family. Niki and I want you boys to always feel that our home is your home, and you're always welcome here."

"Now that we're on the subject, we want the two of you to write to us whenever you can, and keep in contact no matter what the circumstances. And please—please try to visit us as often as possible after you are no longer stationed here. Promise us?" Niki asked.

After both John and David had made their promise, Niki opened a bottle of brandy that he kept in a small cabinet and poured each of them a drink.

"I have been saving this bottle almost twenty years for some special occasion, and what could be more special than to drink to you—our sons. You don't mind us calling you our sons, do you?" Niki said as he raised his glass in a toast.

"Mind? No, we don't mind at all. In fact we'd love to be your sons," John said, before taking a drink from his glass.

"You boys have been the answer to our prayers," Maria added as she wiped away a tear. "Now how about some television and popcorn before we call it a night?"

Around nine-thirty, John and David said good night, and after closing the door to their room, they both undressed and climbed into bed.

"Hey, David, now that we made Maria and Niki our parents, does that make us brothers, and if it does, what's that make our relationship?"

"Incest, my prince," David said, as he burst out laughing. "Now roll over and go to sleep."

The following morning, John awoke to the smell of freshly baked rolls along with the aroma of bacon and fresh-brewed coffee as Maria prepared breakfast.

"Come on, David, sleepy head, you can't be that tired. You'd think the smell of that food would wake you up," John said, as he grabbed David by one leg and started to pull him out of bed.

"I'll get up, damn it, but you're pulling the wrong leg. Here, pull on this, my prince." John couldn't help but laugh as it reminded him of that part about incest David came up with last night.

"Are you boys up?" Niki asked as he opened the door to the room.

"We're getting up. I never smelled anything so good as Maria's cooking. Who could sleep through that?" John said as he finished putting on his shirt and was now slipping into his pants. David had put on one of Niki's bathrobes and had started out the door to the bathroom.

After both David and John were dressed they headed to the small dining room where Maria had already started setting the table.

"Wow! Maria, you're the best mother any two guys could ever want. And we can't leave you out, Niki, you're the best father anyone could possibly have."

"That's the nicest thing anyone could have ever said to us, and it makes us love you boys even more. Now I want you to help yourself and eat as much as you want. Today we planned a picnic. I hope you like picnics as much as Niki and I. We invited several friends who are going to join us, along with a very old friend of ours whom we knew back in Russia. His name's Count Alexandrovich. Feel free to call him Alex, as he prefers it. Later in the day when we arrive back home, we can spend the evening much as we did last night, watching television and enjoying a drink, along with a little Russian treat I prepared this morning while you were sleeping. Perhaps the next time you stay over, or sometime soon, we can have dinner at the wharf."

"Gee, you two think of everything. Sure sounds like you planned a really great day. Can't wait to meet your friends," David said, as he finished eating and pouring himself one last cup of coffee.

After breakfast, John and David followed Niki into the living room where they each lit up a cigarette. Niki turned on the TV and they all relaxed while Maria finished with the dishes.

At last they were on their way. Maria had packed a picnic basket along with a cardboard box which contained beverages for the day. The drive couldn't have been more pleasant as Niki pointed out the many points of interest as they drove down the narrow road.

When they arrived, Niki located a spot directly under a very large tree, which offered shelter from the warm, bright sun. Maria then placed a large cotton blanket on the ground, which she had brought along for the occasion. The grass was soft and green, and nearby was a large clump of geraniums and some smaller yellow flowers, which looked much like buttercups.

"The perfect spot," Maria said. "We've been here before—a number of times, and we like it best. Oh, look, here come our friends now. I'll get our picnic basket out and our friends are also bringing food."

"Good afternoon, Niki and Maria, and also to you fine gentlemen. Please, call me Alex. I am a very old friend of these lovely people."

Alex had arrived with two couples who likewise introduced themselves. At first John and David felt a little uneasy, not knowing these people beforehand.

One well-dressed lady who introduced herself as Olga held out her hand to John, and taking his in hers, she said:"You probably don't remember us, but we certainly remember you. You were both Maria's honored guests at her Names Day. I bet they never had two more handsome young men in the cathedral before, or since for that matter."

As the day progressed, it seemed to John and David that they had known these people forever. It was a beautiful day, and the food was something you'd find at a fine restaurant, but never expect at a picnic. Two of the guests brought wine which John and David drank in preference to vodka; no tables, no chairs, just everyone sitting on the grass or on small blankets or rugs they had brought along. It seemed Niki and Maria had planned everything right down to the last detail.

After lots of friendly conversation, good food and drink, the picnic came to a close, and everyone picked up their belongings, said their good-byes, and went on their way. It couldn't have been any better.

"We have one more stop to make before we arrive back home. I want you boys to meet two younger friends of ours whom we're sure you'll enjoy," Maria said, as they headed back toward town. "Their names are Alexis and Neal. They've been roommates now for several years and live in Carmel. They own a fantastic restaurant and are both excellent cooks. Perhaps you've heard of The Pampered Gourmet?"

"We've never seen it, but we know someone who's been there. I hear it's really great," John said.

It wasn't long before Niki pulled up in front of the restaurant. You couldn't miss the sign which read The Pampered Gourmet in large gold letters, surrounding a goose with a napkin around its neck, eating from a plate.

"Why, Niki and Maria, come on in. I see you brought those two sons of yours you have been telling us about—and they're even better looking than your description."

"Hi, I'm Alexis, and this is my friend Neal. I guess Niki and Maria have told you all about us. We were rather hoping that you hadn't eaten, but knowing Maria as we do, you're probably stuffed from that picnic they took you to. Anyway, we made this really delicious apple cream pie that we're sure you're going to love. We're the only ones that make it, that we know of."

Alexis was rather tall, being a little over six foot, and was quite handsome in a rugged sort of way, with pitch black hair, somewhat rounded face, square shoulders, and large chest. There was little doubt that Alexis might be Russian.

Neal, on the other hand, looked almost the complete opposite with sandy blond hair, deep blue eyes, medium build and he was probably around five foot seven, quite good-looking and a complement to his partner. Both men looked to be in their early twenties.

"Why don't you guys come over and visit tomorrow evening—say around eight? We can meet here and you can ride with us back to the house. It's on a ledge overlooking the ocean, and I think you'll like it," Alexis said, as he poured everyone a cup of coffee.

"Sure, why not?" John answered. "Sounds really great. By the way, how did you come to know Niki and Maria?"

"Oh, we've known them for some time now. My father knew them in Russia. They used to come to his restaurant quite often—that is, before the communists took over. Here's Neal with the pie. Hope you like it. We would have offered you a drink but they're sort of strict here—about age, that is. But never mind—we put some Napoleon brandy on top of the pie. They can't get us for that, I don't think. You'll have to excuse me now. Here comes a group of eight and I have to seat them."

"Aren't they the nicest boys?" Maria said as she finished her pie. "I knew they would like you, and I'm sure you'll like them once you get to know them. By the way, they don't often invite strangers to their home, so I guess you can take that as a compliment."

As they finished eating and were ready to leave, Alexis came to their table to say goodbye.

"The coffee and pie are on the house and don't forget, tomorrow at eight. OK?"

"You can count on that, we're looking forward to it, and thanks for everything," David remarked, as he headed for the door with the others.

It was a little past seven when everyone arrived back at the house. Maria brought in the picnic basket and was busy unpacking, while John and David joined Niki for a cigarette and drink in the living room. For the next three hours everyone watched TV and relaxed.

Shortly before bedtime, Maria went to the kitchen and brought out a tray of pastries that she had prepared for an evening treat.

"Boy, you and Niki sure thought of everything. Can't think of when we had a better time," John said, as he ate one of the small rich cakes Maria had made. "I think if we stayed here much longer we'd be as large as a tank."

That evening John climbed into bed next to David as he did the night before.

"If this were the right time and the right place, boy, could I take you up on a little incest, but I guess I'll just have to settle for a kiss instead. See you in the morning, my prince," David said, as he leaned over and kissed John good night.

The following morning John was again first to awaken, as he had the day before, to the smell of breakfast being prepared in the kitchen.

"Come on, David. We got a long day ahead of us. Got to meet my brother at Yorky's by noon and don't forget, we're invited to Neal and Alexis' tonight." With this said, John ripped the covers away from David and once again started pulling him out of bed by the leg.

"Jesus, John, I'd hate being married to you. You've really turned out to be a nag. Oh, well, you're a sexy nag and I guess I'll just have to put up with you, won't I?"

Before John could answer, Niki had opened the door.

"Come on, boys, it's past nine and time for breakfast. If you need anything, let me know." Niki then pulled the door closed again and departed for the kitchen.

After they were done in the bathroom, John and David finished dressing and were ready to eat.

"Boy, is this good, Maria. What is it?" David asked.

"It's a stradda. I made it last night while you were in bed. All I had to do is pop it into the oven this morning. I thought you'd like it—it's also one of Niki's favorites."

"Come here, Ma," David said. I got something for you." As Maria came to his side, David stood up and gave her a big hug and a kiss on her cheek.

"Now that's for being so wonderful, and that goes for you, Dad," David said as he reached over and did the same for Niki.

"I'm going to cry," Maria said, as she wiped her eyes with a napkin. "Not with sadness, but because I'm so happy." John noticed that Niki was also wiping a tear from his eye as he tried to hold back his emotions.

After breakfast, John insisted on washing the dishes, while David dried. When the task was finished, they retreated to the living room for a cigarette and more conversation before being driven into town to meet Harold and his friends.

"Hi, Harold, see you brought along Bruce and Green. How the hell you been?" John asked as they entered Yorky's.

"Not bad, John. How are you and David doing? Seems you guys are really busy. We don't see much of you lately."

"I'll have to tell you all about it later, Harold, when we're alone. By the way, we can't stay out too long today. We're meeting some friends later on, so we'll have to head out by seven-thirty, if it's OK with you guys."

"Sure, it's OK with us. Hell, that leaves us almost seven hours to kill. I promised Rick we'd drop by for a while. You remember Rick, don't you?" Harold said as he patted John on the back.

"Sure, Harold. We were at his place the other day. We brought along Bill Standish. Rick mentioned you were planning to stop by. Sure is a nice guy, isn't he?" John said, as he looked over at Green to be sure that he wasn't about to grab him by the ass like he had done before.

"What's new, Green?" David asked. You still seeing that broad at the Fort? You know the one with the big boobs that almost got you killed?"

"Shit, no, I might be crazy, but I'm not nuts. I got a new one, smaller tits, but she sure likes to screw," Green said, almost bragging.

"Don't listen to Green, guys," Bruce cut in. "You know he's full of shit. If that broad is screwing, it sure in hell isn't him. The closest thing he gets to pussy is some stray cat that hangs around the barracks looking for a handout, and when it comes to getting some ass, the only ass he ever gets is when he grabs at yours, John."

Everyone burst out laughing, but to conceal his embarrassment, Green did the very thing that Bruce had just said he did. He reached over and grabbed John squarely on his ass.

"Come on, Green, why don't you grab my ass a little. I like it as much as John—in fact you can grab this if you want to, David said, pointing to his crotch." And I'm just a little better padded than John is."

"Where at, your front or behind?" Green quickly added.

"Come on, guys, knock it off before you get so horny you want to get it off. Finish your donut and coffee, and let's head over to Rick's," Harold said, as he drank what was left in his cup.

The walk from the coffee shop to Rick's didn't take long, and as expected, Rick was home.

"Come on in guys." And putting his arm around Green's shoulders, he added, "I see you brought this ladies' man along. How you doing, Green? By the way, John, you should have asked Bill to come with you. I bought some more beer—you know, the kind he likes."

"We would have brought him but we weren't at the base last night. Maybe next time—for sure. OK?" John answered as he went inside.

The evening went much as it did the last time that John and David had been there with Harold and his friends. Lots of bullshit womanizing mixed with booze and sex that never happened.

Finally, it was getting late. Both John and David were beginning to feel their drinks and it was time to go.

"Hey, I know you guys got to be somewhere by seven-thirty. How about me driving you there?" Rick offered. "You other guys can stay here until I return, and I'll drive you back when you're ready. If that's OK with you?"

Everyone agreed, and Rick dropped John and David off at the restaurant with five minutes to spare.

"Thanks a lot, Rick, and you can be sure we'll bring Bill along next time," John said, as they got out of the car.

"Do me a favor, guys, bring him along when it's just the two of you. Don't bring him when your brother is over with his friends, OK?"

David had to smile. "Sure, Rick, we're not exactly stupid, you know."

With that Rick smiled back and drove off, leaving John and David at the door.

"Hi, guys," Neal said. "I'm glad you could make it. Come on in and have a seat. We'll be ready in about twenty minutes. Why not have some coffee while you're waiting?"

"Thanks, Neal. I think we can use it," David replied. "The coffee sounds great and, by the way, we're looking forward to seeing your place."

"I didn't mention it yesterday but we have a really nice pool. We have plenty of bathing trunks but if you want to go bare ass, that's fine with us. We never wear trunks unless we're entertaining, and I don't count you guys in that group," Neal added as he finished the last minute touches before getting ready to close up for the night.

"That sounds fine with us," David said, with a little excitement. We never went bare ass before and I think John is looking forward to it as much I am. What you think, John?"

"Sure, David, sounds really great so long as we don't freeze our peckers off. By the way, you guys aren't some sort of superstuds who just want to show us up once we strip down, are you?"

"Now that's something you'll just have to find out, isn't it? For all we know, it's you two guys who'll turn out to be the superstuds, and not us. I guess that's something that remains to be seen. At any rate, I think you'll like swimming nude. You might even turn into nudists. You never know."

"You're right about that, Neal. You never know, do you? Can't wait to try it, though," David said, as he gently rubbed John's lower back.

At last Alexis and Neal were ready, and everyone made their way out of the restaurant and into the car.

"You know, we never knew that Maria and Niki had any sons until they told us a couple days ago. That must make each of you a prince since Maria is a princess. I guess that's how it works. By the way, since you both have different last names, I'm assuming you were adopted. Of course, that shouldn't change things, should it?"

"No, not really, we're still just John and David. The only time I ever referred to John as my prince was in a private joke we had between us," David said with a laugh.

"Do you think Maria and Niki enjoyed themselves the other day when they were here with you?" Alexis asked. "We hope so, as they're really nice people. I guess you're aware that they know just about everyone."

It was a short drive and Alexis pulled up to what could best be described as a large tri-level home situated on the edge of a cliff. To one side was a rather large deck, which led to a below-the-ground pool. To the side of the pool was a gazebo, which housed a refrigerator, wet sink, and bar. The pool changing area and bathroom was located in the lower level of the house. From the looks of it, they must have hired a gardener to keep up the grounds and someone else to care for the pool.

"Come on in, we'll show you the house first, starting here," Alexis said, as he led everyone into a very large room. "This is our day room, the living room is actually on the next level. We have a small kitchen over there and, of course, a shower and bathroom facilities for the swimmers.

How do you like our bar?"

"Wow, it's as big as any bar I've ever seen, and not many guys have a grand piano in their house. You guys must have some big parties here, at least it looks like it," David remarked, as he wondered how anyone could possibly afford a place like this.

"After I finish showing you guys the rest of the house, we'll head out poolside, if it's OK with you."

"Sure, Alexis, sounds good to us. We've been looking forward to it," John said, as he winked at David.

After they made their way through the house, Alexis took John and David into the kitchen.

"Well, this is the last room to show, but one of our favorites. As you can see, we have almost everything to work with that we have at the restaurant."

"How do you keep it so clean?" John asked as he noticed how spotless the room was.

"Rather easy," Neal answered. "We seldom cook here. You know, having a restaurant, we eat most of our meals there. Sometimes we do a little barbecuing outside but not much else. About the only thing we use in the morning is the coffeepot, except on our day off—and even then we usually eat out."

"It's starting to get a little dark out. What's say we head outside and have a drink? I'll turn the outside lights out, so it'll be just these candles, the stars and the moon. Now how's that for atmosphere?" With this said, Neal led the way to one of the tables surrounding the pool.

"What you guys drink?" Neal asked, as he entered the gazebo with its well-stocked bar.

"How about screwdrivers, unless you have something else you would rather give us," John answered.

"We're having Bloody Marys. Why not try one? You can always switch to something else if you don't like them," Neal offered.

"Sure, Neal. Sounds good to us," John answered. "You don't mind if we smoke, do you?"

"Hell, no. We don't smoke, but we don't mind if you do, just as long as you don't smoke in the pool. I'll get you an ashtray."

It wasn't long before Neal was done mixing the drinks and placing them on the table.

"Here's to the beginning of a great friendship," Alexis said, as he offered a toast. "Good health, long lives, and good living."

"We'll drink to that," John said, "especially that part about long lives and good health. That's important when you're in the Army."

"And good living wouldn't hurt either," David added. "Boy, this drink tastes great. Think I'll stick to this for a while."

After a couple hours had passed with everyone laughing and enjoying each other's company, it was then about time for a swim.

"OK, guys, it's pool time, so everyone strip down and dive in," Alexis said as he started removing his clothes.

It was no doubt the alcohol, but neither John nor David felt the least bit embarrassed as they stripped down to bare flesh before finishing their third drink.

"Jesus, guys, you sure in hell have nothing to be ashamed of. You sure got us beat in that superstud category. Now come on in, the water's great. Ever played water ball before? If we can't beat you one way, I'm sure we can beat you another," Neal said, as he threw a large beach ball into the pool.

David dived in first, followed by John and Alexis.

"Wow, the water's warm. I thought it would be cold at first," David said, as he swam over to John and dived directly under him.

"Damn it, David, these aren't beach balls you just grabbed," John said, as he jumped straight up, then headed to the side of the pool. "Now knock it off. OK?"

Alexis burst out laughing along with Neal.

"Hey, John. How about trying this out?" Neal said, as he pushed a rubber raft toward him. Just climb on top and lie down. I use this thing all the time. That's how I got this suntan all over my body so evenly."

John made several attempts before he finally succeeded in getting on top of the small raft.

"What now? There's no sun, so I couldn't be getting a tan."

"Forget the tan. Just close your eyes and pretend you're just drifting out in the ocean. You won't believe how relaxing it is."

As John closed his eyes, Neal immediately dived directly under the raft, and with one quick shove, pushed it over as he resurfaced. In so doing,

Neal's body brushed against John's, and John couldn't help but feel a flush of excitement in this brief encounter.

"Oh, shit, Neal. You sure got me that time. Hey, David, you can try climbing on this thing next, if you don't mind drowning."

"OK, guys, time for some water ball," Alexis said. "I'll teach you the rules on how to play. You're really going to like it. It can be a really great contact sport, you know."

After about an hour of water ball, everyone was ready to come out and just relax for a while.

"Sit down. I'll fix us a drink. No need to dress unless you want to. It's pretty warm out," Neal said, as he again made his way to the bar.

"You know, this nudist thing isn't so bad. In fact I think I like it. Can't explain why, but I do. What you think, John?"

"I think you like all this bare ass around you, don't you, David? That's what I think. Not that it's so bad. Actually, it is rather stimulating, if you know what I mean."

After a while Neal returned with the drinks. This time he brought along a pitcher filled with Bloody Marys, to save getting up so often.

"Here's to four beautiful young naked bodies enjoying the great outdoors, and may there be many more nights like this to enjoy," David toasted as he lifted his glass.

"We'll drink to that," Alexis added, as he raised his glass along with the others.

Neal turned on the radio for a little soft jazz while everyone continued to drink and talk about anything that crossed their minds.

After a while Alexis turned to John and said, "I don't mean to be getting into your personal lives, but it looks to us like you and David got a little more going than just friends. You don't have to answer if you don't want to, but that's the situation with Neal and me."

"You hit the nail right on the head," David answered. You're sure right about John and me being more than just friends. You can bet your ass we're a hell of a lot closer than any friends could be. Yeah, we're gay, if that's what you're asking. But I'm glad you asked. Now that puts us all in the same boat." With this said, David again lifted his glass. "Here's to four gay guys—good-looking, I might add, sitting next to the pool, naked as the day they were born—except for those of us who were circumcised, that is."

"Let's drink to that, right, guys?" Neal said, as he raised his glass.

"Now that we've broken the ice, so to speak, I often wondered how someone gay in the service could possibly stand it, being with so many men. You know, like when they're in the showers, out in the field, or just lying on the bed next to you. Doesn't that get you sort of hot?" Neal asked.

"Hell, no, you couldn't pay me to go with most of those guys," David said. "Some of them might be really good-looking but after you know them for a while their personalities aren't always that great. Some look like shit, and some are just plain assholes. Of course, some guys look good, and you really like them, but you wouldn't want to lose them as friends, so you keep it that way. We don't just go fucking around with every straight guy we see—or gay ones for that matter. We're soldiers first and gay men second. Like anyone else, we have a job to do, but when we're off base, that's another story. As far as David and I go, it just happened, that's all I can say about it. Does that answer your question, Neal?"

"Sure, John, now I got another question. Do you think that Maria and Niki know about you—your relationship with David, I mean? They know all about us. We told them some time back. Doesn't seem to bother them at all."

"Hell, we never thought about it, but maybe they do. Actually, I wished they did. It sure in the hell would make things a lot easier for us. What do you think, David?"

"Sure, John, it sure would make sleeping with my prince a hell of a lot cozier. But actually we respect them too much to do anything beyond just sleeping together."

"Boy, it's really getting late. How about you two staying over? We got lots of room, you know. We have to get up early to get things started in the restaurant, so Alexis could drive you to your base after he drops me off first. I have a lot to do before we're ready to open."

"Boy, you guys are really great. We'd love to stay over. One thing's for sure—we won't have to bother getting dressed. Seems we're ready for bed just as we are—bare-assed and ready.

"Jesus, David. Take a look at this bed. Ever see something with so much carving? It's almost too nice to sleep on. Looks like something Napoleon might have screwed around on."

"You're right about that, John. Sure is fine, but not so fine as your young ass. Now hop in, we've got business to take care of."

The following morning, Neal got everyone up. "Here, have one of these before we have coffee and a roll," then Neal put two glasses filled with what looked like orange juice at the bedside.

"Gee, thanks, Neal. What is this?" John said, as he took a sip just to taste it.

"They call it a sunrise cocktail. It's champagne and orange juice. You might call it something else, but it's just the thing you need after a night of drinking. How do you like it, guys?"

"Damn, it's really great," David answered. You should have told us about these last night. I think I could drink a gallon of it."

"You might think so, but you'd have one hell of a headache this morning if you had. Now hurry up and get dressed. I'll see you in the breakfast nook, next to the kitchen."

After coffee and a cinnamon roll, everyone got into the car and headed out to work.

"Hey, where were you two last night?" one of the guys asked as they were taking their assignments for the day.

"Nowhere in particular, just out partying all night with some broad from town. Man, do I have a hangover this morning," John said, in an effort to pacify his friend's curiosity.

"Damn, you and David must be the biggest whore-mongers on the base. You guys are always taking off for the night. By the way, don't forget—tonight's the volleyball game. Us guys are playing against those officers from the language school. We should sure beat the shit out of them. We're a hell of a lot better men than they are. What do you think, buddy?"

"I think you're right, Ron. Now how about us heading out to work."

Chapter 9

Early the next day, John filled a small bag with cigarettes and headed out to see if there was any change in duties.

"Hey, guys, what'd you think of that game last night we sure whipped 'em didn't we?" Ron said, as he put his arm around John's shoulders and gave him something of a hug.

"You're right about that, Ron. Now that we won the game I guess that proves we're the real men here on base, doesn't it? We'll be playing them again this week and this time we're going to whip 'em real good. How about the rest of you guys, you going to be up to it?"

"You bet your sweet ass we are," Hartman quickly added.

"OK, guys, payday's not until Friday, so here's a couple packs each of these samples I got last week," John said as he started passing them out. "Those once-a-month paydays sure are a bitch, aren't they? I don't see why they can't pay us twice a month like the Navy does. If they could only see what we go through just to have a cigarette after we've run out of money, they might start paying us like they should. Smoking butts and rolling them in brown paper hand towels is for the birds."

"Hey, Rover and Appleton, you two still cleaning the shit houses or did you get a promotion to KP or something?" Paul asked as he started to laugh. "Haven't seen you two guys around in a couple weeks. Anyway, glad to have you back on the job. We had to take your place while you were gone. Ain't that some shit."

After a few more remarks about last night's game and a little more joking around, everyone got their assignments before leaving for work.

Later that day, John took off for the day room to make a call.

"Hi, Mary. I was hoping I'd get hold of you before you took off someplace. How about meeting David and me at Yorky's—say around six thirty? We miss you gals.

"Sure, John. Sounds great. Joan's been asking about you guys. We can't wait to tell you about our weekend and how things have changed around here."

"If you think you had a great weekend, wait until you hear about ours. Don't want to say much more over the phone. You know what they say, 'the walls have ears.' At any rate, we're looking forward to seeing you," John said as he hung up the phone.

After John met David at dinner and both had eaten, they headed for the barracks to shower, change clothes and make their way into town.

On the way down the hill from the Presidio, John placed his hand around David's waist.

"You know, I like touching you like this even more than I did the first time, David. Do you remember?"

"Sure, John, but we can't keep walking like this or someone will think we're queer. Now we don't want that, do we?"

"Hell, no, not if it means going through what Mary and Joan had to go through. Anyway, we got plenty of time for that, I guess. By the way, do you think that things are really over—I mean with the CID? Guess if it wasn't we'd have heard something by now. When I called Mary, she sounded OK, so maybe it is." With this said, John removed his hand from David's waist as they continued their walk down the hill and into town.

John and David had already ordered coffee and were sitting at a table when Mary and Joan walked in. You could tell from the looks on their faces that everything was fine.

"Hi, guys. Wonderful news, I'll tell you all about it as soon as Joan gets our coffee. We'll love you guys to the day we die."

Joan paid her bill, and took her place at the table with the others.

"Come on, tell us all about it," John asked. "We can hardly wait to hear what's been happening."

"Like I said, it couldn't be more wonderful news. We were called into the company commander's office the day after the party. Would you believe, she actually apologized for what we went through, and after assuring us that Janis Larson was being transferred to another base she asked if we wanted to press charges against her for slander. We said no, and that was that. Friday we took off for Frisco to celebrate. And celebrate we did. By the way, we found that bar you told us about plus a couple others we never heard about before. God, did we have a great time."

"How'd you gals like to go to San Jose with us this weekend and maybe Frisco if we have the time. Gary and Steve are off and Gary just got a car. You're not going to believe this, but he borrowed it from your friend Scott at the bar. Scott said it was his old car and Gary was welcome to use it as long as he wanted. I'll tell you, that Gary must have something really special."

"Sure, guys, we'd love to go. It would be like celebrating all over again. Where do you think we should stay?" Mary asked.

"You remember Bill—Bill Standish? Well, he has a cousin there and I think he might be able to put us all up for the weekend. If not, he's sure to find us someplace we can stay," John said as he lit up a cigarette.

"Is he gay?" Joan asked.

"He's gayer than a pink hairnet or a pink flamingo, if that answers your question," David joked. "By the way, I heard from Steve, and he said that Gary joined The Vet's club. He calls it The dead pecker club. Mostly old men there, I guess. Anyway, he gets lots of free drinks from those guys, and the cops don't bother the place. John and I joined a while back but haven't been there but once. Maybe we had better start going more often."

"You guys are sure something else," Mary said, as she had to laugh about the 'dead pecker club.'

John then went into all the details of the picnic with Niki and Maria. After this he couldn't help but tell them of their adventures with Alexis and Neal.

"Boy, you wouldn't believe what a place they have. Maybe one day when we're feeling loaded with cash we can all have lunch at their restaurant, if you want."

"Do you think you can get Gary and the guys to go back to the club with us tomorrow?" Mary asked. "We really haven't celebrated with you guys yet, at least not with a drink."

"Sure, why not?" John answered. "For all we know, Gary might be there right now with your friend Scott. It seems he's got something going there. At any rate, how about all of us taking a walk down to that ship? If Gary's not there, Steve probably is."

After finishing their coffee, they all walked down to the ship and went aboard.

John poked his head through the hatch, and not seeing anyone, he called out, "Hey, Gary or Steve. Come on out a minute. If you're not dressed you had better slip some clothes on first. Joan and Mary are here."

"Hey, mate, how's it going? I'll be right out. Steve's here too, but he's in the shower. I just finished with mine," Gary said as he slipped on his shirt and pants.

A few minutes later, Gary came out on deck. "What's new, guys? Hey, Joan and Mary. First time you ever been on a ship?" Without waiting for an answer, he added, "I'll pop back in and check on Steve to be sure he's dressed, then I'll make sure everything's shipshape before you come in. We're not supposed to have women on board, but you're in the Army, so maybe that don't count. Anyway, we'll just show you around and spend the rest of our visit out here on the deck, if that's OK with you?"

"Sure, Gary, that's fine with us," Joan said. "Thanks for letting us come on board. In answer to one of your questions—no, we've never been on a ship of any kind before. This is really great. I can't wait to see the inside."

After a while, Gary went back inside to check on Steve, and returned about eight minutes later. "Come on in, guys, everything's OK."

"This is Derek. This is Dale, our cook, and of course you know Steve." Gary said, as he introduced them to some of the crew.

"Thanks, guys, for letting us come aboard. How do you guys keep from getting seasick when you're out in the ocean? I can even feel the motion from the waves, and you're tied up here at the dock," Mary said with a smile.

"Is this neat," Joan remarked, as she and Mary were shown around the ship. "Sort of like in the movies, only this is the real thing. You know, from the outside, you'd never believe there was so much space. I think I joined the wrong service. But don't worry, I have no plans of joining any service again. How you been, Steve?"

"Not bad, Joan. Boy, you and Mary sure look great."

After Joan and Mary finished looking around, everyone went out on deck.

"How about you and Steve joining us tomorrow for a celebration at the club?" Mary asked. "It's on us. By the way, I hear you got a car now, Gary. So between you and Steve, we should all be able to ride there with no problem."

"Oh, you heard about the car already, did you? I'll tell you all about it tomorrow. Sure, I'll come and so will Steve. What time do we meet—six-thirty, like before?"

"Six-thirty's fine. We'll meet at the wharf then. Thanks again for showing us around. Oh, yeah, before we leave, can you and Steve go with us to San Jose this weekend, Gary?" Mary added. "The rest of us are going. That's when we're planning to really celebrate with you guys. We got something special planned for you. It's a secret right now."

"Sure, why not, if it's OK with Steve here. Neither one of us has the duty this weekend."

"Great. I don't have any plans as long as Paul's coming along," Steve replied.

"Hell, yes, you know that Paul's coming, and so is Bill Standish," John answered. "We're hoping his cousin can put all of us up for the weekend. Altogether that will make a total of eight of us, but Steve has a car so with his car and Gary's there should be no problem with transportation."

"Well, that settles that, guys. We'll be heading back now. See you all tomorrow," Mary said, as she started down the ramp.

"Hey, hold up, guys, how about a ride back to the base? Now that I got wheels, I can drop you gals off at Fort Ord, and John and David at the Presidio on the way back," Gary said, as he followed them down the ramp.

The following day, Gary and Paul had parked their cars by the wharf and after everyone had arrived they headed to the Golden Goose as planned. No more had they parked the cars than Scott pulled up.

"Boy, isn't this a pleasant surprise," Scott said as he walked into the club with them and pulled Gary to one side where no one could hear.

"By the way, Gary, you owe me a favor tonight. Let's just call it your weekly car rental fee."

"Don't worry, Scott. I haven't disappointed you yet, have I?"

"No, not yet, but sometimes I worry that you might forget. At any rate, you haven't forgotten me so far. The only thing I wish is that someday we could make a permanent commitment between us, but I guess I'll just have to be satisfied with things as they are for the time being."

"Let's put it this way, Scott, I'm closer to you than I've ever been to another man. Now I hope that makes you feel a little better about the situation. It's just that I get horny so much that I can't make a single commitment to anyone right now. If I could, one thing's for certain, it would be you at the top of the list. Now enough of this talk. I'm here to party with the others. How's this? I love you—now can I join the others?"

"Hell, yes. One thing's for certain, you sure made me feel better than I've ever felt since I first met you. Now for what you just did for me, everything's on the house and I mean that for all of you."

"Thanks, Scott. I really do love you, you're a really great-looking guy, good sex and great personality, and I really mean it. If you can accept my running around on the side, I suppose you could say I belong to you, and you to me. That sounds better than saying we're lovers."

"Holy shit, Gary, you just made me the happiest guy in the world. You didn't know this, but I haven't been able to get you out of my mind for a single day and I never want that to change. Now let's party like we never partied before."

"Hey, Gary, what was all that about between you and Scott?" Mary asked.

"Oh, something personal between us. Something good, and that's about all I have to say about it for now. I see the party's already started."

"Anyone hungry?" Scott said. "It's all on the house along with some hors d'oeuvres and snacks to go along with the beer."

"Here's some change, Joan. How about you playing some songs on the jukebox for us."

"Sure, Gary. Anything special you want me to play?"

"No, nothing special. Yeah, wait a minute—Scott's favorite song is 'Mona Lisa.' How about playing that first, OK?"

"Sure, Gary, in fact I'll play it twice in a row. We should be playing it all night for all this free food and drink he's giving us, but I guess the other customers would complain. You know, Gary, why don't you be the one to play it. I think Scott would appreciate it more from you than from me. So here's your change back."

"You're probably right, Joan," Gary said, as he got up, walked over to the jukebox, inserted the coins, and selected the songs before returning to join the others.

No more had Mona Lisa started playing than Gary looked over toward Scott, who started to smile as he made his way over to their table. Standing close to Gary, he placed both hands on his shoulders, gently massaging them to show his appreciation for what Gary had just done for him.

As the evening wore on, Mary and Joan went into the details of the investigation and its closure. Maj. Jefferies had called them into his office, and after apologizing for what he referred to as a terrible mistake, he personally destroyed every bit of evidence associated with their case.

"God, what a relief that was," Mary said, as she proposed a toast to Gary without whom they would have gone through further hell and probably eventual discharge. Another toast was proposed to everyone else who had a plan for helping them through this very trying ordeal.

"Now one more toast," David proposed. "Here's to good friends, long life, and happiness."

"We'll all drink to that," John said, as he raised his glass along with all the others.

"Here's to our everlasting friendship," Steve added, as he once again raised his glass in a toast to each and every one of those present.

Mary made the final toast. "Here's to Scott, a really good friend and someone special to all of us." With this, everyone stood up, raised their glasses, and loudly voiced: "To Scott."

With this final toast, Gary got up, placed his arms around Scott, and squarely kissed him on the cheek. "Now that's from all of us, and especially from me." Scott couldn't have been more pleased, as this was the first time in public that Gary had ever shown any affection toward him whatsoever.

"Come on, Scott, pull up a chair and join us. You can sit next to me," Gary said, as he motioned the others to make an extra space.

It was now getting late, and to assure that Gary would stay over, Scott asked to go along as Gary dropped off the others. This way he would be certain that Gary would drive him back to the club and stay over for the night.

After Scott and Gary returned to the club, closed it for the night, and drove the short distance to Scott's home they went directly to Scott's bedroom.

"Tell me something, Gary, and be truthful. Did you really mean it when you told me how you felt about me?"

"Let's get one thing straight between us, Scott—if I told you I loved you then I really meant it. When I said I'm yours, I meant it, and now I'm letting you know that you belong to me as much as I belong to you. Is that clear enough? The only thing you'll have to understand, like I said before, is that I fool around on the side, but that won't change our relationship unless you let it. Maybe one day I'll be more settled and that won't be a problem anymore. Just remember this, no matter who I might go out with or who I might sleep with, it's only a temporary release and I'll try not to let you know about it. But one thing's for certain—you'll always be the only one I really love and care about. Can you accept this, Scott?"

"Sure, Gary. You're damned right I can accept it. Now let's go to bed and make good on what you just said."

The following morning was Thursday and Gary was up early so that he could be back to the ship for duty.

"We still have time for breakfast, Gary. There's a nice little place just a block away. What do you say? You'll still be back on time."

"Sure, Scott, sounds great. By the way, you were really super in bed last night. I think the best you've ever been. Keep that up and I might quit running around."

"In that case I'll have to try to outdo myself next time," Scott replied.

After breakfast, Gary dropped Scott at his house, and made his way back to the ship.

Friday, and it was payday at last.

"Hi, Maria, Guess what? David, Gary, Steve, Paul, Bill, our friends Mary and Joan, and I are all going to San Jose this weekend. We'll all be staying at Bill's cousin's for the weekend. He's got a really big house and should have no problem putting us all up. We're leaving tonight right after work so that we'll have a couple nights there before we have to come back to the base. How's Niki? Tell him I miss him and actually I miss the both of you when I'm away."

"You must know, John, that Niki and I are becoming closer and closer to you and David each day. I hope you're not offended but we regard you as our sons. Like we said before, we never had children, you know, and its too late for that now. From what you've told me you were both orphans at an early age. Oh, how I wish we'd had the opportunity to adopt the both of you back then."

"You know, Maria, David and I have always wished we had parents and a home to come back to, especially now. I hope you know that the both of us have come to love you just like you were our parents already. It's possible, you know, to adopt us, if you and Niki really wanted to."

"Oh, praise God in heaven. Yes, there is nothing more that would give us greater pleasure and meaning in life than to have two wonderful sons such as you and David. Please, John, bring David here when you return on Monday and we'll talk this over more at length at our home after work. Have a wonderful time this weekend, John, or may I call you son? You'll never know what this means to us. It's an answer to our prayers."

After John finished with his work, he and David quickly ate dinner, then returned to the barracks to pick up their shaving kits and a few other items that were already packed.

"I've got something really important to tell you, David. Remember the day we discussed how much we loved Maria and Niki and wished they had been our parents?"

"Yeah, I remember, but why are you bringing it up now?"

"Because they feel the same about us and want to adopt us. This way we'll have a real family and, if nothing else, I can at least love you as my brother. They couldn't call it incest because we came from different parents. Anyway, how do you feel about it?"

"This might surprise you, John, but I think it's great, and hell, yes, I'll take Niki and Maria as my parents anytime and especially you as my brother. As soon as we get back tell them yes, OK? Now let's get a move on or we'll be late."

Shortly after their brief conversation, they met Paul and the three of them drove down to the wharf to wait for everyone to arrive.

About fifteen minutes later, Gary drove up next to Paul's car as they waited for the others.

It wasn't long before Steve, Mary, and Joan had arrived and it was decided that Paul, Mary, and Joan would ride with Steve, while the others would ride with Gary.

The ride to San Jose was pleasant enough with lots of conversation and laughter, and since they were in no great hurry, they made a couple stops for coffee and latrine relief.

"You guys don't mind if we take you to a couple women's bars, do you? We met a few really nice gals there and we'd like you to meet them," Mary asked.

"No, not at all, as long as you don't mind going to a couple men's bars. Not that we know anyone there, but that would even up things between us," Paul said with a smile.

"After what you guys have done for us, we'd go to the ends of the earth for you," Mary answered.

After a lot more conversation and a few jokes both cars finally pulled up in front of Art's house.

"Boy, you were sure right, this certainly is one big house."

Bill got out of the car, walked up the stairs, rang the doorbell, and was greeted by his cousin who appeared at the door.

"Come on in, everyone. I got everything arranged, and something really special for you two gals."

After everyone grabbed their belongings and entered the house, they saw that Art had already arranged for a catered meal which would arrive about an hour after they had settled in. In the meantime everyone was offered drinks and made to feel at home.

Shortly before the meal arrived, the doorbell rang and two fairly attractive women in their mid-forties arrived.

"Hi, I'm Sarah and this is my friend Rose. I take it you're Mary and Joan. Whether you know it or not, you're going to be our houseguests this weekend and I can tell from the start that we'll become good friends."

"Great. I'm Mary and this is my friend Joan. I can see that Art has arranged everything to make us feel comfortable while we're here. I'm sure we'll become good friends," Mary said, as she walked over and gave each of the two women a brief embrace.

"We live right next door so that should make things easy for all of us. Art thought you'd be a lot more comfortable around other women and the men more comfortable with men: he's so thoughtful. Guess that's why we just love him so much," Sarah said as she sat down next to Joan. "Anyway, how about you and Mary grabbing up your belongings and we'll take them next door before the food arrives. We'll show you the house and your bedroom later, if that's OK with you?"

"As far as we're concerned, Art couldn't have made a better arrangement for us women, and I know we're going to enjoy each other's company."

"By the way, the real reason we're here is that we owe these guys a super celebration for something they did for us and something we'll never forget. Hope you two don't mind going along with the celebration. We can't tell you the reason for the celebration other than we love these guys like they were our brothers."

"Fine with us," Rose commented. "We're always ready for a good party and good friends. Anyway, let's get a move on it or the food will arrive before we get your things over to our house. Hope you brought along some civilian clothes. If not, I'm sure we can find something for you to wear. We got tons of clothes in just about any size you can imagine, as we go up and down in weight." A little later Mary and Joan grabbed up their belongings and followed Rose and Sarah next door.

"Thank God," Gary said. "Now we don't have to worry about the women seeing us bare ass or us seeing them the same way, or worse."

Shortly after, the women returned and the caterers arrived with the food. Everyone dug in like it was their last meal.

Later that evening Art said, "OK, guys and gals, time for bed so we can all be up bright and early for breakfast. I found a really nice new place and the meal's on me, so you better take advantage of it and order whatever you want," as he ushered the women out the door.

"I think you can guess who you'll be sleeping with, Bill, and you'd better be at your best—I've been waiting a long time for a repeat performance," Art said, as he grabbed Bill by the hand and led him off to his room. "By the way, guys, there are two other bedrooms and a den with a couch that makes into a bed, so take your choice. Incidentally, I'll expect you up by nine, shaved, dressed, and ready to go. Now how's that grab you?" Art said, as he and Bill made their way to Art's room.

As the others picked out their rooms and prepared for bed, David turned to John and said, "You know, John, the more I think of this adoption business, the more I like it. I never had a family that I ever knew of—but you did, and we really need someone to care about us, and care about what happens to us. Do you feel the same as I do, John?"

"Sure, David, you know I do. And you know what, I can't think of anyone better to be our parents than Niki and Maria. I already feel like I'm their son, how about you, David?"

"Yeah, John, I feel the same as you. I don't know why, but somehow it's like they were always our parents and for whatever reason we're finally getting together. Hell, yes, I can hardly wait to get back to the base and let them know how much this means to us. This will be the first time that I'll finally have someone to write to other than you, who cares about me. You know another strange thing, John, I think Niki and Maria know how close we are toward each another, and it really doesn't matter to them just how close we really are."

"I think you're right, David, and maybe that's one of the good things that will come out of this adoption. Anyway, we can talk about that later. Right now I'm thinking about a little premature incest. How about you, David?"

"I've been thinking about that from the moment we hit the bed. What's say we get started?"

The following morning Art was up and, without knocking, he entered John and David's room, pulled down the sheet that covered them and announced that it was time to get up and get ready.

"Jesus, we haven't been asleep that long. Do we have to be up so early?" David asked.

"Hell, yes. If you two hadn't been making out all night you'd both be rested up by now. Anyway, I've made coffee, so get your asses up, throw on a robe, and come on down and join us. Maybe a good cup of coffee will get the two of you back into shape. Damn, they should have glued you two together the way you carry on. I don't even have that much energy. Incidentally, the girls are downstairs having coffee with us, so maybe you better put on your undershorts just in case your bathrobes happen to expose the better parts of you. If the women weren't downstairs there's no way I would have insisted on the undershorts. I'll expect you down in about five minutes. Got it?"

"Yeah, we got it. We'll be down as soon as we can.

Maybe less than five minutes. Now how's that for timing?" John said, as he slipped into his shorts and started putting on his robe as David followed suit. It took less than five minutes before both John and David arrived at the dining room, sat down, and poured themselves coffee.

"Excuse my manners," John said. "Good morning, everyone, and a special thanks to our host Art for having the coffee ready so early in the morning,

Immediately after coffee, John and David returned to their room, took a quick shower, shaved, and brushed their teeth, then quickly got dressed so they could join the others for breakfast.

"No need for a car. It's only down the block or so, and the walk will do us all some good. "Whatcha say? Let's head out," Art said, as he opened the door and motioned everyone to step outside.

After arriving at the restaurant, two tables were placed next to each other so that all eight could be seated together.

"Like I said, order whatever you want. Breakfast is on me," Art again reminded everyone.

"How 'bout David and I having the steak and eggs, orange juice, and coffee? Is that in the deal, Art?" John asked as he reviewed the menu.

"Like I said, have anything you want. That is, except that young cute guy behind the counter, he's mine. You might not believe this but I've already been with him about five times and he's really something—I mean really something. Making out with him is almost as good as making out with my cousin here. Come on, Bill, I'm sorry I'm embarrassing you," Art said, as Bill's face became a little flushed.

"Jesus, Art, you don't have to tell everything, do you?" Bill asked.

"Sorry about that Bill, I won't mention it again—at least for today."

"You mention it again, and you'll be sleeping alone, that is unless you can get your little friend over there to take my place," Bill said, somewhat agitated with the conversation.

"I'll be good from now on, I promise. I sure don't want to spoil a good thing when I have it," Art said as he prepared to place his order.

After everyone had eaten Art suggested that they walk about four blocks farther to watch the early morning runners as they got in their exercise for the day. After this they would return to Art's place where they would map out the remainder of the visit.

It was decided that the museum, the zoo, a couple movies, and several bars would fill the time quite nicely. Of course, there was the Veteran's Club hall that Mary and Joan had rented for a special celebration on behalf of all those men who offered to help or did help in solving their problem with the CID. Needless to say it was to be a celebration to end all celebrations. Sarah and Rose had rounded up just about everyone they could possibly get in contact with and likewise Art must have drained the local bars for men to participate.

"Everyone give a big hand to Mary and Joan for arranging the rental of the hall, and as for me," Art said, "I'll probably go broke, but everything, including the food and drinks, is on me tonight. Now come on now, let's party like we never partied before."

By the time the celebration ended and everyone arrived safely back home, John and David could hardly wait to go to bed and prepare to leave for the base the following morning.

The ride back to Monterey was filled with all the pleasant memories of this fantastic get-together. Mary and Joan had met new friends with whom they would continue to keep in contact, and although it was really great fun, everyone was happy to be on their way back.

Four weeks had passed, and the paperwork had been prepared and processed. Niki and Maria had arranged for John and David to be off that Thursday and Friday to appear in court in preparation for the legal adoption that would take place.

"It is my understanding that you, John Earl English, and you, David Eduardo Marconi, desire to be adopted as the legal sons to Maria Anastasia Romanoff Nevski and her husband, Nikolai Petr Aleksandr Nevski, on the date hereon set upon this document. It is further understood that you have the legal right to change your last names to that of your adopted parents at any time of your choosing, or you may retain your current last names until you choose to do otherwise. I understand that for the time being, you, John, and you, David, have elected to retain your birth names and reserve the right to use the name of your adoptive parents at special functions, or on any occasion that you might wish to do so. If all parties are in agreement, please sign your legal signatures in the spaces provided. When you have accomplished this you shall be legally bound one to the other as a family consisting of two sons and two parents."

After the documents were signed, the judge congratulated Niki and Maria along with John and David on the legal joining of them together as a family.

Immediately, Niki and Maria kissed both John and David, now their legal sons and certainly the most important young men to have ever entered into their lives.

"Your honor, we would be pleased if you were to come to San Francisco next week to celebrate this greatest and most beautiful event in all our life," Niki asked. Our dear friend Misha has arranged a magnificent banquet in celebration of this wonderful event. We will again be guests at our friends the count and countess. The following day the bishop will join us together as mother, father, and sons in a most splendid and spectacular ceremony. This union shall acknowledge both you, John, and you, David, as princes in the eyes of the Church and the Russian people, by virtue of your relationship to your mother, Princess Maria. Following the church service the banquet will be held in the cathedral hall."

"I should be honored to attend these ceremonies," the judge said before leaving the room. "Please advise me or my secretary of the times these events will take place."

Immediately after returning home, Niki opened a bottle of vodka which he had brought from Russia when they left to sail to the United States.

"I have been saving this bottle all these years for a most special occasion—it was the finest vodka in all of Russia," he said as he opened the bottle and poured each of them a drink into four small glasses. "Here's to our wonderful sons, John and David. May they enjoy long life, happiness, and prosperity."

"And here's to our wonderful parents, Niki and Maria, may they also enjoy long life, happiness, and prosperity," John said, as everyone raised their glasses to toast the occasion again.

At this point, Maria informed John that his name in Russian was called "Ivan" and that David's name was pronounced "Daveed." This was important to remember, as they would be so addressed at the church, and later at the banquet that would follow, by most of the Russian guests.

"I think we like John and David a lot better," John said. "Wasn't there an Ivan the Terrible? But we'll go along with it on occasions such as this." John and David had arranged for a week's furlough to attend the ceremonies that lay ahead.

The following day, John, David, Maria, and Niki left early in the morning for San Francisco to visit first the count and countess. Later they would attend the celebration at the church service, to be immediately followed by the banquet at the cathedral hall that Misha had prepared.

"Welcome my dear Princess, John, David, and General Nevski," the count said in greeting them. "It's an honor to have you again as guests at our home. Of course, this time it's even a greater honor than before, as you bring with you your two sons who are now legally bound to you now and forever. Please make yourselves comfortable as we await the church service, followed by the banquet that has been arranged in honor of both you and your sons. Misha has assured me that it will be one of the most splendid events that he has ever prepared. Even more spectacular than your Names Day banquet not so long ago."

Finally the big event was to take place. John and David were dressed in tuxedos that the count had graciously provided for the evening, and were seated next to Maria and Niki, who were also elegantly dressed for the occasion. Niki wore the uniform of the Russian imperial general staff, while Maria wore a most elegant gown and jewels provided by the countess. John and David were seated to the front of the church, alongside their parents Niki and Maria

The service was conducted in Russian and after what seemed a lengthy start the bishop left the altar and took his place in front of John and David. First in Russian, and then in English, he said: "From the day of your birth, this union between you, Ivan, and you, Daveed, to your parents Nikolai and Maria, was preordained by God and therefore has always been. With the acknowledgment that by virtue of Maria's birth, and her direct relationship to the late Czar Nicholas II of Russia, both Ivan and Daveed being the legal sons of Princess Maria and General Nikolai Nevski are now and henceforth to be considered princes in the eyes of the Church and to all those here present."

Fortunately, the service did not last beyond an hour and after anointing with holy water, incensing with frankincense and myrrh and extending all the blessings of the church upon the union of this newly created family, the bishop left with those in attendance and the service came to an end.

Immediately following the service, Niki, Maria, John and David were escorted to the banquet hall and seated at a table elevated on a platform, to the front of the hall.

One by one, countless guests passed by offering their best wishes and good health to Princess Maria, Prince Ivan, Prince Daveed, and General Nevski.

"Here's to Princess Maria," Misha said. With this proposed, everyone raised their glasses and drank the contents.

"Here's to General Nevski." Again, everyone raised their glasses and drank the contents.

After once again refilling their glasses, Misha again proposed a toast. "Here's to Prince Ivan and Prince Daveed. May each of you, as well as your parents, have long life, happiness, and prosperity in the days and years to come."

Next, David stood up, and smiling he lifted his glass and said, "On behalf of my brother Ivan, and myself, I propose a toast to our parents whom we love and honor above all others."

After everyone finished toasting their honored guests, Niki offered a final toast to the bishop and especially to Misha for preparing this magnificent banquet.

"Please, everyone be seated," Misha announced. At this point the waiters entered the dining area with many of the dishes that would be served throughout the evening.

Russian dancers provided entertainment, along with several vocalists who sang Russian songs of the past. There was no doubt that this was the most beautiful and most spectacular event that John and David had ever experienced before or since.

Following the banquet, John, David, Maria and Niki were chauffeured back to the Count's home to spend the evening. They would leave in the morning to return to Monterey after breakfast with their hosts.

Chapter 10

"David, guess what?" John said, looking somewhat depressed, "I just got orders to report to Fort Worden, Washington, the first week in August. At least at The Presidio we could see each other every day, but now I won't be able to see you at all. Lord, am I going to be lonely without you—my brother Harold, Niki and Maria, and my friends—but especially you. Do you remember that fortune you got in Chinatown? Something like you were going on a long trip. Well, it looks like it came true for me and not for you. I guess we all knew that something like this could happen, but I never thought that much about it—that is, until now.

"Holy shit, John! I don't know what to say except I'm going to miss you more than I've ever missed anyone else in my life. You're the closest I've ever been to anyone—or ever will be, for that matter. God, I'm going to miss you. Anyway, today's April the 20th, so that gives us a little more time together. What do ya say we meet with all our friends next Saturday at the Golden Goose for sort of a going-away party? I'll call Mary and Joan to see if they can make it—I hope they can. God, I'm going to miss you John. Sunday, we can take Niki and Maria to the Pampered Gourmet for dinner. Don't worry, I got the money, as I've been saving up to take all of you out, anyway. We can visit with Alexis and Neil at the same time.

How's that sound? At any rate, we'll have to tell Niki and Maria tonight. This is really going to be hard on them, you know. I'll ask Steve to drive us to the house as they've both left work and should be home by now."

"Promise me you'll write to me often. Will you, David?"

"Sure John, you knew I would, even without your asking."

"Before I actually leave, we'll have to make up some code words to use in case someone should read one of our letters. You know, something like signing off the letter with your friend followed by your name. This could actually mean I really miss you a lot, and you mean more to me than any-one I've ever known, or ever will. We could also figure out some other code words to use. What do you think about this plan, David?"

"I think it's great, John, and you're right about keeping our letters safe from others."

Shortly after calling Steve, he arrived on the base, and after John and David got in the car, they headed for Niki and Maria's house. That is to say also John and David's home now that Niki and Maria were their parents.

Upon arriving at the house, Steve accompanied John and David inside.

After introducing Steve to Niki and Maria, John said, "Guess what? I've got something important to tell you. First off, we all knew that one day either David or I might get transferred someplace other than Fort Ord. Well, to make a long story short, I'm being transferred to Fort Worden, Washington. Actually, that's not too terribly far from here, as it's right next to Seattle, Washington. One thing's for sure, I'll write at least once a week and I'll call whenever I can. I love you both, and you know I'm really going to miss you, just as I'll miss David while I'm away."

"Come now, John Earl English, why don't you have a seat with David and your friend while Niki pours you a drink to celebrate your continued health and happiness. You probably know that since this Korean War, Niki and I have been just scared beyond belief that you might somehow be transferred there. Well now, I had better not think about it or I'll start crying. We don't ever want to lose you or see you hurt."

"Don't worry, Mom, nothing's going to happen to either David or me, you'll see."

"John's right, you know. We're a family now and nothing can break that up—nothing," David said in agreement with John.

"Thank you, Steve, for bringing my boys home tonight. Niki and I really appreciate it, and you've been such a good friend to both of them that you're welcome here anytime."

After Niki handed everyone a glass of tea into which he'd added strawberry preserves and a double shot of vodka, he proposed a toast. "Here's to both John's and David's safety and good health. And should they both be transferred at some point, I ask the Lord to bring them both back to us safe and sound. I only want to add to this that, as Maria and I have already said before, both you, David, and you John, are the gifts from God that we have so long prayed for. Everything we have is yours, you are our sons and we love you both more than anything else in this world."

"Now enough of this sentimental talk. Let's celebrate all those things that we have to be thankful for," Maria said, as she started toward the kitchen to prepare some snacks to go along with another drink that Niki was now preparing to serve.

"If you don't mind, Mr. Nevski, I'll just have tea without the shot this time. I have to drive back to the ship, you know."

"Why don't you stay here tonight, Steve?" Maria asked. "You can sleep with John and David, if they don't mind being a little crowded. I'll get another pillow and Niki can provide you with pajamas and a bathrobe. I would have suggested the sofa but it's a little too short and would be much too uncomfortable."

"We don't mind sharing, and you know you're more than welcome to stay," David said. "None of us have to be up early with tomorrow being Saturday. Anyway, you'll love Maria's cooking. So what do ya say, Steve?"

"Sure, why not? Paul has a weekend assignment at The Presidio, and can't go out. Guess I can have a double shot, after all," Steve said, accepting the invitation.

After watching TV for the remainder of the evening along with snacking and a couple more drinks, David, John, and Steve were more than ready for bed.

"Gee, guys, wait until I tell Paul that I spent the evening sleeping with the two of you. I wonder what he'll think of that?"

"My guess is he won't give it a second thought," John said. "Paul knows that David and I don't fool around. He also knows that we respect his relationship between the two of you. I must admit that you are one really cute guy and if David and I weren't together you wouldn't be safe tonight. How's that for a compliment? Now let's all get some sleep, OK?"

After the three had undressed and changed into the pajamas Niki had provided for them, they got into bed. Steve slept on one side of the bed next to David. Suddenly, David grabbed both of Steve's hands, pinning him to the bed, and laughingly said, "Now I got you where I want you." Then immediately letting him go, he added, "Let that be a lesson to you not to accept this type of invitation from strangers." All three started laughing so much that they could hardly control themselves.

"OK, guys, we'd better stop laughing and get to sleep before Niki comes in to see what's going on," John said, still trying to hold back the laughter himself.

After a while all three drifted off to sleep and the joking around had ended for the evening.

The following morning, after knocking briefly on the door, Niki entered the room. "OK, boys, time to be up. Breakfast will be ready soon. Maria and I are done in the bathroom so you're welcome to use it now. I left a new toothbrush for you, Steve, and if you want to shave you can use John's or David's razor. I'm sure it would be OK with them."

After Niki had left the room, David once again pinned Steve to the bed, saying, "You can use the bathroom after we're done with you." Then David released him almost as quickly as he had the night before. Once again they all started laughing.

"No more grab ass, I promise," David said as he gave John a swat on the butt and started climbing out of bed.

"I'll go first," Steve said. "That way I can get a head start on the two of you. Anyway, I'm getting hungry, so the both of you had better be just as fast as me or there won't be anything left for you to eat. By the way, I'm really enjoying my stay. If you don't mind, could I stay again tonight?"

"Sure, Steve. You know you're always welcome and it's sort of fun having you stay over," John said as he started to get dressed.

After everyone had used the bathroom and finished dressing, they started toward the kitchen.

By this time the smell of fresh-brewed coffee, bacon, eggs, pancakes, pork chops, and fried potatoes with onions was enough to get all three moving, and it didn't take long before everyone was seated at the table and ready to eat.

"Good morning," Maria said as she started to pour coffee for everyone. "Now be sure to eat as much as you can. I've prepared plenty and we don't want it to go to waste—now do we?"

Following breakfast, the three of them sat around engaging in conversation with Niki and Maria. After a while Steve said, "How about me giving you guys a ride back into town. We could spend some time with our friends from the Ship and The Presidio. Boy, are they going to be surprised to hear about your transfer, John."

"Sounds good to me," David said. "That way we can tell them about our plans to meet at the Golden Goose next Saturday and have a sort of farewell party for John." And turning to Niki and Maria, he added, "You know you're both welcome to join us if you want."

"Thanks, David, but I think we'll leave that day for you and your friends to enjoy. Anyway, we have you here at home the rest of the time," Maria said, as she started clearing the table.

"Now you know if you change your mind you're always welcome to join us," John added. "Anyway, don't make any plans for next Sunday as we have plans for the four of us; it's sort of a surprise, OK? Oh, yes, Steve asked if he could stay over again tonight, if it's OK with you."

"Why, thank you, John. You can be certain that Niki and I will be looking forward to Sunday, and of course Steve is always welcome to stay over."

After about an hour had passed following breakfast, Steve, John, and David excused themselves and drove into town to meet up with their friends.

"You know, John, I think we had better not ask Harold and his friends to join the party next Saturday, and I'm sure you know why," David said as they made their way to the ship to see Gary. "I think they'd go nuts if they saw the way Steve and Paul carry on after they've had a few drinks, and I guess that not only goes for them, but for the rest of us as well. Anyway how 'bout us inviting them somewhere else to get together on Friday? I'm sure Rick wouldn't mind the bunch of us coming over. If he can't have us over on Friday, there's always The Vet's club. By the way, I think we should also invite Rick to join us on Saturday, but we'll have to tell him to keep it a secret from Harold and the others."

"Sounds good to me," John said.

"Me too," Steve added.

Friday evening everyone arrived at Rick's shortly after six to get together prior to John's leaving for Fort Worden on Monday. Rick was looking forward to this gathering as Bill had agreed to stay the night with him after everyone had left.

"I'm really going to miss you, little brother," Harold said. "And I'm sure that goes for the rest of us. Anyway, it was bound to happen one day so let's party and make the best of it." Rick had bought several cases of beer and Green brought wine. Harold provided the chips and other snacks to go along with the drinks. As before, conversation revolved around women, with real or imagined stories of their female conquests.

It was well past eleven when the party ended and everyone but Bill had left for the night. "Well, John, we survived that ordeal alright. Didn't we?"

"We sure did, David, but I'm glad we were able to get together with Harold and the others. Tomorrow should be fun. Joan and Mary said they could make it, and they plan to stay overnight at a motel so that they can really enjoy themselves and be completely sober when they drive back to San Francisco the next day."

By six-thirty Saturday evening everyone, including Rick and Don from Fort Ord, had arrived at the Golden Goose where they were met by Joan and Mary. After a while Scott came over to the tables that had been placed together for them and, after putting his hands on Gary's shoulders and gently rubbing them, he said, "Drinks and everything else is are the house if you're staying with me tonight, Gary. Actually, I'd do it for John even if you said no, but I hope your answer is yes. Whatcha say, Gary?"

"You didn't have to ask, Scott. I already planned on staying with you— you're sort of growing on me, you know it. Hope you're good at giving a massage. I could really use one tonight to limber me up."

"Sure, Gary, I'll give you a massage like you never had before—one that'll cover every inch of your body."

"Sounds great, Scott, but while you're rubbing my shoulders just massage my back a little right now."

After several pitchers of beer arrived at the table and everyone was poured a drink, Mary proposed a toast to John, "Here's to our good friend John. We're all going to miss you. But Fort Worden, Washington, doesn't sound too bad. At least you'll have a chance to see Seattle, and I hear Washington is really beautiful this time of year."

The evening couldn't have been better. Everyone was having a really great time. Rick and Bill seemed to be hitting it off and it appeared that Bill was becoming more interested in Rick than he had been in Gary. One thing was for certain, Mary and Joan, and the guys had become so close that they were like family. John was going to miss them as much as they would miss him. After a wonderful evening together, everyone said their goodbyes and made their way back to town. After dropping John and

David off at home, Steve stayed the remainder of the evening with Paul at the church and would return to the ship the following day.

Around 5 P.M., David asked Niki to drive the four of them to The Pampered Gourmet as he had something special planned for them.

After they arrived at the restaurant and were escorted to their seats, they were greeted by Alexis and Neil who both came to their table. "What a pleasant surprise this is, to see the four of you again. Is this some sort of celebration?" Neil asked.

"No, not actually a celebration, but rather a going away dinner for John. He got transferred and he's leaving for Fort Worden, Washington, this week," David answered. "I was planning on taking Mom and Dad out for dinner anyway and I figured this was the best time to do it—that is, while John was still here to be with us."

"Wow, I know that's really going to be hard on all of you—and Alexis and I are going to miss him also. Now don't worry about a thing, everything's on the house. It's sort of our farewell gift to John."

"Gee, thanks, Neil, but we really didn't expect you to do this. I have the money to pay," David said.

"You might have the money," Alexis added, "but we want to do it—and that's that. I recommend prime rib, which is the special for the day." Niki and Maria had had it before and it was the best they ever ate.

"That sounds wonderful, and if everyone is agreeable that would be just great," Maria suggested. John and David were also pleased with the selection, and shortly after placing their order, dinner was served. Following the meal Alexis and Neil both found time to join them for dessert and some pleasant conversation. This was to be the last time that the four of them would go out together before John was to leave for Fort Worden and an uncertain future.

Amid sad and tearful farewells John boarded the bus that would take him to Seattle and from there he would report for duty at Fort Worden.

"Sir, PFC John Earl English reporting for duty, sir."

"Well, English, you will be assigned to the base hospital, as I see your MOS indicates you are a medic," Lt. Lester said. "Sgt. Easton will take you to the barracks where he will assign one of the men to show you around. Tomorrow morning you will report to Mrs. Gilligan, a civilian nurse at the hospital. We don't have an Army nurse here, but you will regard her as though she were an officer. At any rate, welcome to Fort Worden and I think you'll enjoy your stay here," the lieutenant said, ending the brief interview.

On the way to the barracks Sgt. Easton said, "My name's Kelsey. Anything I can do to help you, let me know. By the way, we're not that formal here so forget the sergeant when we're alone like this."

"Sounds fine with me, and you can call me John, OK?"

Kelsey hailed from Texas, was only nineteen and already a sergeant. Perhaps his promotions were due in part to his deep, commanding voice, as well as being over six feet tall, and rather muscular. This was complemented by his rugged good looks.

The walk to the barracks was short and soon John was introduced to Pvt. Piper. "Hi, I'm Alan, Alan Piper. Glad to meet you, John."

Alan was born in Michigan but moved to California when he was still a child. He was about five foot-seven, of medium build and had light brown hair with a short-cropped haircut. He had a full face, pleasant smile, and was attempting to grow a mustache.

"Guess I'm supposed to show you around the place, so we'd better get started," Alan said. "I hear you're being assigned to the hospital. Boy, that sounds like an easy job. How'd you get to be a medic, anyway?"

"You're not going to believe this, but while I was at The Presidio, they assigned me to work in the dispensary shortly before my transfer. Not much to do there but I did learn a few things," John said as they continued touring the base.

"What do ya do for excitement around here, Alan?"

"Actually, not much, there's a few bars outside the fort but other than that we usually spend the weekends in Port Townsend or Seattle. If you're into women, I know a really nice little bar we could go to tonight. Whatcha say, John? I got a car. Actually, most the guys here have cars, otherwise it would be a little hard to get around."

"Sure, Alan, I'd be glad to go out with you tonight but I'm not twenty-one yet and, as for the women, I'm engaged—and so far I haven't been cheating. In fact, I don't intend to, if that's OK with you."

"Boy, you sure must be in love. I'm married and I screw around—when I can, that is. My wife lives in Portland with her parents, so that makes it easy for me. Anyway, I have to respect you for being faithful. Not many of us are, you know."

"What ya do for entertainment here? I mean, like a theater," John asked.

"Yeah, I'll be showing you that soon, and if you like water, we always have the ocean. Sometimes we have maneuvers. You'll see the landing craft when we get down to the beach. You play volleyball? We got that, handball, and tennis if you're interested."

"Sure, Alan, I played volleyball back at The Presidio and I used to play handball a lot. Never played tennis but I'm game for a try."

After a couple hours had passed, the tour was over and it was time for lunch. "Food's not bad here. Could be worse, you know. I usually sit over there with Kelsey and four other buddies," Alan said, as they made their way over to a table nearest the serving area.

"This is Adam. This is Brice. This is Carson, and last but not least, this is Barney. Of course, you already know Kelsey."

Adam was a twenty-year-old from New York with a Brooklyn accent. He had dark brown eyes, heavy black hair, an elongated face, and was tall and exceptionally thin.

Brice was from Kansas and had actually been stationed at Camp Funston for basic training at the same time that John had been there. Actually, that's about all they had in common, as they had been in different companies. Brice had straw-colored hair, deep blue eyes, average build and height, nice-looking aside from a mild case of acne.

Carson's mother was Japanese and his father was Caucasian. They had met and married shortly after the war. He had a slight oriental look to his eyes, rounded face, dark brown eyes, coarse black hair, was five foot-eleven with a muscular build, and a skin tone similar to that of an Italian. This ethnic combination made him quite an attractive man.

Barney was born in Australia and came to this country when he was twelve. He had a definite accent, which seemed to make him interesting to the others. Aside from being over six-foot, he appeared to be of average looks, build, and weight. Like Brice, he had straw-colored hair and deep blue eyes.

"OK, guys, this is John English," Alan said as he introduced John to the others. "He just got transferred here from The Presidio of Monterey—California, that is."

"Boy, I sure wouldn't mind being stationed there," Brice cut in. "What do ya say the six of us pick up a case of beer and head out to the park as soon as we're off-duty? Alan can pick it up—he's twenty-one. We'll eat first and after chow we'll head out, if it's OK with you guys."

"OK with me, and I guess that goes for the rest of us," Adam said as he continued eating.

After everyone had emptied their trays and returned to the barracks they quickly changed from their fatigues into civvies, while a few wore their uniforms.

"We'll only need one car, so what's say we take my station wagon. It's got plenty of room," Carson offered.

Thanks, Carson. We'll chip in on the gas, and don't forget, guys, when Alan picks up the beer we all have to divvy up. Maybe we'll pick up some chips to go with the beer," Kelsey said as the six of them left the barracks and started toward the car.

After a short drive, they arrived at a seldom-used park and made their way to a nearby picnic table. After placing the beer and chips on the table and taking a seat, Kelsey passed each of the men a bottle of beer and said, "I got the opener, and if you gotta take a leak, go over there by those trees.

There's no john here—there's no women here either so you'll have to take care of that problem another day. Anyone know any good jokes?" It seemed everyone knew a joke or two and this helped pass the time. As they drank more beer, the conversation naturally turned to women just as John thought it would. Much like with Green and the others it was questionable as to what was truth and what was fiction. It was to some extent true that the more a man bragged about it, the less he actually got.

At any rate, by the time the men had consumed four beers each, they were ready to head back to the Fort. One thing's for certain, the tree nearby sure got a good wetting as each in turn left the table from time to time to water it with their urine.

The following morning, John reported early to the base hospital, where he met another medic who was also assigned there.

"Hi, my name's John. I just got transferred here from The Presidio of Monterey. What's your name?"

"Cpl. Jarvis. You can call me Marty—glad to meet you. I usually work the afternoon shift, but the guy I relieved was transferred to Fort Lawton. Guess you'll be taking his place. Mrs. Gilligan, the nurse, will be here shortly. You'll like her."

Marty looked to be in his early twenties, slightly on the heavy side, with thick lips, rounded face, and a rather large nose. His hair was already receding in front, and the sloppy manner in which he wore his uniform did not add to the way he looked. At any rate, he was pleasant and more than anxious to show John around.

"This is the nursing station," he said, pointing to a rather small area which the nurse usually occupied. "That area over there is the treatment room, and that room over here is the ward. As you can see, right now we got sixteen guys in the ward, mostly with a really bad cold or the flu. Hope you don't get it. I already had it and it sure was hell."

The ward was the largest room in the hospital and this was where John was to spend most of his time.

Shortly after eight, Mrs. Gilligan arrived. "Hi there. I guess you're the young man being assigned to take Cpl. Horne's place. My name's Mrs. Gilligan. I'm the nurse. As you can see, I'm not in the Army although I used to be during the War. I understand your name is John English. Am I correct?"

"Yes, ma'am," John answered.

"Well, John, I'm happy to meet you and I hope you enjoy working here. Capt. Falconetti is the base physician. He usually makes rounds around ten. We call it grand rounds. Cpl. Jarvis will show you what you have to do. If I can be of any help please don't hesitate to ask." Mrs. Gilligan then took her place at the desk and Marty introduced John to the patients on the ward.

Mrs. Gilligan appeared to be in her early to mid-sixties with gray hair which was pulled back into a bun. She wore a starched white uniform and cap and was fairly thin. This combined with her pleasing smile, and gentle manner, seemed to add to her grandmotherly appearance.

Later, after the doctor arrived, John walked behind Marty as the doctor stopped at each patient, removed the chart hanging at the foot of the bed, and carefully went over the mans condition as well as his plan of care. This was the first time that John had actually received so much medical information and he could hardly wait to learn more. One of the patients required an IV to be started and Marty instructed John in the procedure.

That evening after John had returned to the barracks, he sat down at his bunk,m and placing a piece of paper on an old magazine, he wrote a letter to David. "Dear David. I started my new job today. I met Mrs. Gilligan, the nurse, Dr. Falconetti, who I'm sure is Italian, and a Corporal named Marty who will be working the afternoon shift—sort of reminds me of Green. Had my first introduction into what I'll be doing here. Oh, yeah, yesterday I met the commanding officer and later on, six of the guys in the barracks. We went out together and had a few beers in the park nearby. Seem like nice guys but I still miss all of you back home. I hear that Seattle is a lot like San Francisco, and is also on seven hills. I plan to be going there soon with some of the guys. Give my love to Ma and Dad, my brother Harold, and the others. Your friend, John." After finishing with the letter, John placed it in his footlocker, undressed and, placing a towel around his waist he proceeded into the latrine to take a shower, brush his teeth, and prepare for bed.

Two weeks after arriving John had become proficient in starting IVs, monitoring vital signs, sterilizing gauze and instruments in the autoclave, and had given two injections under the direct supervision of Mrs. Gilligan. There was much more to learn, of course, but John proved to be an eager learner and a competent practitioner.

"Hey, John, wanna join us? We're going to Seattle tomorrow for the weekend. It's a good thing we just got paid. We'll be going by boat unless you're a good swimmer. Ever been there before?" Alan asked.

"No. Never been there. How is it?" John asked.

"Great. Lots of places to go and lots of women to choose from. By the way, if you promise never to tell, I'm going to show you a place where you can get a new ID card. Promise?"

"Sure, Alan, I promise. You know damned well I'd never tell anyone. I'm not exactly stupid, you know."

"I knew I could trust you, now take a look at mine," Alan said as he pulled out his wallet and took out his ID. "What do ya think of this? I'm really only nineteen. Pretty good, huh?"

"Hell, yeah, you could sure fool me. How do I get one?"

"When we get in Seattle, we all split up. You and me can stick together and I'll show you the place. All you have to do is pay for it. Anyway, it's not that much," Alan said as he returned his wallet to his back pocket. "Later on we'll get a room together, and after that I'll show you a couple good bars where I know a few women. If I manage to pick one up would you mind if I brought her up to the room for about an hour? You could wait in the bar and I'd meet you back there as soon as I was finished. You don't mind, do you?"

"Hell, no, I don't mind as long as you don't take too long with her," John said in an attempt to convey his approval.

"You don't have to worry about that. I get off so quick, it's usually over in fifteen minutes unless she goes for a little foreplay. Anyway, the reason I say an hour is that sometimes I manage to get off twice."

"Boy, Alan, you're one horny sucker, aren't you?"

"I'm probably no more horny than you. It's just that you don't play around the way I do. Just as well, at least you'll keep your pecker clean. There's all kinds of shit you can catch out there."

The following day, Alan, John and the rest boarded the ferry that took them to Seattle. It was strange but John now felt a close attachment to Alan, although not sexual, that was nonetheless close. This relationship was a great help in relieving the depression he had felt after leaving The Presidio.

"OK, guys, we're here. What do ya think? Quite a town, isn't it?" As the guoup paired off and went their separate ways, John and Alan headed for the photo ID shop.

Upon receiving his new ID card, John along with Alan found a hotel where they paid for a room.

"You don't mind, do you John—I mean sharing with me. All they had was a double bed.

"No, it won't bother me, if it don't bother you, just as long as we both sleep with our shorts on. Anyway, I know I'll be safe from you and you'll be safe from me. Alan had to laugh. "You know damned well I'll have shorts on. I don't believe in taking a turn in the barrel. If I hoard the covers, just yank your half away from me. "

After checking in, they made their way to a local bar where western music was played and the customers dressed as though they had just came off a ranch in Texas. With the Korean War going on, uniforms proved to be quite popular with the women and it wasn't long before Alan had hooked up with one of them.

"See you in about an hour," Alan said, as he and the woman left for the hotel. John wasn't quite sure if Alan was paying, or getting it for free. At any rate, it really didn't matter one way or the other.

"Hi, soldier. Mind if I join you? I see your buddy just left with Cora. You married?"

"No, but I'm engaged."

"What's that supposed to mean—like you don't fool around? By the way, my name's Grace, so if you want company, I'll be sitting over there."

"Don't bother with her, buddy," the guy sitting next to John said. "She's a hustler, and I hear she's got the clap. How about a drink, it's on me soldier? I was in the Army during WWII. Sure in the hell glad I got out when I did or I'd be in this Korean shit right now. By the way, my name's Tex."

"Thanks, Tex, I'll have a beer. Any kind is OK. Whatever you're drinking is fine with me, and my name is John. Thanks for cluing me in on Grace. One thing's for sure, I don't need the clap."

"And watch out for that one over there. She's a looker all right—but nothing but a prick teaser. All she does is take a guy for drinks, but never puts out. She'll even rub your leg to lead you on. But I guess you've seen that type before."

John sat there sipping slowly on his drink so as not to have too many before Alan returned. Strangely enough, John didn't feel at all uncomfortable in this setting and the conversation between Tex and him shifted from one topic to another.

"Excuse me, buddy, time for a piss call," Tex said as he got up and headed to the latrine. Just as Tex left, Alan returned and ordered a beer.

"Wow! Was she hot and guess what? I got it for free. Turns out she's married to some guy who can't get it up. What a shame—for her, that is. But for me it couldn't have turned out better. Anyway, I'm sorry I took so long but I actually came three times. Of course, the third one was a dry run." John couldn't help but laugh at the way Alan had put it.

By this time Tex had returned to his seat and after introducing Alan to Tex, they had one more beer before leaving for a nearby café.

After they had eaten, Alan and John took in one more bar before winding up the evening and returning to the hotel.

"If you don't mind, I'll shower first?" Alan asked as he started to undress. "I need it after all that action I had earlier."

"No, go ahead, I'll go next" John answered as he too undressed, wrapped a towel around his waist and waited to shower next before calling it a night.

After both were in bed, Alan casually remarked, "I'm glad I met up with you, John. I think we're going to be really good buddies. What do you think?"

"Yeah, me too, Alan. Now what's say we call it a night? Oh, by the way, thanks for getting me that ID card."

Although Alan was quite good-looking, John remained devoted to David. Even if he hadn't been, he wouldn't have approached Alan sexually, as he valued his friendship far more.

The following morning both were up early and after shaving and brushing their teeth, they were ready for breakfast and a day of sightseeing which would be later followed by another evening of hitting the bars. Alan made out once again, and the night ended much as it had the day before.

Everyone made it back on time, thus ending John's first weekend in Seattle, and the beginning of a close and honest friendship between Alan and himself.

After returning to the barracks, John again started a letter to David, followed by another letter to Niki and Maria. In writing these letters he was careful to omit those details that he knew he couldn't and shouldn't write about. There were nonetheless lots of interesting things to say.

During the next four months John continued to learn as much as he could while assigned to the hospital. So far he had assisted with giving blood on two occasions, performed many IV sticks and IM injections. Mrs. Gilligan had given him several books from which he could continue learning. One was a book on anatomy and physiology, another a book on pharmacology, and one on medical surgical nursing. When not going off the base he would read these books, absorbing as much as he could. Where he had questions he would ask either Mrs. Gilligan or Dr. Falconetti for advice.

So far he had been to Seattle four times and to Victoria Island in Canada once. Of course, John and Alan remained close friends, often going out to different places together or joining with the others who had also become his friends.

Twice there had been maneuvers on the beach and one involved the use of a couple landing craft, which were operated by sailors stationed nearby.

One day while having lunch, Carson and Barney informed the others at the table that they had received orders to report to Fort Lawton on the outskirts of Seattle. It was no secret that their next stop would be Japan and then Korea.

"Boy, that's some really bad news, guys, and we're really going to miss you. Looks like they're trying to break up the old gang, doesn't it?" Alan said.

"Sure does, and it won't seem the same without you guys around here. We're sure going to miss going out, having fun, and joking around with you," John added. "Today's Thursday, so what do ya say we all go out together once more before you guys leave. How's this Saturday sound to everyone?"

"Sounds good to us," Carson answered for the others. "Guess it'll be Seattle again. It's the best place to have a good time. How about us all staying at the 'Y' this time—that way we can sort of stick together. We could get three double rooms in case we want to sit up and talk. Anyway, double rooms are cheaper and there's two beds to a room."

"I can go along with that except for one thing. You're talking about the 'Y' and there's no way to get a woman up to your room," Alan remarked in response to the suggestion.

"Come on Alan, you can do without it for just one weekend, can't you?" Kelsey asked. "Anyway, you seem to get all you need at that bar outside the fort."

"Guess you're right, Kelsey. Yeah, the 'Y' is OK with me if it's OK with you guys. It'll be rough, but remember, I'm giving it up this time because you're my friends."

"Jesus, Alan, you make giving up pussy for a couple nights something like committing a mortal sin. Anyway, your prick could probably use the rest. If you're not screwing you're probably pulling on it," Kelsey said with a laugh.

"I'm not doing anything the rest of you guys don't do, although I admit I do a little more of it than the rest of you. Now whatcha say we finish eating and get back to work. See you guys at dinner, then I have a date tonight," Alan said as he finished with his tray and continued with his coffee.

The trip to Seattle proved to be a lot of fun. Alan smuggled in some whiskey, which they mixed with soft drinks they had brought in with them, and all six men spent a good portion of the evenings in Carson's room, drinking, telling jokes, and laughing a lot. At one point the guy in the room next door—a sailor—came over to complain and was invited to join them. He did, and both that night and the next, there were no further complaints.

By the time they had returned to Fort Worden they had been bowling, roller skating, had taken in a flick at a nearby theater and also went dancing where they were charged for each dance.

The following Monday Carson and Barney said their last farewells, boarded the boat and left for Seattle for the short trip to Fort Lawton. There was a certain and definite sadness in seeing them go, and were it not for Alan and those who remained, John would have experienced some of the depression he'd felt on leaving David and the others behind when he left The Presidio.

Next to go was Kelsey, and just one month later John received his orders to transfer as the others had already done. It was now early November and getting quite cold.

"Mail call," Pvt. Nelson called out, as he started to pass out mail to most of those who had gathered. "You got four letters, English. You sure must be popular."

John took his mail and while alone he read first the letter from Niki and Maria. Next from Joan and Mary, then from his brother Harold, Finally, he carefully opened the letter from David, which he had saved for last, and began to read it:

"Dear John:

I don't know if Harold has told you or not, but Harold, Green, and several others including myself have all received orders for Fort Lawton. Being that you're stationed at Fort Worden, we'll finally get a chance to see one another again. I had planned to take a furlough and visit you this Christmas, but I guess this way it won't be necessary, as we'll be nearby. I've been staying every night at home with Niki and Maria, and they always say how much they miss you. I haven't told them yet, but I only have one week left before the transfer. I hate to tell them, as I don't know how they'll take it with both of us gone. Everyone back here asks about you all the time. Call me one evening this week at home. I miss talking to you.

Your Friend,

David"

Later that evening, John called home and after having a pleasant conversation with Niki and Maria, he asked them if he could talk to David alone,

"Go right ahead, dear, I know you boys have a lot to say between yourselves," Maria said, as she and Niki made their way into the kitchen.

After they had left David took the phone and said, "Hi John. How you doing? I miss you."

"Boy, it's great talking to you, David. By the way, I got your letter the same day I got one from Harold. Strange he didn't mention the transfer. Maybe he didn't know yet when he wrote to me. You're not going to believe this, David, but I also got orders for Fort Lawton, so we'll probably be meeting up there around the same time, so be sure to look for me, and I'll be looking for you and the others. I can't talk much longer as I'm running out of change. Give my love to everyone and I'll see you soon." At this point the operator interrupted and John had to hang up. One thing was for certain—by fate, luck, or misfortune they were all bound for Korea together in the very near future.

Chapter 11

As Harold continued to recall the events surrounding his brother, and John's relationship to David, his eyes watered slightly and he stared off into space for a moment, as though deep in thought.

"It was in November of 1951, and it was cold as hell when John, David, Bruce, and I got our orders and were transferred to Fort Lawton, Washington. As we would soon find out, Fort Lawton was located just five miles northwest of Seattle and was the center for embarkation. You might call it fate, but by whatever strange coincidence, we all ended up there together. It was Korea and we knew it.

"John and I were put in a Quonset hut, a long oval shaped single floor barracks made of corrugated metal that was heated with an oil stove fed by a barrel outside. Unless you stood right by the stove you never really seemed to get warm. One of the guys changed the barrel when it got empty. How he knew what to do, I'll never know.

"A couple days went by and we were told to stand in another long line while we waited to see the medics," Harold continued. "We got the same shots we had at Camp Funston, plus several others that we never had before; so much for sore arms. This was followed by short arm inspection. I guess you'd call it a pecker check. You stood in front of this guy, pulled out your dick, and milked it down—like milking a cow with only one stroke allowed. Checking for VD, they said. God forbid they should ship you out with the clap. You gotta die clean, you know. David arrived a few days after we did, and ended up in the barracks next to us. It's a wonder he even found us with so many men waiting to be processed for shipping out."

Again, Harold stopped to recall those days that seemed like only yesterday, and yet were so very long ago.

"Jesus, John. I thought I'd never see you again. I hear that Harold's here also," David said, as he grabbed John and hugged him for almost a minute before letting him go. "When they shipped me here, I sure in hell knew why. Everyone that I ever talked to, all said the same thing—if it's Fort Lawton, your ass is off to Korea. Hey, what do you think of these chow lines? I never saw anything so long or so slow. By the time you finally get in the mess hall you could have froze to death."

"How long do you think we'll be here, David?" John asked. "I hear some guys have been here as long as a month—maybe even more."

"Well, let's put it this way, John. As long as we're here, we're not over there—getting our ass shot off, that is."

"I guess you're right about that, David. We sure in the hell don't want our asses shot off. Do we?" John said, as he had to laugh at the thought of it.

"You'll never believe this, John, but guess what, Bruce is a couple barracks down from me. Wait till Harold finds out. He'll sure be glad to see him. Oh, yeah, saw a couple other guys we know. Green's in with Bruce and you'd never guess who they put in with me—Big dick Dickson. You remember him from Basic, don't you? Hope the poor guy don't get his pecker shot off—by a bullet, that is."

"Damn, David, maybe if we keep looking we might find everyone we know waiting here to ship out. Boy, you have no idea how much I missed you while you were still at the Presidio."

"Come on, John. You couldn't have missed me any more than I missed you. What do you make of this place? It's like being sent to hell, only in reverse. A guy could freeze his balls off here. One of the guys said that 'If you think this is cold, wait until your ass lands in Korea.' How would he know?—he just got here himself—same as us."

Later on we all got passes and headed into Seattle to kill some time and have a little fun. Seattle was like San Francisco—same hills, same atmosphere. It was sort of like old times. Bruce, Green, John, David, Dickson, and I, all together again at least for one more time in town.

"You guys in the mood for Chinese? We could eat in that restaurant over there if you want," Bruce asked, as he pointed to a sign with big red letters, The Golden Dragon. "We can figure out where to go from there."

"Fine with me," David answered. "But I think I'll pass on those fortune cookies. I didn't like my fortune that time we were in Chinatown. Remember, John? The last thing I need is another fortune like that."

Everyone followed Bruce inside and took their place at a table next to a fountain and a statue of Hoy Tin.

David lit up a cigarette and handed it to John. He than lit another for himself. Soon after they were seated, a waiter arrived at the table and gave everyone a menu and a glass of water.

John ordered sweet and sour pork while David ordered almond chicken, which they planned to share between themselves. Harold, Bruce, Dickson, and Green, after carefully reviewing the menu, decided on dinner for four. First came wonton soup and an egg roll, which was soon followed by the main course.

"Boy, this is really great," Dickson commented, as he started eating. "You guys won't believe this but I never been to a Chinese restaurant before. In fact, I never been much of anyplace before. Coming from a farm you don't get to see too much of city life. Sure am glad you guys let me come along."

"Anyone heard anything? About being shipped out, I mean?" Green asked.

"No," David answered. "When it's time, they'll let us know. In the meantime let's make the best of it. Man, this almond chicken is really good. They sure in the hell give you a lot of it. How do you guys like what you ordered? The way you're scoffing it down, yours must be really good, Green."

"Yeah, it's great," Green answered, in between bites. "What's say we try to pick up some women before we head back—we might get lucky. Got the rest of the weekend to find them. What do you think—Bruce?"

"If you want my opinion, there's no way in hell we'll ever find a woman with this many guys sticking together. What do you say we break up into groups of two later on? We could all meet at the A&R Café a couple doors from here, if that's OK with everyone. How about Sunday at noon?"

"I'll go for that," Harold added. "How about Bruce and me, John and David, and Green and Dickson pairing off ? That should be one way of improving our chances."

"That sounds like a pretty good idea to me, Harold. But before we break off in pairs, how about all of us just walking around and checking things out? I'm sure there's a lot of things to see here in Seattle," Dickson commented.

"Sure, Dickson. I didn't mean that we had to separate right away. Maybe we can take in a movie on Sunday after we all get back together. In the meantime let's just finish eating before we get going," Harold remarked, as he poured another cup of tea.

"Why'd you put me with Dickson?" Green asked.

"Because he's got four times as much of what you haven't got. And maybe if you're lucky, he'll find a woman and get her so excited she won't notice you jumping in for leftovers," Bruce said, as everyone burst out laughing.

After they had all finished eating, the waiter brought a bowl of fortune cookies to the table.

"Come on, David. Take a fortune. This time it might have something good to say," John insisted, as he placed one of the cookies into David's hand.

"What the hell—why not?" David answered, as he broke open the cookie to read his fortune. "'A thoughtful man is a good man. You are both.' Wow, that's a nice change. At least it didn't say I was going on a long trip or something like that."

"Guess what? That was my fortune. You know, the one about the long trip," Bruce said, as they all started laughing again.

After everyone was ready, they paid the bill and started on their way.

"You guys ever been to the museum?" Bruce asked. "Now that was a stupid question, wasn't it? Except for John, the rest of us just got here. Anyway, how about giving it a try? It's something to do and we'll probably like it."

"Sure, why not?" Dickson answered. "I never been to a museum before. I hear they got all kinds of great stuff in those places."

"We could take the bus but the museum isn't that far away, so what do ya say we try walking it instead of taking the bus?" David suggested.

"Sure why not, I'm game if the rest of you guys are," Bruce answered as everyone started walking toward their destination.

After about twenty minutes everyone arrived at the museum and entered the building.

"Wow, this place is a lot bigger than I ever thought it would be," Green said as they made their way inside.

"Hey, Green, take a look at this," John remarked as he pointed to a painting of a rather large hipped woman with extremely big breasts. "They must have known you were coming when they hung this one up."

"What do you say we take in the Greek exhibit first, the Roman next, and the Egyptian after that?" Harold asked as they made their way in that direction?

"Sounds really great to me," Dickson answered. "I read a little about those people back in school. Wonder if it's true that those Greeks went around naked half the time?"

"Guess part of it's true, anyway. Take a look at these vases with all the naked men. And look at that statue. He's naked too. How'd you like to have been in the army back then? Take a look at those guys. They're wearing helmets and hardly anything else. If they were stationed here, they'd freeze their balls off. What do you say we move to the next room?"

"Sure, Bruce. Let's see how the Romans lived," John asked. "Remember Julius Caesar and Mark Antony? Didn't they both have something going with Cleopatra?"

"Sure did. She must have really been something, from what I read about her," Harold answered.

"Wow, look at all the statues. Maybe one day I'll make it to Rome," Dickson commented as he moved about the room fascinated by everything he saw. "Boy, I can hardly wait to see all that stuff from Egypt. Especially the mummies—if they got any."

Finally everyone entered the Egyptian room with its collection of amulets, carvings, necklaces, and bracelets. Dickson seemed almost hypnotized by it all, especially by the painted wooden sarcophagus, four canopic jars, along with the mummy of a young man in the same glass case with two mummified cats, a baboon and an ibis.

"OK, guys, we better keep moving," Bruce remarked. "We got the medieval and Chinese rooms to see yet. I don't know about you guys, but I want to see those two places before we leave. What'd you think of that Egyptian stuff, Dickson? Hope you don't have nightmares."

"Yeah, that Egyptian stuff was really great. I'm sure glad you guys let me come along or I'd probably never have seen it by myself."

"Man, look at that armor. I bet it's heavier than hell. Can't you just picture us guys trying to fight in something like that?"

"No, Green, I can't imagine it. Our field packs are heavy enough, without being weighed down with all that steel," Bruce answered.

"Jesus! Look at the size of that sword. Now who in hell could handle anything that big? Whoever it was had to have muscles like one of those weightlifters you read about. And take a look at that," Green continued, as he pointed to a spiked mace. "How'd you like to be hit over the head with that thing?"

"For my part, I don't want to be hit by anything. Now let's move on to the next room," John said, as he started toward the next exhibit.

"OK, guys, this is the last one. After we see this oriental stuff we can split up in twos and see if we can't find us some women for the night."

"Sounds good to us, Bruce. Let's see, tomorrow's Saturday, so that means we won't get back together until Sunday at noon. Now before we all split up, what's say we go someplace for coffee together?" David asked.

"Did you ever see so many statues of Buddha before? Looks like most of them had a pearl or something in their foreheads. Guess someone stole them, 'cause they're not there now. They sure knew how to carve things, didn't they?" Dickson remarked, as they made their way around the exhibit.

"Well, seems like we've seen about everything, so I guess we'll head out and find us a place to have coffee together," Harold said, as he headed toward the door. "Glad we came here. It was really interesting. Wasn't it?"

"Hey, Harold, let's stop in there," John said, pointing to a corner restaurant. "By the looks of all those people going in and out, it must be a pretty good spot."

"Sure, why not? After we have our coffee, we can split up until Sunday. OK?"

"Boy, this place is really something. Did you ever see anything like this before?" Dickson asked. "Look at this. I put in a dime and this crazy box asks for my selection. Just like one of those disc jockeys on the radio. Wonder how they do it?"

"Beats me," Green answered. "How about this, 'The Little White Cloud That Cried.' It's by Johnny Ray. Ever heard that song before? He sounds just like a woman, but he's really a man."

"No, can't say that I have," David said, as he lit a cigarette, handed it to John, and then lit one for himself. "Hey, Green. Look over there. That looks like your type for sure—big boobs and big hips. Why not give it a try? You just might luck out."

"You think I won't, don't you? Watch this."

Green got up and walked over to the table where two women were sitting and asked to join them.

"Look, soldier boy, I don't know what you're looking for, but if it's what I think it is, you'd better shove off and look someplace else. By the way, if I were interested, I'd pick either one of those two," as she pointed toward John and David.

"I got a friend you might be interested in. He's sitting over there and he's got something so big he could satisfy both of you at one time," Green said, as he pointed to Dickson.

"If it's that big, soldier boy, try shoving it up your ass. You look like you need it more than we do. Now shove off before I have to get up and kick the shit out of you."

Green stood at the table a little longer making a feeble attempt at conversation before he finally got the message and returned to his seat with the others, who were roaring with laughter.

"Boy, Green, you sure in the hell know what to say to a woman, don't you? You're one stupid son of a bitch. No wonder you never get any pussy. I can see now that Dickson will have his hands full putting up with you," Bruce said as he finished his coffee. "Now let's head out before those two broads cause us some trouble."

"That Green sure is something else. Am I glad he's not hanging out with us."

"You can say that again, David," John said, as the two of them made their way down the street. "What do you say we check in at the 'Y'? We could get a double cheaper than a hotel room."

"Sure, sounds good to me, John. I feel sorry for those poor guys: They'll probably spend the whole night out there, hunting women, while we already got what we want. Now where can we go to get a drink? You've been stationed near Seattle for almost a year now, so you should know where to go by now."

"I can do one better than that, David. Take a look at my ID card. It says I'm twenty-one."

"Jesus, where'd you ever get it?"

"There's a place here in town. They make passports and ID cards. For ten bucks they'll make one so good, you'd think it was the real thing. Come on, I'll show you where it is."

About twenty minutes later, John and David arrived at the place John had referred to. A short, fat, middle-aged man with thick-looking glasses was at the counter.

"What can I do for you boys?"

"Barney sent us. My friend needs a new ID," John answered, knowing that "Barney" was the code word the man was waiting to hear.

"After I take your ID photo you can have a seat over there. I'll have your card ready in about fifteen to twenty minutes. That'll be ten bucks for the ID and one dollar for the lamination. That's a total of eleven bucks in advance. By the way, keep your mouth shut about this. As far as I'm concerned, I've never seen you guys before." David handed the man the money and took a seat next to John as they waited for the finished product.

"How'd you ever find this place? I bet you've sure been around with that ID, haven't you, John?"

"Not long after I got stationed at Fort Worden, one of the guys told me about this place. He never did tell me how he found out, and I never asked. You're right about one thing though—I've been around all right but I've never been to bed with any of those guys, as it could never be the same as it is with you—if that's what you mean."

"Sure, John, you know that's what I meant, and it's been the same with me. I was never that close with anyone else like I've been with you. I sure in the hell missed you after you got transferred—I missed you a lot. Think I'd have gone nuts if hadn't been for Steve, Gary, and the others. That's the problem with this man's army, you get close to someone and they're sure in hell going to find a way to separate you."

"OK, soldier, here's your ID. Like I said before, keep your mouth shut about where you got it, OK?"

"Goddamn, if I didn't know any better, I'd swear this card was issued on base. Now that we're both legal, what's say we head out and find us a place to get a drink."

"Sure, David, and I know just the place. I've gone there quite a few times. They call it The Back Street Tavern. You're really going to like it. At first glance it looks a little rough, like one of those shit-kickin' western bars, but it's really more gay than straight. I met a lot of really great guys there."

"As long as it's safe—no cops and no MPs—then it's OK with me, John. I've heard about these places but this'll be the first time I was ever in one. How'd you find it, anyway?"

"You know the guy who told me where to get the ID card? He's also the one who told me about this place. I met him shortly after I arrived at Fort Worden. He was assigned to showing me around the base. Anyway, we became friends and started chumming around quite a bit after that. His name is Alan. I didn't mention him in my letters that I wrote you because I tried to be careful what I said. Remember all that shit that Mary and Joan went through? Well, I just didn't want it to happen to us just because someone got hold of one of my letters and read it when they shouldn't have, or put something into it that wasn't really there."

"How much farther is this place?"

"We're almost there, David. It's just around this corner and to the rear of the street. Guess that's how it got its name. We enter through the back door."

As John and David made their way into the bar, they were stopped by a really big guy who asked for their ID, then allowed them to enter.

It was still quite early, but almost every seat at the bar was taken. John and David grabbed a table not far from the jukebox, which was playing one of those western songs that didn't seem to make much sense. They had barely sat down when the waiter came over to their table.

"Hi, soldier, who's your friend? Just curious, but are you two together?"

"This is David, and in case you forgot, my name's John. Yep, we're together alright but that don't mean we can't be friends, if it's OK with you."

"Sure, why not? Now what do you guys want to drink?"

"Two glasses, a pitcher of beer, and some chips if you have any," John said, as he lit two cigarettes, and handed one to David.

After about ten minutes had passed, a rather good-looking guy wearing a western hat, boots and tight jeans came over to the table. "You guys mind if I join you? I just got out of the service about three months ago. It was a damned good thing my time was up or I'd be in Korea right now."

"Sure, have a seat. My name's David and this is my friend John. What's your name?"

"Ed Stinson. I've been coming here for about two weeks now. Haven't seen you guys here before, but if you don't mind, how about me getting the next round?"

"Gee, thanks, Ed. Hey, waiter, how about a glass for our friend Ed," David said, as he motioned the waiter over to the table.

"Where you guys stationed?"

"Fort Lawton," John answered. "Actually it's not like we're stationed there. We're just waiting for orders to ship out."

"You mean to Korea?"

"Yeah, so far as we know. Anyway, David and I plan on making the best of it while we're still here. Before this, we were stationed together at Fort Riley, Kansas, and then the Presidio of Monterey. I got transferred to Fort Worden, Washington, about six months ago, and David just got transferred from the Presidio last week. Anyway, we're together again, and that's all that counts. Do you live around here?"

"Just two blocks. That's one of the reasons I like this place. If I have too many, I can just walk home."

"Do you live alone or do you have a friend—like a lover, I mean?"

"If you mean another guy, I had one, John, but things just didn't work out somehow, so mostly I come here looking. Maybe I'll find someone. You never know. Anyway, I got plenty of room if you guys need a place to stay."

"That sounds good to us, Ed. We were planning to stay at the 'Y,' but your place sounds like a lot better deal to me," David said, as he started pouring another round of beer.

"Drink up, everyone. We got another pitcher coming before we leave," Ed said. "See that guy sitting over there? I've been with him a couple times—maybe three—but I'm not sure if he wants a relationship or not. He claims he's looking for someone but I'll just have to wait and see."

"Why don't you see if he'll join us," John asked. "I noticed that he keeps looking at you."

"Sure, if you guys don't mind, I'll go over and ask him. Maybe if things turn out, he might be sleeping with me tonight."

"I'll be right back," Ed said as he started to walk to his friend's table. "Hi, Jason, I see you're sitting over here by yourself. Why don't you join us? If you're wondering about those two soldiers I'm with—they're together. I've invited them to stay over at my place tonight. How about you staying over too? You could sleep with me," Ed said, as the two of them headed over to where John and David were sitting.

"I was hoping you'd ask. Sure—great. Now how about introducing me to your friends."

"This is John, and this is his friend David."

"Hi, guys. I'm Jason. Looks like I'll be staying over at Ed's tonight, so that'll make the four of us. I live about an hour from here, so that means I don't have to drive home tonight. Where you guys from?"

"Detroit," John answered. "That is, that's where we came from; but we plan on moving to Monterey when we get discharged. We got a lot of good friends and a lot of good memories in Monterey. Where you from, Jason?"

"Right here in good old Seattle, same as Ed. Gets a lot colder here, but we like it—not as expensive as San Francisco or Southern California."

The next couple hours passed quickly as the four of them talked about almost everything they could think of.

"OK, guys, what say we down our beer and take off for my place. There's a store at the end of the block so I'll pick up some beer on the way home."

After leaving the bar, the four of them stopped briefly to pick up beer, then continued to Ed's apartment.

"Well, guys, this is it. How do you like it?"

"Boy, this is really neat," David remarked, as he took a seat on the sofa.

The apartment was decorated with a wide variety of furniture. The walls couldn't possibly have held another picture or item of interest.

"You guys ever try this?" Ed said, as he offered John and David a small hand-rolled cigarette.

"What is it?" David asked.

"Weed—reefers. Ever tried it?"

"I doubt it. Never heard of it," David added.

"Here's a light. Go ahead, try it. You hold it with this hairpin and you smoke it like this," Ed suggested, as he and Jason lit up and inhaled deeply, holding the smoke in as long as they could.

"Wow, this stuff is really something," John remarked as he continued to puff on what he thought was some strange cigarette. "What's in this thing, anyway? I feel like I'm floating. Maybe it's the beer. Anyway, I'll have just one more, then I think David and I have had enough for the night."

After John and David smoked one more of those strange cigarettes, John started to get up from where he was sitting. "Jesus, am I drunk. Where's the bedroom before I pass out?"

"It's back here," Ed said laughingly, as he led John and David to a nearby room occupied by a dresser and two single beds.

"You guys can sleep on that bed, and Jason and I will be sleeping on this one. Being in the Army, you shouldn't mind sharing the room with someone else. Now should you? Here, I'll help you guys get undressed."

With this said, Ed started undressing first John, and then David, who were already half asleep. "Boy, you guys are sure built," Ed remarked as he stood by the bed just watching John and David as they lay there naked. After removing his own clothes he started to climb in bed between them when Jason entered the room.

"What the hell, Ed! I can't believe you're doing this. If you want me to stay over with you, you'd better leave them alone and get in your own bed right now."

"Sure, Jason. I had a little too much myself. I thought I was getting into my own bed."

"A likely story," Jason said, as he finished undressing and climbed into bed next to Ed. "From the look of it, I doubt those guys ever smoked a reefer before."

The following morning Ed got up first and went into the kitchen to make coffee and get breakfast together. Jason soon followed, leaving John and David alone in the room.

"Oh, shit, John. I feel like I've been run through a meat grinder, and what the hell do you make of this? We're both naked as jaybirds. This might sound strange but I seem to remember Ed pulling off my clothes last night. How about you, John?"

"To be honest, David, I don't remember a thing after coming to bed. One thing's for sure, I never sleep naked with other people in the room—like when I'm a guest somewhere. By the way, it just came to me, those cigarettes they called reefers—isn't that another name for marijuana?"

"Hell, I don't know. I've never smoked one before, but by what we experienced last night, I think you're right."

"Well, let's get dressed. Smells like they're fixing breakfast, so after we finish eating, we'll head out. One thing's for sure, we're staying at the 'Y' tonight. If we sleep naked, there won't be anyone else in the room but us," John said, as he started putting his clothes on.

"You guys getting up? Breakfast is ready in about five minutes. Hope you like omelets," Ed said in a loud voice.

"Sounds great," David answered as he finished dressing. "We'll be in, in a minute. You wouldn't happen to have an extra toothbrush would you?"

"Sure. You'll find a couple new ones in the medicine cabinet in the john. I always keep extras for overnight guests."

"Thanks, Ed, we appreciate it," David said, as he and John headed to the bathroom.

After they were finished, John and David made their way into the small dining area next to the kitchen. Jason was already having a cup of coffee when Ed brought the omelets and toast to the table.

After they were finished eating, Ed asked if they'd like to stay again that night.

"Thanks a million, Ed. We'd love to, but we have to report back to the base later today, and we're not sure if we'll even be in town tonight," John said, as he and David prepared to leave.

"Well, anyway, I'm glad you guys could stay last night, and anytime you need a place, you know where I live."

After leaving Ed's, John and David headed straight for the 'Y' where they managed to get a double room.

"What's say we both have a nice shower and rest up a bit before we head back out? And, by the way, John, that was some pretty fast thinking you did when you told Ed we had to be back at the base today. I don't think I could have taken another night at his place. I hope to hell he wasn't in bed with us. Not that he wasn't good-looking, it's just that I got what I want," David said, as he put his arm around John's shoulders and pulled him toward his chest.

"Come on, David, you can do better than that, can't you? No one can see us with our door closed, you know."

"Yeah, you're right, John," David answered, as he started removing John's shirt. "We have to get undressed anyway if we're going to use the showers. All we need to go down the hall in is a towel wrapped around us. This way, we'll have a head start," David said with a smile as he unbuckled John's belt.

"One thing's for sure, we might get that shower but I don't think we're going to get much rest," John said, as he returned the favor and started to remove David's shirt.

After both men were undressed, John lay down next to David and pulled him as close to him as he could. "You know, David, this is the first time we've been together like this since I got transferred, and last night don't count. You have no idea how good this feels. I really missed you, David."

"Yeah, John, you couldn't have missed me any more than I missed you—and I do have an idea how good this feels. Now let's finish what we just started."

After an hour or so had passed John fell asleep on David's arm, while both men rested up before the shower.

"Did you ever wonder why they always put you half-way down the hall from the latrine?" David asked as he and John finished shaving, stepped into the shower, and turned on the water.

"Yeah, it sure seems that way. Guess they just want to see how fast you can run when you have to take a leak real bad. By the way, I found my toothbrush in my shaving kit. Well, we got a long day ahead. Got any ideas?"

"Sure, John, to start with we could stop by the USO for a while and then make our plans from there. Anyway, we'll run into other guys there who might have some ideas."

After John had turned off the water and was bending over to wipe his legs, David gave him a quick snap across the butt with his towel, causing John to jump from the spot.

"Jesus, David. What was that for?"

"Just testing your reflexes, and you sure got a lot of action there. Now let's get back to the room and get dressed, so we can get started."

After John and David returned to their room they realized they had left the key on the dresser and the door was locked.

"What the hell, David. We're locked out. Now you'll have to go down to the lobby and get them to open our door."

"What do you mean me," David said as he started to laugh. "It was you who forgot the key, remember? And by the way, make sure you tuck that towel in tight or you might get raped before you get back."

"Very funny," John said as he made his way into the elevator.

About five minutes later John returned with a clerk from the front desk.

"You men have any proof that this is your room?" the man asked.

"Not unless it's tattooed on us," David said, as he started laughing."

John almost doubled up with laughter. "You can see we don't have anything on but a towel. Anyway, you'll find our uniform in there and we have ID in our wallets. My name's John English and this is David Marconi.

After they were back in their room and the man had left, John and David were still laughing as they finished dressing.

After making their way to the lobby, John stopped at the desk to ask where the nearest restaurant was.

"If you're looking for something inexpensive, how about trying Don's Diner. It's just around the corner," the man suggested.

"Gee, thanks. We'll give it a try," David remarked, as he and John started toward the door on their way out.

The diner turned out to be an old streetcar which had been converted into a restaurant of sorts, with booths on one side and a long counter on the other.

"Come on, soldiers, have a seat over there," as the waitress motioned them to a booth next to a window. My name's Ethel—what can I do for ya?"

"We'll have the breakfast special, and how about coffee while we're waiting?" John said, as he lit cigarettes for David and himself.

"Boy, does that sun feel good. It sure in the hell beats those cold, drab days we've been having. I wonder what Harold and the guys are doing right now? Just out of curiosity, do you think they might have got lucky?"

"I don't know, John. I doubt that Dickson did, with Green hanging along. Anyway, I hope we don't run into any of them at the USO. I really don't want to get back together with 'em until tomorrow—like we planned."

"I can go along with that. Now what's say we finish eating and head on out. We can just walk around a while before we stop off again."

After eating John and David started walking in the general direction of the USO.

"Do you think we'll be shipping out anytime soon, David?"

"Hell, I don't know, and I don't think they know either. One thing's for sure, I hope they ship us out together and don't separate us somehow. If you're there, I want to be there with you. By the way, when we meet the others tomorrow, do you mind if I spend a few hours alone with my brother. I got a few things I have to discuss with him—sort of personal, so you don't mind, do you?"

"Hell, no, why would I mind? It's not like you were with a stranger. How about later in the day, that way we could do whatever we had planned together, like taking in a movie or whatever. You and your brother could meet afterward, and I could meet you back at the base."

"Thanks, David. Yeah, that sounds fine with me. By the way, I know a couple guys who live here in Seattle. I had almost forgotten about them. Haven't seen them in three or four months, maybe we'll stop by and visit later on. How's that sound with you?"

"Sounds good to me. Boy, being stationed at Fort Worden sure helped you to know your way around Seattle."

"Here we are. Let's go inside. They serve coffee here. Sometimes they have donuts. Those USO volunteers are sure nice people," John said as they entered the building.

"Hi, I'm John and this is my friend David."

"Glad to meet you. My name's Marge and these two young men standing near you are Brain and Clay. Clay's the sailor and Brian's the Marine. Can I offer you some coffee and a donut?"

"Gee, thanks, Marge," and turning to Brian, John asked,—"Are you two guys stationed here?"

"Yeah, we're at the recruiting station around the block. We usually come here on our breaks. We're off today, but thought we'd stop in anyway. You guys stationed here too?"

"Nope, we're at Fort Lawton—waiting to ship out. We had the weekend off, so we're just bumming around. You guys know of any good places to go?" David asked.

"Sure, lots of 'em—that is, if you guys like bars. You're old enough, aren't you?"

"We're old enough alright, but we're not into bars with a lot of shit going on," John answered, as he tried to figure out where Brian was coming from.

Clay was rather on the thin side with thinning sandy blond hair, blue eyes, fine features, pale skin with poor complexion, and looked to be around twenty-four. In contrast, Brian, in his dress blue uniform, appeared to be on the husky side, with dark brown eyes, thick black hair, nice complexion still retaining a tan, and he had a rather handsome face with a small cleft in his chin. Brian was probably in the same age group as Clay or possibly a little older.

"You don't have to worry about the bars we'll take you to. We haven't had any trouble yet. Why don't we all have a seat over there, and get to know each other a little better before we head out, OK?" Brian said as he led the way to a corner table. "You guys play pool? If so, you can play a couple games with Clay and me."

"Yeah, we play a little—just for fun and no bets, OK? How about eightball?" David asked.

"Sure, eightball is fine with us, and we don't gamble on pool, either. You guys are probably just as good at this as us," Brian said, as he started racking the balls for a game.

"You guys into a few free drinks? If you are, we know just the place to get 'em. We call it the wrinkle room. Bunch of old men mostly—some straight, some gay. Some just want to relive their youth through you and some just want to have you. Anyway, it's good for your ego, and most of them are nice. You can meet some really interesting people there if you guys are game to give it a try."

"Sure, Brian. We're not exactly cherries, you know," John said, as he waited for Clay to start the game with the first break.

"I didn't think you were—cherries, that is. You can answer this if you want, and don't answer if you don't want to. But are you two guys close? I mean super close, like going together?"

"Yeah, guess you could say that," David answered, a little taken aback by the question.

"No problem, and now that that's straightened out, so are we—together, that is. I met Clay the day I got assigned to the recruiting station. Sailors turn me on, and I thought he was the sexiest guy I ever met. We hit it off right away and have been together ever since. How long you two been together?"

"Since basic training. That's been almost two years now," John answered. "Boy, I'd never have guessed about you guys. Especially you, Brian. You look like any man's idea of what a man should be. You're not only well-built and good-looking, but you look like you could beat the shit out of anyone if you had to. I'm really glad we stopped in when we did, or maybe we'd never have met you guys."

"Thanks John. By the way, I can beat the shit out of anyone, not that you guys have to worry. I think I've met more straight sissies than I have gay ones. Anyway, when we finish this game, maybe we can head out to that bar I was telling you about. It opens at noon, and it stays busy."

After the game was over the four of them made their way out the door, and started toward the bar.

"I still can't believe it. We won two out of three games. I was sure you guys would win," David said, as he offered a cigarette to everyone.

About fifteen minutes later, Brian pointed to a building with the name The Tender Trap written over the door. "OK, guys, we're here. We'll all sit together, but act like you're available. One buck on whoever gets the first drink bought for him; you guys game to bet?"

"Sure, Brian, but it looks pretty much like an uneven bet," John answered. "They seem to go more for sailors and tough-looking marines then they do for soldiers."

"Well, it won't be long and we'll find out," Brian said with a grin.

The four of them had no more than sat down before the waiter came over to the table. "What are you guys drinking? This round's on the gentleman at the end of the bar—that is, after I see your ID."

"How about four glasses and a pitcher of beer," Clay quickly answered. "That way we'll last longer than if we drank hard liquor. By the way, tell the guy who bought these, he's welcome to join us if he wants.

After checking IDs and stopping only long enough to joke around a little, the waiter left to fill the order.

Shortly after the beer arrived, a man who was probably in his early sixties came over to the table.

"Thanks for inviting me. I was hoping you'd ask, but I actually didn't believe you would. My name's Benson. I own the place. Sorry I can't stay, guys, but when I saw four good-looking men sitting where you are, I couldn't help but buy you a drink. By the way, I'll send the waiter over with another pitcher before I leave. If any of you are still here later on, I'll be back."

Shortly after Benson had left, a drink was sent over for Brian.

"OK, guys, I won—those first drinks didn't count. That'll be one buck from each of you. Guess whoever bought this has a preference for Marines—that is, besides Clay. I'm going over and thank the guy. I'll be back shortly."

About ten minutes passed, and the waiter was back, this time with a drink for John.

"The gentleman over there wants you to join him for a drink."

"Go ahead, John. Must be someone who likes good-looking soldiers," David said. "Maybe someone will be buying one for Clay and me if we sit here long enough."

Before David could finish his beer, an old man sitting at the bar sent over another beer for both of them.

"Should we join him, Clay?"

"Hell, no. The last time I was here he couldn't keep his hands off me. I told him I didn't drink much and didn't want it, but he insisted anyway. How about you telling him that Brian and me are going together, and that he's really jealous."

"Sure, Clay, if you think it will help," David said as he got up and walked over to the man.

"Thanks for the beer, sir, but see that big Marine over there? Well, he's jealous as all shit, and he and that sailor are together, if you know what I mean."

"Well, how about you, soldier boy?" the old man said as he reached over and groped David before he could move away.

"Hey, enough of that, old buddy. And the same goes for that soldier over there—he's mine. We can be friends, but none of that shit. OK?"

The man never answered and just turned his barstool in another direction as David started back to his table.

"How some of those hustlers can do this for a living, I'll never know. Actually, I'd just as well not have the drinks if I had to put up with that. I can understand how some of these old guys are lonely. And I really don't mind talking with them for a while, just as long as it don't go any further than that," David said, as he lit a cigarette and poured himself another beer.

"Sure, David, I can go along with that. I think that if I ever went out with one of these guys, Brian would kill me, and if he didn't kill me, I'd probably wish I were dead when he got done with me."

David had to laugh, and so did Clay when he realized what he had said. After a while, John and Brian returned to the table and when everyone had finished their drinks, they decided to leave and meet up again later.

"How about meeting us back here in about four hours? I could use a little sack time," Brian said, as they left the bar and started in the direction of the "Y."

"Sure, Brian. With all that beer, I think John and I could do for a little rest ourselves. In the meantime, thanks for everything, and we're glad we met you guys. See you later, OK?"

After returning to the "Y," both John and David could hardly wait to lie down and sober up a bit before going back out.

It was close to seven when David woke up and sat on the side of his bed.

"Hey, John, you awake yet?"

"I wasn't, but I am now," John answered, as he took a look at his watch.

"Holy shit, we've been sleeping for almost three hours. You hungry, David? I sure am."

"Yeah. How 'bout you and me heading over to that diner and grabbing a bite before we start out again. We can stop at the Tender Trap first, and see if Brian and Clay are there. If they're not, we'll check out those two guys you told me about. How's that sound with you, John?"

"Sounds fine with me, David. Now I think we should take a shower and brush our teeth before we go. The shower should liven us up a bit, don't you think? By the way, no more grab ass, or snapping my butt with your towel, OK?"

"Sure, John. Just don't drop the soap while I'm in there with you," David said, as he moved over to where John was lying, and grabbing hold of his wrists, quickly positioned himself on top of him.

"Right now I need this a hell of a lot more than I do a shower. The shower can wait until after we're finished and by then we'll both have a reason to take one," David said, as he gently kissed John on his cheek and then on his lips.

"Yeah, David. I think you're right."

An hour passed and David got up from the bed, wrapped a towel around his waist and yanked the sheet off John.

"Get up. I'm not showering by myself, at least not here. The place is crawling with guys who'd love to catch you in the shower alone."

"Hold on, I'm up. Hand me a towel."

Instantly, David removed his towel and handed it to John, who started laughing.

"I didn't mean your towel, fool. I meant any towel other than the one you were using."

David grabbed another towel and the two of them headed for the showers to get ready for another night on the town.

"Do you think Brian and Clay are at the bar? At any rate, we'll stop there first just to see if they are," John said, as he and David returned to their room to finish dressing.

"Come on, David. Let's get a move on. We're already late, you know."

As John and David entered the bar, Brian and Clay were nowhere to be seen.

"Hey, waiter, remember that Marine and sailor we were with earlier? Have they been back in lately?"

"Yeah, they just left about a half-hour ago. Here's their address and phone number. They said to give it to you if you came in. If you need a place to stay, give them a call."

"Thanks, buddy. We'll have a draft, and then we'll see where we're going from there," David said, as he and John sat down at the bar and ordered a couple beers.

"Jesus, talk about luck, look who just came in. That's that old coot that groped me when we were here this afternoon. There's an empty seat right next to me and I hope to hell he don't sit there. Oh, shit, wouldn't you know—that's right where he's sitting."

"Bartender, give these two handsome young men a drink," the man said, as he placed his hand next to David's leg.

"Come on, buddy, I thought we went through this once today. Like I told you then, I'm telling you now—none of that touching stuff. Hey, bartender, cancel those drinks he just ordered for us, we gotta run."

John and David finished their drinks and left the bar, hoping they might find the two guys at home that John had mentioned earlier.

After a brief walk, John pointed to a large house situated next to a complex of row houses.

"That's the house over there. We might as well give it a try."

After John knocked on the door several times, a man wearing only a large towel wrapped around his waist answered the door.

"Well, hi, John. You'll have to excuse me. I just got out of the shower and haven't had time to get dressed. Who's the soldier you brought along with you?"

"Oh, this is my best friend, David. David, this is Kelly."

Kelly looked to be in his mid-to late twenties with long sideburns that came down to his chin. His intensely blue eyes seemed almost in contrast to his dark brown hair.

"Come on in, guys. Chico's in the basement repairing a chair. He'll be up in a minute. Let me get you a beer, before I go up and get dressed. I'll be back in a few minutes."

Shortly after John and David had sat down and started drinking the beer Kelly had brought them, Chico came up from the basement.

Chico was around the same age as Kelly. They'd met one winter in Puerto Rico while on vacation. Chico's skin looked as though he had one of those perpetual tans and there was something very sexy and sensual in the way he looked, and it wasn't difficult to understand why Kelly brought him back to live with him.

"Hey, John. What's new?"

"Not much, Chico. I want you to meet my buddy, David."

"Hey, David. I've heard so much about you, I feel like I know you already. I can see why John talks about you all the time. You're one good-looking stud, and if you're as good in bed as you look, you'd wear a man's ass off."

"Gee, thanks, Chico, and I could say the same for you. I've heard about you Puerto Rican guys and how you go at it from morning to night. By the way, are you and Kelly going out tonight?"

"Sure, David. We're going to a party. You guys want to join us? You're welcome if you do. I just have to run up and shower first, and then we'll be ready to leave. Sound good to you guys?"

"Sure, Chico, why not? Sounds like fun," John answered, as he lit a cigarette then continued to sip on his beer.

After a while both Kelly and Chico were dressed and ready to go.

"Come on, guys. My car's out front. I'm driving to the party, but Kelly will be driving us back. He drinks maybe two beers, and that's about all he ever drinks when we're out. At least one of us is sober enough to drive back home."

"Where you guys staying tonight?" Kelly asked. "If you don't have a place, you're welcome to stay with us. We got plenty of room, you know."

"Thanks, Kelly, but we're already checked in at the 'Y.' By the time we get up, shower, and shave, then have breakfast, it will be time for us to meet John's brother and some of our friends. Weekends sure fly by fast, don't they?" David asked.

"Yeah, they sure do. And as far as I'm concerned they fly by too damned fast," Kelly answered, as they turned down Sparrow Street.

"What do you know, we're here already. That was sure quick, wasn't it?" Kelly remarked, as the car pulled up in front of a large four-family flat.

"Boy, from the looks of it, there sure must be one hell of a lot of people here. You guys can get out. I'll have to park someplace at the end of the block."

Everyone got out of the car and waited on the steps of the building until Chico returned, then they proceeded to enter and mix with the crowd.

About four hours had passed when Kelly came over to where John and David were standing.

"You guys having a good time? I hope you don't mind, but I was thinking that we might be heading back. Chico is really getting loaded, and I'm getting tired of standing. There's hardly a place to sit around here. Anyway, it's getting a little late and I know you guys want to get some rest before tomorrow."

"Gee, thanks, Kelly. We were hoping you would be heading back pretty soon. We're getting tired ourselves. One thing's for sure, we had enough to drink."

After Kelly had convinced Chico that it was time to leave, the four of them got into the car and, with Kelly driving, they headed toward the "Y."

"Thanks a lot, guys. We really had a great time. I'll say one thing, your friends sure know how to throw a party," John said, as he and David sat in the back seat keeping an eye on Chico, who had already fallen asleep with his head resting against the door.

After a brief ride, John and David were back in their room and ready for bed.

"We better both use the latrine before we turn in for the night, or we might piss the bed after all the beer we drank at that place," David advised.

"Sure, David. You're right about that," John answered, as the two of them headed to the bathroom down the hall, relieved themselves of much of the beer, and returned to their room.

"Good night, David. If you wake up before me, make sure I get up when you do. If I'm up first, I'll wake you up, OK?"

"Sure, John. Now go to sleep. I'll see you in the morning."

The following morning, John woke up first and glanced at his watch. It was already past nine. After getting out of bed, John walked over to David and gently shook him until he was awake.

"We better get started. By the time we piss, shit, shower, and shave, we'll have just about enough time to get dressed, have breakfast, and meet the others at that café by noon."

"Forget breakfast, we can eat when we get there. I need another half-hour of sack time. You can wake me up then," David said, as he rolled over and fell back asleep.

John wrapped a towel around his waist, grabbed his shaving kit, and headed down the hall, making sure he took the key in case he had a hard time waking David when he returned.

While in the shower, John turned his back to the entrance briefly while rinsing, when suddenly he felt the touch of someone's hand against his thigh. Instinctively he pulled away. Turning around, much to his shock and dismay, there stood the very same old man who had groped David at the bar. He was naked as all hell, and looked like a wrinkled prune perched upon a pair of spindly legs.

"Jesus, don't ever walk up on me or touch me like that again. What the hell's wrong with you, anyway? Don't tell me you're staying here too?"

"I just stay here on the weekends. That's when the best lookers check in. You never know when you'll get lucky, now do you?"

"Well, one thing's for sure, this isn't your lucky day. Now get your ass out of this shower, before I kick it out."

With this said, the man made a hasty exit and John was able to finish his shower without any further advances. After shaving, John returned to his room to wake David and tell him what had just happened.

"OK—OK, I'm up. You mean to tell me you ran into the groper? Shit, in that case, I might as well shower on the next floor."

"I don't think you have to worry about him, David. If he thinks I'm still there he won't be back for a while. I threatened to kick his ass."

"OK, I'm on my way. You can keep the key. So let me in when I get back," David said, as he grabbed a towel and started out the door bare ass.

"I think you'd better wrap that towel around you, David, or you might get raped on the way to the shower."

"You're right about that, John. I'm still too tired to think, I guess."

As David entered the room, he looked carefully to see if anyone was hiding in one of the stalls or in the shower itself. After he was assured it was safe, he quickly showered and shaved, then returned to his room to get dressed.

"Hell, that old buzzard wasn't anywhere to be seen. You sure must have scared the hell out of him. It's a damned good thing you did, or I might have actually kicked his ass myself, if he had come on to me the way he did you."

"This must be my unlucky day for the hands-on approach," John said, as a snicker turned into a loud laugh just thinking about the incident in the shower.

"How's this for the hands-on approach," David said, as he gently pushed John down onto the bed, and started running his hands across and down his body.

"Oh, shit. Now I know we're going to be late for sure," John said, as he made no effort to stop what had already started.

It was just past noon when John and David turned in their key to the front desk, and proceeded to the Café where they were to meet Harold and the others.

"I was beginning to wonder," Harold said. "It's a good thing we waited like we did, or we'd have missed you guys. You're not going to believe this, but every one of us made out, even that screwball Green. Crazy as it sounds, he finally got some—that is, after Dickson was through with it. Now Dickson will never get rid of him." Harold could hardly contain himself from laughing, just telling about it. "OK, here's the plan. First, we're having breakfast here, then we're taking in a movie. Matinees are always the cheapest. We can smoke if we sit in the balcony. From there, we thought we'd hit the amusement park, and that should take up most of our day. How's that sound with you guys?"

"Sounds really great to us, Harold. I can hardly wait to get started," John said, as he followed the others into the restaurant to order breakfast.

The day proceeded pretty much as planned and after leaving the amusement park it was agreed that everyone was now on their own to spend the rest of the day whatever way they wanted.

"If you don't mind, Harold, I'd like to spend the rest of the day with you. I have some things that I've been meaning to tell you for some time now. Now that we'll be shipping out fairly soon, I thought I had better say it now. How about us just walking through the park to start with, OK?"

"Sure, John, we haven't spent much time alone together so this might be a good time to start."

It was a short walk to the park, and John seemed nervous and anxious at what he had to say.

"Well, this isn't easy, but I guess I'll start with David and me. I guess you know how close we've become. Well, to be honest about it, we're more than close. I hope you can understand that I love him, Harold. I think I love him more than anyone or anything. In fact, I know I do. Now the next thing that you need to know is that just before I got transferred, Niki and Maria from the Presidio legally adopted David and me. Neither one of us had parents, you know, and I needed them probably more than they needed me. The same goes for David. We have their names on our records so that if anything happens to us they will be notified along with you. We had the option of changing our names but we chose not to—at least for now. This was fine with Niki and Maria. Another thing is that we saw a lawyer and had our wills made out. We're going to Korea, you know, and that's why we did it. If either one of us were to get killed, we want to be cremated and our ashes taken out not far from The Wharf, and near the Presidio, to be emptied into the sea."

"That thing with Niki and Maria is what really comes as a shocker to me. As far as you and David go, I suspected it all along. I'm not exactly blind, you know. Guess what, if it had to be someone, I'm sure in the hell glad it was David. He's probably the best thing that ever happened to you. One thing's for sure, he's managed to pull you out of that quiet little corner you were in, and made a man out of you. This might come as a real surprise to you, but I had an affair with a guy once. I even thought I loved him. It surprised the hell out of me because I've always been one for women. I guess what I'm trying to say is that I understand how it could happen, and I feel the same for you as I always did. You're my brother, and I love you. As a word of caution, you know how the Army feels about this sort of thing, so don't ever get caught. By the way, with this adoption business, I wonder if that makes David my brother also?"

"Gee, I never thought of that, Harold, but I guess he is your brother—at least I think so," John answered.

In the passing of the next couple hours John pretty much brought Harold up to date on his relationship with David.

"Gee, Harold, you have no idea how much better I feel with you knowing the things I just told you. Right now I feel like you and me are closer than we've ever been before. Like you said, you're my brother, and I love you."

Chapter 12

Early the next morning, a sergeant came into the barracks with a ciga-rette in one hand and a clipboard in the other.

"All right, men, up and at 'em. You heard me, I said, rise and shine. I want your bunks stripped and the mattresses rolled forward. Put your sheets and pillowcases in the laundry hampers at the center of the room. Fold your blankets and put them on top of your mattress. Put everything you own into your barracks bag, place them at the foot of your bunks, and tag them with one of these large white tags. You will put your name, rank, and serial number on the tag. Someone will be by later to pick them up. After breakfast, I want everyone outside, lined up and ready to go. You have exactly two hours to be ready. Immediately after roll call, you will board buses and be taken to the pier to ship out. Is that clear to everyone?"

Most of the men answered yes, some nodded and some just grumbled, as everyone commenced to get ready.

"Jesus, they sure in the hell don't give you much warning," the guy next to John said, as he got up and started pulling the sheets from his bunk, while attempting to get dressed at the same time.

"Hey, Harold, do you think the other guys all made it back OK?"

"Don't know, John, but we'll find out soon enough. You had better eat a good breakfast. It might be a while before we eat again."

"I was sort of hoping we had a little more time here, but since we don't, I'm sure glad I was able to have that little talk with you last night," John said, as he lit a cigarette in a futile effort to calm himself.

"I'm sure glad you told me everything you did, John. Now if anything should happen—and I sure in hell hope it don't—I would at least know what to do. Now let's hurry and get down to eat. We could stop and check in with the others on the way back, that is, if we don't run into them at the mess hall."

John quickly finished what he was doing, and both of them made their way to breakfast via one of those long lines that had already formed.

"Damn. By the time we finish eating and get back, those buses will already be loading," John said, as he waited in line with the others. "It will be at least fifteen minutes before we finally reach the serving line, and another ten minutes before we finally get around to eating. Knowing that we're shipping out, you'd think they would have let us in the mess hall before the others."

"I don't know, John, maybe all these guys are shipping out—just the same as us."

Just as John had predicted, it was a little more than fifteen minutes before they finally got into the building and out of the cold. Breakfast was nothing special. Shit on a shingle, scrambled eggs, grits, coffee, and toast. At least you could say it was warm, filling, and really not that bad considering the number of guys who had to be fed.

"I see Green and Dickson over there," John said, as he pointed to where they were sitting. "And Bruce is heading toward our table right now. I don't see David anywhere, maybe he's still back at the barracks. I'll ask Dickson before he's finished eating. He should know, they're in the same barracks together."

"Hey, guys, mind if I join you?" Bruce asked, as he sat down across from Harold. "Guess you heard the news. We're shipping out today. Not that I'm anxious to get shot at or anything like that, it's just that I'm getting tired of this friggin' place. By the way, I just got done talking to Green and Dickson. According to Dickson, David didn't make it back last night. If he doesn't get back in an hour or so, we'll be boarding those buses and heading for the pier. Don't ask me where he went after we all split up. He went his way and I went mine, that's all I know."

"Damn, I hope nothing's happened to him. It's not like him to do something like this," John said, as his face took on a worried look that reflected his deep concern.

"Don't worry," Harold said, in an effort to calm and reassure John that everything would be OK. "By the way, Bruce, did Green and Dickson score again last night?"

"They didn't mention it, so probably not. I didn't, that's for sure. You almost done eating, Harold? If you are, we'd better be starting back to the barracks, OK?"

"Sure, Bruce, as soon as we finish our coffee we'll be ready. I see Green and Dickson are about to leave. Green's already up, and heading over there with his dirty tray," Harold remarked, as he hurriedly sipped the last of his coffee and glanced at John, to see if he was ready to go.

On the way back to the barracks, Bruce and Harold discussed the events of the weekend. The more they thought about Green, the more reason they had for laughing and joking around.

"Boy, they sure don't waste much time when it comes to getting those buses out front, do they?" John said as they approached the barracks.

"Well, here we are. I wonder how much longer we have left before we board the buses, Harold?"

"The way I see it, John, we should be getting ready to go any time now. See that sergeant over there? It looks like he's checking to see if everyone is back from the mess hall."

By this time everyone had returned to the barracks and, shortly after, the sergeant reappeared to issue more orders.

"OK, men, we'll be boarding the buses in just ten minutes. If you've gotta use the latrine you had better do it now. It may be a while before you have a chance to take a leak again, so if you don't wanna piss your pants, you'd better start pissing before we leave. In the meantime the corporal here will pass out mail."

Harold received two letters and after a number of other names were called, the corporal gave John his mail.

"Wow, look at this, Harold, I got three letters. Let's see, this one is from Niki and Maria, this one's from Mary and Joan, and would you believe this, this one's from Bill Standish."

John opened Bill's letter first, as he couldn't believe Bill wrote it.

"Dear John: (and this isn't a Dear John letter)

Things haven't changed much here except that we all miss you. Gary and Steve said to say hello. Gary gets a letter from Mary and Joan every couple weeks. I see Rick Taylor every now and then. I introduced him to my cousin a couple weeks ago and it looks like a marriage in the making. I'm not much for writing so will close for now. Hope this letter gets to you before you ship out. If you see anyone else I know, say hello for me. Good luck, Your buddy, Bill."

John read Mary and Joan's letter next, saving Niki and Marie's to be read later on.

"Dear John:

As you already know, Joan and I received honorable discharges some months ago and are now living in San Francisco. I can't tell you just how wonderful it is. Joan got a really great job at the post office, and I found work as a secretary. At present, we're renting a small apartment but hopefully, we'll be able to save enough money for a down payment on a house in a year or two. I think that as long as we live, we'll never forget just how wonderful you and the other guys had been to us when we really needed it. We received your last letter in which you said that you were being transferred to Fort Lawton, and from there to be shipped to Korea. One thing you may always be assured of and that is, that our prayers are always there for your safe return.

We love you, and God bless you.

Your (sisters), Joan and Mary."

"OK, men, move out for roll call." With this said, the sergeant took his place near the waiting buses as the men began to fall into formation. After everyone was outside, he picked up his roster and briefly checked it over.

"When I call off your name I want you to say 'present' then board the bus as quickly as possible. We'll start with Adam, Bernard L. Are you here, Adam? If you are, then speak up."

"Present. Sorry I didn't hear you, Sarg."

"They should have fitted you with a hearing aid if you're that damned hard of hearing. Now hurry up and get your ass aboard the bus."

Finally, it was John's turn, and the sergeant called out his name: "English, John Earl."

John quickly answered, "Present, Sarg," then left the ranks, and stepped aboard the waiting bus to save a seat for Harold.

When all the others were accounted for, the sergeant came aboard, made one final check, then took a seat up front before the bus proceeded to its destination. Most of the guys were laughing and joking around, or just talking in idle conversation.

It was a short ride to the pier, and as they left the bus everyone was directed to form ranks near the waiting ship. Nearby was an Army band, which had started playing, in preparation for their departure. Red Cross volunteers were standing close by with coffee and donuts for anyone who wanted some. There was even a guy passing out samples of Lucky Strike cigarettes to all the men who smoked, as well as to those who didn't.

"Isn't that the largest ship you ever saw," John said, pointing to an old Liberty Ship from the Second World War. "I guess that's the ship we're leaving on," John added, as he made out the name on its side, Pvt. Sadio S. Munimori. "I wonder who he was. He had to have a Medal of Honor to get his name on a ship. What do you think, Harold?"

"Don't know, John, but you're probably right. They don't name anything after privates unless it's something like that."

"Boy, this nice hot coffee sure comes in handy on a cold day like this," John commented, as he placed his hands tightly around the cup in an effort to keep them warm.

"Holy shit, from the looks of it they got all of Fort Lawton waiting down here to ship out with us. I wonder how in the hell they'll ever get us all aboard?"

"Guess that ship's a hell of a lot bigger than it looks from here," John answered, as he tried to imagine what it looked like from inside.

Finally, after what seemed an eternity, but in reality was only a couple hours, roll call was again taken and instructions were given on boarding.

After a second and final check of the roster, each man finally made his way on deck and was further ushered into what were called the holds.

The holds were fairly large rooms with stacked bunks which were so close to the others that you could touch the guy sleeping next to you just by turning from side to side.

Once everyone was situated and received some basic instructions, permission was granted to go up on deck to witness the ship leaving port.

"You know, Harold, I heard that that stuff about getting seasick was all in your mind. If you think you're going to get sick, you probably will. Anyway, I hear they got a pill to prevent you from getting sick. I think they call it Dramamine."

Finally, as the band played "Anchors Aweigh," the ship pulled up anchor and started slowly moving from the pier.

"I wonder how fast this ship can go?" John asked, as he watched the people waving on the pier, which was slowly moving away, with the people getting smaller and smaller.

"I heard ten knots at top speed, which comes to ten nautical miles an hour. Don't ask me how fast that is compared to regular miles, because I don't know," Harold answered, as he attempted to light a cigarette with the wind blowing in his direction.

Ever so gently the ship started a gradual rocking motion which intensified as they left Puget Sound and entered The Strait of Juan de Fuca.

"Oh, shit, I'm getting sick to my stomach. I think I'm going to throw up. How about you, Harold?"

"I was getting sick not long after we left the pier, now I'm really sick," Harold said, as he leaned over the rail and emptied his stomach of everything he had eaten that day. "Let's go down below. Maybe we'll feel better when we can't see the ship moving back and forth in the water."

As John and Harold made their way through the hatch and down the ladder into the hold, they were immediately aware of the smell of vomit, as men were throwing up all around them.

"Hey, you, I want you to report to the galley for KP" a sergeant said, as he grabbed hold of one of the men who promptly threw up in the sergeant's face.

Eventually, several men who somehow managed to keep from being sick were selected for the much-dreaded KP duty that awaited them.

Through the stench of vomitus, which spilled onto the deck as well as nearby bunks, John and Harold somehow managed to survive into the fourth day without food, and very little water. Miraculously, on the morning of their fifth day of misery, the sickness that had plagued them from the first day of the trip suddenly vanished.

"What I need right now is a shower, and from the smell of it so do a lot of other guys here," John said, as he made his way to the latrine.

"Jesus, how in the hell do they think we'll ever get clean with salt water? You can't even get the soap to make lather and the water's cold as hell," John remarked, as he quickly showered along with a few other guys brave enough to give it a try. Shaving was not much easier, and brushing your teeth tasted like hell. "Thank God I'm not a sailor; I couldn't go through this every day," John said, as he made his way back to join the others.

"Oh,shit, am I hungry. How about you, Harold? I haven't had a thing to eat in four days. I think I'll find that store they were talking about. Maybe I can get myself some candy bars."

"Sounds good to me, John. Hold on, I'll go with you. I'm just as hungry as you are—maybe even more so."

Candy bars were to be the first solid food that John and Harold could tolerate, and better yet, hold down, since they started out on this lengthy journey.

After a while, John pulled a somewhat wrinkled envelope from his pocket and began to read the letter from Niki and Maria.

"Our dear sweet son:

Both Niki and I pray every day that you will remain safely in God's care. We have arranged with the bishop to say prayers at every service, every day, until you and David return back home to be with us again. By the time you receive this letter, you may have already transferred to Korea or may be yet en route. I received a letter from David a week or so ago in which he said that you should be shipping out very soon. As we have said many times before, the both of you have come to us as the gifts that we have so often asked of God. Now in this time of separation we are deeply saddened that you cannot be with us each and every day. Please be careful, both you and David, and come back safely home when you have finished over there.

With our deepest love and affection, we remain your grateful parents, Niki and Maria."

John carefully folded the letter and placed it back in his pocket, to be read again and again with the others.

Later that day, John and Harold ventured for the first time into the galley for dinner. The ship was still rolling and they had to be especially careful not to fall on the slippery deck.

"How in the hell do they manage to cook in those big brass pots or on those grills with the ship rocking around like this—you'd think the stuff would spill over?" John asked, as he held onto a rail to keep his balance. I hope to hell we never end up on KP You'd need hazard duty pay just to work in there."

As they made their way down the serving line they were given large helpings of roast beef, mashed potatoes and gravy, corn, and apple pie for dessert. Apparently, from the size of the servings, there were still many men who remained sick and unable to eat.

After dinner, John and Harold climbed the ladder to the main deck and into the fresh sea air. As the evening wore on, the setting sun was one of the most spectacular events they had ever seen. And later, as nighttime fell and the sky turned dark, it seemed as though a million stars shone far more brightly than they ever had before. This was to be one of many such evenings that John and Harold would share together as the ship continued sailing toward Japan, the first stop before Korea.

Not a day went by that John didn't think of David, and wondered when, and if, they would ever see each other again.

The journey seemed as though it would never end but like everything else in life, it did. At last the ship arrived in Japan and docked at Yokohama, its final destination. Camp Drake was the next stop before continuing on by train.

"Wouldn't it be great if we could go into town, Harold? From what I've heard, there's a lot going on and all kinds of things to do there."

"Sure would, John, but I don't think we'll be going anywhere except to where they're sending us—and you know where that is."

Camp Drake was a pleasant break from the monotony of the ship, the food wasn't bad, and at last there was the luxury of a warm, fresh-water shower. The stay there was all too brief and early the following morning, after another roll call, John and Harold, along with the others, were marched off to the side of the tracks at the nearby rail station. From there they were ushered aboard a train on which they would take the long journey across Japan to Sasebo, where they would board another ship bound for Korea.

"Boy, this is the slowest train I've ever seen—or been on, for that matter. Did you ever see anything quite like this before? If you stretched your arm out the window you could touch the buildings or the people standing just a couple feet away."

"Nope, it's all new to me," Harold answered, as he lit up a cigarette and leaned back in an effort to relax.

As the train traveled toward its eventual destination, John's eyes seemed fixed on everything that went on outside the open window.

"Boy, take a look at that," John said, as he pointed to the local farmers working small, squared-off plots of land that extended into terraces cut into the hillside.

As they continued on their journey vendors approached the train whenever it stopped in an effort to sell whatever they could to GIs, eager for souvenirs, to send back home.

Above the seats was a long green net provided for baggage, which no one had, so some of the men climbed up and used it as a hammock to stretch out and rest. Others played cards, engaged in endless conversation, or just dozed off periodically in an effort to pass the time with sleep.

Around noon, box lunches consisting of two sandwiches, several cookies, and an apple or an orange were passed out along with coffee, juice, or bottled water.

"Wait until you use the latrine," John said as he returned to his seat. "They got four holes cut into the floor with a pair of feet painted next to them. And there's just one roll of toilet paper on a small table along with a basin of water to wash your hands. Bet you've never seen anything like that before."

"Nope, don't think I ever have," Harold commented, as he tried to read an article from the Reader's Digest that he had purchased from a vendor at one of the stops along the way.

After what seemed an endless journey, the train came to a final stop and everyone debarked in preparation for the next means of transport that would take them to their destination.

Once again everyone formed into ranks to be accounted for.

After a while a lieutenant came to the front of the group and "attention" was announced by a nearby sergeant.

"Listen up, men," the lieutenant began, "this will be your last move before Korea. You'll be boarding a ship, which will take you from here to Pusan. It's an old Japanese ship from WWII, so don't expect anything special. You will remain in Pusan until you receive further orders. Some of you will ship to the front, and some will remain in the rear. Whatever your assignment—Good luck, and come back safe and sound."

After the lieutenant finished his announcement, the men proceeded to the ship and commenced to board.

"Take a look at this, Harold. Did you ever see anything quite like this before?" John asked, as he pointed to individual straw mats, one next to the other, covering most of the deck. Each mat was just big enough for one man to lie down, provided he was no taller than five foot-ten.

"Now I've seen everything," Harold answered. "It at least gives you something to write home about."

After everyone was aboard and took a seat on one of the small straw mats, a sergeant had a few more announcements to make.

"First, I want to say that if you have to take a leak, you will have to piss in those buckets at the head of the ship. If you have to take a crap, there are two buckets located to the rear of the ship. As you can see, this ship was strictly for carrying troops and not meant for luxury.

"Secondly, if for some reason we should hit rough seas or experience rain, everyone will go below to the hold, which will provide standing room only.

"Lastly, you are responsible for your weapon, which was assigned to you before you came aboard. All weapons are to remain unloaded and anyone caught fooling around will be subject to discipline."

"How long do you think we'll be in Pusan, Harold, I mean, before we're shipped to the front? Maybe if we're lucky it'll be a while."

"I haven't the slightest idea. Like the lieutenant said, some of us will be shipped to the front and some of us will be staying in the rear. Doesn't look like it's bothering Green any. Look at him. He's sound asleep over there. Looks like Bruce is down by the other end. I'd go over and say hello, but I'm afraid I'd step on someone just trying to get to him. Might as well just sit back and relax until we get there. Thank God I don't have to take piss or worse yet take a crap. I'd step on someone for sure."

After a while, John turned onto his side and, using his helmet as a pillow, he managed to fall asleep for the remainder of the trip.

"OK, men, on your feet—we're here," the sergeant bellowed out. "After you've left the ship, I want you to form into ranks for roll call. Once everyone is accounted for, you will be taken to a replacement center where you will receive further orders. Any questions?"

A couple men answered no, but most remained silent as they rose to their feet in preparation for debarking.

Once every man was ashore and roll call was taken, John and Harold were marched off along with the others, to await further instructions.

Upon arrival they were greeted by a young lieutenant who looked like he just got out of high school.

"I want you men to form up over here. The medics have a couple shots to give you. When you're done there, line up by one of these tables and give your name, rank, and serial number, after which you'll be given your assignments. Some of you will move to the front and some will remain behind, at least for the time being. When we're finished with this, we'll break for lunch and report back here again immediately after. Do I make myself clear?"

Lunch consisted of some sort of stew, dehydrated potatoes, bread, butter, and coffee with canned fruit cocktail for dessert. Actually, not really that bad considering what they might be getting in the future.

After lunch everyone returned for further instructions and orders.

This time a Maj. Barkley introduced himself and quickly got into the details of sleeping assignments and combat preparedness. "When you are assigned a building and a bunk, I want every one of you men to field strip your weapons and clean them like they've never been cleaned before.

Make sure your bayonets are where you can get at them in a moment's notice and I have no objections to a sharpened edge. Let's get one thing straight right now—these aren't war games we're playing. You finished with that the moment you arrived here. If you don't kill them, they sure in the hell will be killing you. Some of you may think you've seen everything in life but, believe me, you haven't seen anything yet. Take a good look around you. Many of you have been the best of friends throughout your time in the Army. Not all of you will be coming back, and that should be enough to scare the living shit out of any man. Now let's look at it this way, if your buddy should get it, I want you to get mad as hell and get out there and kill those bastards that killed him. At least this way you won't have time to feel the fear and the loss, because you'll be motivated by hate and anger. You'll be seeing men with their arms and legs and even their heads blown off and their brains and blood even spattered on yourself, You'll be seeing men with spinal injuries who can no longer walk, or move, for that matter. You'll see men with their guts hanging out from their stomachs. You'll be seeing men who have gone blind or deaf. You'll be hearing men crying in pain and absolute agony. There will be times when you can't stop to help these guys and these are the times that you think you'll go mad. I know, because I've been there.

"You probably remember all that stuff you learned in Basic but this is now the real world. You won't be bayoneting a straw dummy, throwing dummy grenades into a marked-off area, or shooting blank shells in mock battles. The real truth is that you will be shooting to kill, bayoneting, slitting throats, garroting necks with wire or anything else at hand. You'll be throwing grenades, bashing in heads with rifle butts, hitting them with flame-throwers, and using any and every other means of killing to keep from being killed. If you desert your buddies, I can assure you that you will pay with your life. There's no room for cowards here. If you think I'm out to scare the hell out of you, you're right. And if by my doing so it saves your life, goddamn it, that's what I am hoping to do. Now with all this said, I suggest you spend a little time writing letters and getting ready for tomorrow. Good luck to each and every one of you guys. I'm sure you'll all be fine soldiers."

After Maj. Barkley left the men were given a free carton of cigarettes along with a cigarette break—and they sure in the hell needed it. Not much more happened after this except that they were given temporary assignments and allowed to visit a nearby Quonset where they were given two cans of beer each. For those guys who didn't drink, they shared their beer with their buddies. For those who didn't smoke, they likewise shared their cigarettes.

After John and Harold found their assigned Quonsets, John sat down and started writing a letter while drinking the first of his two beers.

"Dear Maria and Niki. I'm hoping this letter finds you both well. Harold and I received our initial orders and it looks like we will be staying here in Pusan for a little while yet. Somehow David missed the ship and I'm sure he'll be on the next one here. I really miss him. Believe it or not things aren't really so bad here. The food is fairly good, and they have been assuring us that this whole thing will soon be over. I just received a letter from you in which you mention that you and Niki want to get a bigger house so that David and I will have rooms of our own. There is really no need for separate rooms so why not consider twin beds? To be honest with you, we actually found no objection to sleeping together in that nice old double bed. There's plenty of room, and of course, if it worked out so well before, there is no need to change it now. By the way, please don't worry about us. We'll both be coming back and you'll have your family back together safely again.

Love to both of you. Your son, always, John"

Initially, Harold and John got stuck with road construction. This consisted of a bulldozer clearing the roadway, and then a dump truck poured hot asphalt onto the newly cleared road. Harold, John, and the others were responsible for raking the asphalt to an acceptable depth, to be rolled by yet another machine. It was already getting fairly cold and large, heated barrels of oil were required to keep the asphalt from sticking to the rakes.

This job lasted a couple weeks until John finally got assigned to the 12th General Dispensary, a venereal clinic located close to the pier and not far from the heart of the city. Harold managed to be assigned to an office in the replacement center. Fortunately he had learned to type and run a mimeograph machine while at Fort Ord.

Christmas proved to be a depressing day for John as he had not heard from David. Niki and Maria had not yet received a letter from him, and John was extremely worried. It was cold as hell and even though the troops had done their best making ready for the season, and the cooks had prepared turkey with all the trimmings, it just didn't seem right without David there beside him. New Year's Eve was not much better and John wondered if he'd ever see him again.

Three months had passed, and one day David unexpectedly arrived at the dispensary.

"John, am I glad to see you," David said as he came up from behind and gave John a big hug and a kiss on his cheek.

"Jesus, it's you, David. What in the hell happened that you missed the ship? I was so damned worried I thought I'd go nuts. No, don't even tell me what happened. I'm just so glad you're here right now. By the way, what's that badge you're wearing?"

"Just got off the line, that's where I've been for the past three months, John.—sort of an R&R. You know, rest and recuperation. This is the combat medics badge. Pretty neat, isn't it?"

"Sure, David, it looks great on you. One thing's for sure, you know I'm proud of you. I just wrote a letter to Maria and Niki, and I'm sure in the hell going to write them again tomorrow if not tonight and tell them the good news. I don't know if you wrote, but they didn't mention it in their last letter. God, I missed you. You'll never know how much I missed you."

"Guess what, John? I got orders to report to C Company for front line duty again," David said, as he once again gave John a big hug. "What kind of duty did you get?"

"I got assigned to a dispensary but I'm sure in the hell not staying there if you're being shipped to the front again. I know this corporal in head-quarters and I'm sure he can arrange to get me shipped out with you. I'm also sure Harold will want to go along. I'll ask him. We're not going to get separated again."

"You guys must be nuts," Cpl. Ditter said, as he lit up a cigarette and pushed a stack of papers to one side of his desk. "Just because this David guy is shipping out don't mean you have to go with him. You don't know how lucky you are to be back here. At least you're alive. But if that's what you want, consider it done. I owed you a favor once for giving me a shot for the clap and not reporting it. Now this is one hell of a way of repay-ing it. You might as well start packing now. You'll be leaving Monday."

Monday morning, following breakfast and roll call, John, Harold, and David boarded the trucks, which were to leave Pusan and head north to the front lines. Prior to leaving, box lunches were provided for the trip and several stops were scheduled for rest and latrine relief.

"Well, David," John said, as he put his arm around David's shoulder, "it looks like we're all in it together. Guess you knew that I couldn't stay behind while you shipped up front, and Harold wouldn't stay back with me going along."

"Thanks a million, John, but your coming along is the last thing in the world I would have ever wanted. Not that I wouldn't want you along, but I just can't stand worrying about you."

"Come on, guys," Harold broke in, "we're here and that's the way it is. Let's put it this way, we'll be fighting for one another. That way we'll all stay alive. Now give me one of your cigarettes, David, and let's stop talk-ing about it, OK?"

"Sure, OK with me. Think I'll take a little sack time while we're mak-ing our way there. Little bumpy and it's sure in the hell cold, but I think I'm about tired enough to sleep through anything right now," David said, as he leaned back on John's shoulder and closed his eyes.

The trip seemed to go on forever, and would have been almost unbearable had it not been for the many stops along the way. Finally, in the distance they could hear the sound of the larger guns firing at what was no doubt the enemy.

"Jesus, you mean we're finally here?" one of the guys on the truck said, as he attempted to stretch his body from being cramped up so long. "One thing's for sure—I'm sure in the hell glad to get out of this fuckin' truck, even if it means walking."

"Alright, men, out of the trucks and form up here," the sergeant said, as he indicated the area that they would be moving to. "From here, it's all on foot. We'll be forming two columns, one on each side of the road. Any indication of enemy action, both columns will hit the side of the road closest to them and stay close to cover. Do I make myself clear?"

Each man indicated he understood as the trucks all unloaded and the full complement of C Company was now formed into a single group.

It seemed almost as long as that march at the end of Basic before they finally began to experience some real action. The reality of it never really struck home until suddenly a private walking next to John stumbled a bit and fell face down with blood gushing from his neck. Everyone had heard the gunfire but never really thought that it was now directed toward them. The private who was no more than eighteen died almost the moment he fell to the ground and another soldier, with tears in his eyes, dragged him to the side of the road. There was no doubt that this was his buddy, and the loss was almost more than he could bear. A sergeant removed the dog tags as he lay there, pushing one between the dead man's teeth for identification and placing the other one into his pocket as a record of the death. Because of increasing gunfire the private was left behind. This was no doubt the first really hard lesson that would be only one of many in this godforsaken conflict. Many of the men had tears in their eyes but somehow they all managed to keep moving on.

"Jesus Christ, it's cold," one of the men remarked as he held his hands over his nose and blew warm air into them in an effort to warm his face.

"How in the hell do they expect us to sleep in this kind of weather? If we don't freeze our asses off we're liable to never wake up. Mentioning sleep, I'm getting on the tired side right now."

"Let's get one thing straight—no one's sleeping, at least for now. If you get tired, I've got some amphetamine to keep you awake. One thing's for certain, you try sleeping out here and you're dead for sure," the corporal stated as he passed out two amphetamine pills to anyone who thought they might need them. The leaves had all fallen from the trees and it was still dangerous as hell due to the large mounds of dirt and hills that surrounded the countryside and easily gave shelter to the enemy.

"Damn it, David, seeing that private get it back there, I've really been nervous—scared is more the word." With this said, David suddenly reached over and took hold of John's hand, probably to reassure and comfort him. Whatever it was, something more intense than words themselves had passed between them. The anxiety seemed to leave John's face as he held tightly to that grasp, and David did this without guilt or shame. It was like two children, one leading the other by the hand as they proceeded past a rather large hill.

"You scared, Harold?"

"Yeah, I'm scared, John. Who isn't?"

"You know, Harold, I'm not so much scared for myself but for David and you." John's face suddenly took on a saddened look. "Don't know what I'd do if anything happened to either one of you—I couldn't take it, and I don't know how in the hell I'd be able to go on."

Strange, but both David and Harold felt the same. Even though they didn't express it.

Just as they passed a hill they encountered rapid gunfire. Before they could hit the dirt, David was struck several times in the chest and John stayed back long enough to pull his friend to a nearby ditch.

Blood was not only oozing from David's chest but also running down the side of his mouth. Immediately John opened his first aid kit and attempted to stop the sucking chest wounds with gauze and tape.

"I love you, John." And these were the last words that David said before he later died. It was strange but this was the first time that either John or David had ever told the other that he loved him, and they should have done so many times before. God, how John wished that he had said "I love you, David" long ago.

For a long time, it seemed a very long time, John just seemed to gaze in shock. He had already grabbed David up with his arms wrapped so tight around him, holding him close, like a child. His eyes had swelled into tears, then he started sobbing, which proceeded into an uncontrollable episode of crying. He kissed David several times on his cheek and once on his mouth. By this time blood had already soiled John's uniform as he held David so closely to him.

Then in a soft and almost whispering voice, he said, "Don't go, David. Please, God, don't let him go. I love him."—But David was already near death. Over and over John kept saying. "I love you, David." Finally he screamed at the top of his voice, "Those bastards, those bastards. I love you, David." Maybe three or four more times he said it. Then after a pause, his voice became soft, almost a whisper. "I know you can hear me, David—I know. I promise you, I'll never forget you, not even for a day. I'll never love anyone as I have loved you—it's a promise, David, and when my time has come, I'll join you, and this is also my promise to you."

It was strange but no one made any attempt to initially help or comfort John. Somehow they all knew what he was going through. They understood, but just weren't able to help. Their silence was their expression of sympathy and understanding.

John continued to hold David close and was attempting to pull him along with him so as not to leave him behind. Finally when they had to move on, several men standing nearby approached John, and after pulling him away from David, they gently hugged him and offered their hands, much like David had done for John before. This was their attempt to comfort him and show their support.

Leaving David behind, and watching as they forced a dog tag between his teeth, like they'd done for the private before, was probably the greatest pain beyond David's death that John would ever again experience.

Chapter 13

"Come on, men, get a move on it. We're coming under heavier fire. Cpl. Pryor, try calling in for some backup or we're not going to make it. Get a move on it, goddamn it. The rest of you guys keep low to the ditch until we get out of this goddamn area."

Before the lieutenant could finish what he was saying, the company was hit with even heavier gunfire, this time killing three more men and wounding another four who weren't quite fast enough to make it to the ditch for cover.

John moved from man to man as quickly as possible, risking his own life in pulling the men to cover and administering whatever aid he could.

"Jesus Christ, Lieutenant, the closest help is about an hour away, with Alpha, Bravo and Easy companies. The only thing we can do is keep low and pray to God that they don't decide to bring in a direct attack," the sergeant said as he kept low to the ground.

"Corporal Vance, you start spraying them with the BAR while the rest of you guys give them all you got with your rifles. Maybe they'll think we got more than we have. Damn it, I wish we had some mortars right about now. I can't believe it, but we don't even have grenade launchers," the lieutenant said, as he started making his way down the ditch to check out the wounded.

As C Company poured in as much firepower as they could, suddenly they were receiving enemy fire from their left flank and were being rushed by at least half a platoon.

"Holy Christ, we just got about four more guys hit bad—if they start coming from the forward or rear position we're all dead. Keep firing only if you have to so that we don't run out of ammo, and concentrate on the ones that are rushing us. The major line of heavy fire is coming from behind that hill to our right, and there's not a fuckin' thing we can do about it right now," the lieutenant said, as he appraised his future options.

John continued to render whatever medical support he was capable of giving with his now limited supplies. He was down to one morphine syrette and gauze dressings were about exhausted. Suddenly, John grabbed four grenades, a carbine and ammunition, then ran like hell toward the hill, moving in a zigzag pattern, firing at the enemy to his left flank, while all the while gunfire was directed toward him from the hill. Before he could approach the hill he was hit once in the leg and took a grazing wound to his neck. Now standing just below the hill, he threw two grenades directly over the top, and the shooting there stopped momentarily. He next circled around the hill, and after throwing one more grenade he shot the two remaining survivors. As he made his way back to his company he continued to fire at the enemy to his right, while his company, who were still holding out in the ditch, directed as much protective firepower as they could. Quickly moving toward his company, he managed to throw his remaining grenade at the enemy, killing four, before taking one more bullet into his thigh. On reaching cover, he jumped into the ditch as fast as he could.

"Son of a bitch, you could have been killed," Harold said, as he helped his brother with bandaging his wounds. "What in the hell made you do it? You're a medic, not a goddamned rifleman."

"You asked why I did it? It's because I am a medic and I'm responsible for saving lives and not standing by while they die. Let's say I did it for David, and I did it for those other guys who were killed, and let's just leave it at that."

With no further action from the hill, the company could now direct its full attention to the left. After a five-minute gunfight Easy Company arrived along with Alpha and Bravo, and the enemy disappeared as quickly as they had arrived.

"If it weren't for you, English, do you mind if I call you John?" the lieutenant said, "we'd all be dead men. If we get out of this alive, and I think we will, I'm recommending you for the highest award this Army can give. You're one hell of a soldier and I've never seen one that could ever compare with you. And by the way, I'm really sorry about your friend David. I know how much he meant to you. You may think I don't, but I really do."

"What the hell went on here, Lieutenant East? Looks like you really ran into some heavy shit."

"Do me a favor, Captain, and get my wounded to the rear as quickly as possible to get treatment. As for the dead, let's get them back also. I'm going to send one of my men to help you locate two others who were killed earlier as we made our way here. One's a Corporal David Marconi and the other is a Private Edward Nixon. You can identify them by the dog tag between their teeth. Handle them gently, it means a lot to me and to my men."

"You don't have to worry, Lieutenant, my men are already loading the wounded into the truck."

"By the way, Captain, have you got a pen and some paper? I have to write a recommendation for the Medal of Honor. You can understand that if I get killed at least someone will be able to see that this recommendation gets through."

"Sure, Lieutenant, take your time and be sure to leave nothing out, because if you do they may not consider it. You sure it's not the Silver Star rather than the Medal of Honor you need to be requesting?"

"I know the difference, Captain, and it's definitely the Medal of Honor. For my part, I could never settle for less, and there's not a man in this company who wouldn't agree with me."

After John and the others were loaded into one of the trucks, they then proceeded toward the rear. The dead were to be transported in the same vehicle as the living, as trucks were in short supply.

All the way back, John placed his hand near David as he tried his best to keep from crying out loud. Because of John's wounds the captain had provided another medic to render aid to those in need. Silently, John kept saying over and over, I love you, David, I'll always love you.

At last the truck arrived at the field hospital and a team of doctors and nurses immediately prepared the tent for surgery. John, like the others, would remain there for the next three weeks. At that time it was decided to fly them to Japan for further treatment and evaluation.

John's stay in Japan was rather brief, lasting only another four weeks, and from there he was returned to Pusan, Korea, for reassignment back to the 12th General Dispensary. Not long after his arrival he was joined by Harold and some of the other guys he knew.

"God, am I glad to see you, Harold," John said, as he gave his brother a big hug that seemed to last for at least a minute. "Got any news about all the guys we were buddies with?"

"Well, so far as I could find out, Green was the only one who got it. They say he died almost instantly. I guess only you can understand how much of a loss this is to me. I really loved the guy even though he was a little on the goofy side. I'm sure in the hell going to miss him. By the way, John, how you holding up with losing David? You don't have to answer if you don't feel like it right now. Believe it or not, I really do know how much you loved him and how much he loved you. On the brighter side, we won't be going back to the front again. I got it in my hip, of all places.

Could have been worse. Could have got it in the crotch. I see you got assigned to the clap shack, and I got assigned to office duty again."

"I wrote a letter to Niki and Maria while I was in that field hospital, but it was so hard to tell them the bad news about David's death," John said. "I Just got a letter back from them yesterday, which I think you might want to hear."

After Harold had finished, John took a folded and obviously much read letter from his pocket.

"To our dear son John:

Thank you so much for your letter while being treated in that field hospital, we have prayed for you every day since. By the time that you read this letter we can only describe the events of David's funeral. We were notified by telegram even before we received your letter. 'It is with deep regret that we must inform you that your son David Marconi while in the defense of his country was killed in action while serving in Korea.' The telegram went on to say when we should expect his body to arrive so that we could make the necessary funeral arrangements. For our part, we felt that we had died along with him.

When his body arrived, a soldier assigned as his escort and wearing a black arm band stood by his casket throughout the entire funeral. A military honor guard fired their rifles and this was followed by a bugler playing taps. I was presented with the folded flag which was removed from the casket along with his medals, and this was the saddest day of our lives. In accordance with his wishes, David was cremated and we shall await your arrival before proceeding further. We should like to say at this time that we have always fully understood how deeply you loved David and how deeply he loved you, for this reason we understand what a great loss this is to you. Our only consolation is in telling you that we also love you dearly and you must come back safely as you are all we have left.

With love to you, our son,
Niki and Maria."

"I'm really glad you read me that letter, John, because I know how much it means to you. I know I can't do much, but you can always count on me to help you in any way I possibly can. In the meantime how 'bout you and me going into town and just bum around a bit. We get off duty in about a half-hour and we'll go right after chow. OK?"

"Sure, Harold, it might help me take my mind off David for at least a while."

"Oh, yes, there's a bar on the pier, sort of like an EM club. We'll have a few beers there before we start out, if that's OK with you?"

"Yeah, Harold, a few beers might do me some good. Let me just say one thing before I forget to get around to it. You're my brother, Harold, and I love you even more than I can put into words. I'm thankful to God that you made it back like you did and we're back here together. Sounds a little mushy, but I'm saying it from the heart."

"Thanks, John, not many men could say what you just said, and I love you even more for saying it."

John and Harold remained in Korea for another six months, during which time they were able to finally experience some warm weather and meet new friends. At last it was time to board a ship bound for Japan, where they were given a "homecoming" meal consisting of steak, mushrooms, and all the trimmings. This was followed by a sundae for dessert, which tasted like real ice cream and nothing like the stuff they served in Korea.

Military script was exchanged for greenbacks and the following day, John and Harold were assembled along with what seemed hundreds of other men for the return back to the states. The trip back was somewhat uneventful and believe it or not, not many men got sick. Maybe you only get sick once. Who knows?

Finally, there it was, the Golden Gate Bridge. Sort of made you feel much like those guys returning home from the Second World War. From there it was Camp Carson, Colorado for discharge or reenlistment. John choose reenlistment while Harold could hardly wait for his discharge and eventual return back home.

John could hardly believe the orders—he was being assigned back to Fort Riley, Kansas, the very place he had started out in. He had decided to take two weeks vacation, spending it with Niki and Maria, and would take the rest of the money that he had in cash, along with his reenlistment bonus to start a bank account.

"Sir, John Earl English reporting for duty as assigned," John said, as he entered the captain's office.

"Have a seat, Corporal English. I have something to say to you that I have never had the honor of telling any other man before. Congress has awarded you the Medal of Honor. You have no idea what a great honor this is, and what an honor it is for me to be the one to tell you."

"Thank you, sir, but whatever I did, I did it because I had to."

"To start with, you will be going to Washington, where the president will personally award you the medal after an officer reads the citation. When this ceremony is accomplished you will be returning back to my company temporarily, until you are assigned to a dispensary or the base hospital. Congratulations and good luck to you, Corporal English and I wish you the very best in your military career."

The trip to the capital was uneventful, and when he finally arrived and the ceremony began, John could hardy hold back the tears, not so much from pride, but from thoughts of David who could not be here with him, as the president placed the medal around his neck. Over and over in silence he thought, I did this for you, David, I did this for you. This medal is as much yours as it is mine. I love you, David. I'll always love you.

"Congratulations, Corporal, or should I now say Sergeant English. It's a real honor to have met you and presented you with this nation's highest award." The president then shook John's hand and left with many of those in attendance. John was now free to return to Fort Riley to continue with his career.

Three months had passed, and John was wanting more and more to return to the Presidio of Monterey to be with his friends, and also with Niki and Maria. Finally, he put in a request of transfer, but instead received orders to proceed to Easy Company, 63rd Infantry, Fort Ord, California. Being that Fort Ord was so close to the Presidio, John was thankful just to be so near to the place that held so many fond memories.

The train ride to California was rather long but nonetheless enjoyable, as he passed much of his time in the dining room and the club car, where he met other servicemen who had much in common with him. This left little time for the unpleasant memories that he would have otherwise been plagued with.

"Won't you join me for a drink, Sergeant? I see by your ribbons that you have earned the Medal of Honor. My name's Major Hartman. What's your name?"

"Sergeant English, sir. That is, John English."

"Well, John, I'm not going to ask you what you did to earn it, as I'm sure you're tired of going through it again. Anyway, I'm not the only one on this train who has noticed that you're wearing that ribbon. There's a corporal here who was stationed at Fort Riley, who knows you—not personally, you know, but you were pointed out to him as having earned the medal. Do you mind joining me for dinner after this drink? It's on me and I'd really be honored if you did."

"Thank you, sir. It would be my pleasure, sir."

After dinner, John again thanked the major before rejoining the other enlisted men he had been sitting with.

At last he was there, Fort Ord, California—the base where his brother had been stationed along with Green and some of the others. After meeting the company commander of his new company he was instructed to report to regimental headquarters to meet with Lt. Gen. Allan.

"Segeant English reporting as ordered sir," he said, as he entered the room adjacent to the general's office.

"One moment, Sergeant," the lieutenant said as he knocked on the general's door and announced John's arrival.

"You can go in now, Sergeant English, the general is expecting you."

"Sir, Sergeant English reporting as ordered"

"Have a seat, Sergeant. The reason I called you here is that you are only the second Medal of Honor recipient that I have had the honor of having in my command. I personally want to welcome you here and if there is anything that I can possibly do to make your stay a pleasant one, you can call on me at any time."

"Thank you, sir, and it was my privilege to meet you, sir." John once again thanked the general and left the room to return to his assigned company.

"Sergeant English, you are to report to Lt. Col. Strump's office at battalion headquarters after lunch," the company clerk said, after John had returned to the company.

"Did he say why I was to report there?" John asked.

"No—maybe for the same reason you had to report to the general's office. I just get my orders and pass them on, you know."

"Sir, Sergeant English reporting as ordered, sir."

"At ease, Sergeant, and have a seat. I just wanted you to know that I heard a somewhat disturbing rumor, and I know it's only a rumor, and nothing but a rumor, that you had some sort of close affair with another soldier while in Korea. What I'm trying to say is that this relationship was a little more than just good buddies. Now what I'm asking you is quite simple. All you have to say is that the rumors are exactly that, rumors and nothing more.

"You know how gossip gets around and I want to put a stop to it before it gets any further. By the way, the name of this soldier was David Marconi, according to the rumor. All I'm asking you is to just say it isn't true and we'll get the guy who started this whole lie. What do you say, Sergeant English. Sounds easy enough, doesn't it?"

"Yes, it does sound easy, Colonel, but the truth is that it's not a rumor. I did love David, I still do, and I will always love him."

"Come on now, I know he was your buddy and you know how you can feel when it comes to your best friends. I'm sure that's what you mean. Now isn't it?"

"No, sir, what I mean is, I'll never forget him. I really loved him. He loved me, and I'll always love him."

"Jesus Christ you're a goddamn queer. I gave you every chance to deny it but you didn't, and won't. You know that medal you got? Well, I'm going to make sure that I get it taken from you. Corporal Bates, I want you to go to general headquarters right away and request that they inform General Allan that I have some very important information that they should be aware off."

About an hour passed before the general arrived and was escorted into the colonel's office.

"Sergeant English, it's a pleasure seeing you again, the general said. Now what is it that's so damned important that I had to rush over to your office, colonel? You know the rules. You were supposed to contact the colonel at regimental headquarters and ask permission to see the major general and from there to see me. It's not the other way around."

"I apologize, sir, I didn't intend to have you come personally to my office, but rather that you be informed of the situation."

"What situation, Strump?"

Well, sir, it seems that this Sergeant English had a lover, I mean another soldier while stationed in Korea, a homosexual affair, and I think that we should start proceedings to have his medal removed and prepare him for discharge."

"What the hell's wrong with you, Strump? Who really gives a shit who he had an affair with. The truth of the matter is he is a Medal of Honor recipient, and that's one thing you will never be able to take from him.

Before I go any further I'm going to ask that everyone leave the room until I finish my conversation with you, Strump."

After the room had emptied except for the colonel and the general, General Allan first lit up a cigarette and began by talking loud enough for those in the other room to hear. "Now get one thing straight, you stupid son of a bitch—if you have any ideas that you will transfer this man or in any way punish or harm him, or if I hear one more word coming out of that big fat mouth of yours, you can kiss those silver oak leaves on your shoulders goodbye. I already have enough in your file to assure that you will never reach the rank of bird colonel. Do I make myself clear? Do you have any idea what this kind of publicity could do to the Army? It sure in the hell would hurt us more than it would ever help us. Now get this straight, he will transfer when he chooses to do so, and he will stay if he chooses to do so. He's one hell of a good soldier and I don't give one shit who he loves or who he sleeps with. And for that soldier, David, well for your information he was John's brother, and a goddamned good soldier and he died in Korea along with a lot of other good men just like him. Another thing, Sergeant English is welcome to come to my office any time he chooses to do so. You will instruct your staff to say nothing more about this matter to anyone, and I do mean anyone. Do I make myself clear, Colonel?"

"Yes, sir, perfectly clear, sir. Consider the matter closed, sir, and I assure you it won't be brought up again, sir."

"Incidentally, before I leave you have told me absolutely nothing that I was not already aware of. If it didn't bother me, it sure in the hell should have never bothered an idiot like you." With this said, the general left the room and on his way out he stopped momentarily to ask Sgt. English if there was anything he wanted before he left.

"Yes, sir. I would like a transfer back to The Presidio of Monterey if it is at all possible sir."

"Consider it done, Sergeant. I'll take care of it the moment I return to my office. Once again, it's my privilege meeting you and always feel free to visit me should you need my help."

"Thank you, sir, and it's equally my privilege to have met with you, sir." With this said, the two men went their separate ways and John felt good that he was now able to return back to the Presidio, which held so many fond memories.

Later that afternoon John received his orders to transfer to the base hospital at the Presidio of Monterey. He could hardly wait until the following morning, when he would at last return to a place filled with so many happy memories. That evening he spent his time watching a movie at the base theater, and then having a few drinks at the NCO Club.

Early the next morning, John finished breakfast and was ready to leave when a Jeep arrived to drive him to The Presidio. The driver identified himself as General Allan's chauffeur. "The general said to tell you good luck in your military career and to feel free to contact him at any time."

Up until then, John had not notified Niki or Maria that he was back in California and was saving this as a surprise.

According to his orders he was not to actually be assigned to duty until four days from his date of arrival. This would give him Thursday, Friday, Saturday, and Sunday to spend with Niki and Maria, as well as his friends. After reporting to the base hospital he was assigned quarters where he quickly dropped off his belongings and immediately went to the building where Maria worked.

"Hi, Maria, it's me, your son, John Earl English. I'm back. Come on over and give me a great big hug and a kiss. I've really missed you and Niki."

Maria burst into tears as she almost ran to John and held him in her embrace for quite some time. "Oh John, praise God he saved you and allowed you to return safely home. You know, of course, that I can never get over the loss of David, and both Niki and I know how deeply you loved him. Tell me now, where will you be working? I know you won't be cleaning offices like before; and look at that—you're a sergeant now.

When they told us about your winning the Medal of Honor it was all we could do to contain ourselves from bragging to everyone we knew. You would think we had won the medal ourselves. You have no idea how proud we are of you."

"I'm sure you know, Maria, that I would have given up this medal in a flash if it meant that David could have lived. In fact, I would have sacrificed my life for his. I'm so lonely now that sometimes I think I'll go mad. Maybe after I see some of my old buddies this evening it might help to cheer me up—at least a little. Would you mind if I didn't come home with you tonight? I need a lot of time to think and get myself together."

"Sure, John, I understand and I'm sure Niki will also feel the same. Now go out and start looking up your old friends, John Earl English."

"Hey, Paul, I'm back. Come on over here and give me a big hug. I really need it right now. Do me a favor—I can't walk down that hill alone since David was killed. I'll need you with me for support. OK?"

"I'll be ready to go in about an hour. Why not go over and see Bill while you're waiting. He's working in maintenance and, by the way, congratulations on your promotion to sergeant. Damn, look at all those ribbons and, holy shit, is that what I think it is? That blue one with all the stars? Goddamn, you got the Medal of Honor. I don't believe it. My best friend is a real life hero. Hell, yes, I'd be honored to walk down that hill with you. Wait until I tell all the others, they won't believe it either. By the way, John, I'm really sorry about David. I knew how much you two guys loved each another. I really did. Anyway go check on Bill, will he be surprised. Maybe we'll all walk down to town together. Of course, we have to stop by and see Steve and Gary. They ask about you all the time."

"Hi, Bill. How's things going? As you can see, I'm back. How's your cousin, and did he hook up with Rick? You said it looked like a marriage in your last letter."

"Well, so far as I know they're still going together, and Rick's really built—if you know what I mean, so I guess it looks like the real thing. By the way, word gets around here fast, and I hear you're some sort of hero. In fact, the colonel is planning a parade in your honor next week."

"Jesus, that's the first I've heard of that," John commented as he put his arm around Bill's shoulder and gave him a quick embrace. "How 'bout you joining Paul and me and head into town today. I need the company since David was killed. OK?"

"Sure, John, and thanks for asking. Should we eat first or grab a bite in town?"

"My treat. It'll be the Fisherman's Wharf. I also want to invite Gary and Steve to join us. I'll give them a call so they don't eat first. I got some money from my reenlistment bonus. Meet us in front of the mess hall and you, Paul, and I will walk down together. OK?" John said, as he gave Bill another big hug before leaving.

After John said hello to a number of other guys he knew, Paul and Bill were standing in front of the mess hall and ready to go.

As they started down the hill, tears welled up in John's eyes. "Do you mind holding my hand, Bill, while Paul puts his arm around my shoulder? It will remind me of how David and I used to do that when we walked down this hill together. You know, I still can't believe he's gone. You'll never know how much I loved him. I just can't seem to get over it. If it weren't for you guys, I think I'd go nuts. Guess I'll get used to walking alone after a while, but for now I really need your support."

"Don't worry about it, John, either Paul or me will always be around to walk with you. We're your buddies, John, and that's one thing you can always count on. Here, use my handkerchief, it's clean, and wipe your eyes. You don't want Steve and Gary to see you've been crying, do you?"

"Thanks, Bill, but that's no guarantee they won't see tears before the night's over. I can't help it. I just can't stop thinking about David. We had so many good times together. I wanted to come back here where we had so many memories, but I'm not sure I really made the right decision. It's turning out to be more painful than I thought it would be."

When at last they reached the wharf, Gary and Steve were waiting. First Gary and then Steve gave a long and welcoming hug to John, then offered their sympathy in the death of David. Once again, John's eyes welled into tears as he tried unsuccessfully to control his emotions.

"Hope they have the same waiter," Steve said, as he put his arm around John's shoulder in an effort to console him. "You know, the one who serves the wine without asking for proof of age."

"No problem for me, Gary added, "I'm twenty-one now, and I guess we'll all be of legal age in a few more months."

"What's say we head on in and order. I'm starving. Why don't we just order fish and chips? I hear they have really great whitefish here, and the fries are huge," Paul suggested.

"Sounds good to me if it's OK with the rest of you guys, that is, of course, if we can order wine with the meal," John answered.

"It's OK with us, so let's head on in and order," Bill said, as they made their way into the restaurant.

The wine arrived well ahead of the meal, and after toasting to John's return and good health, Paul raised his glass again and said, "Let's toast to Joan and Mary who will be here this Saturday. We're all going to The Golden Goose just like before. I called them just before I quit work today and they can't wait to get together. We'll meet at Yorky's."

"You guys are the best friends anyone could ever ask for. Thanks for everything and thanks for being with me, especially today. I really needed you," John said, still a little teary-eyed as he recalled David also dining with them in the past.

"One last toast before we eat, Paul said, raising his glass. "Here's to our best friend, a real hero, and winner of the Medal of Honor."

"Jesus, is this for real?" Gary asked.

"Yeah, Gary, it's for real but let's not ask John to go into it right now. Maybe another time, if he feels like it. Right now, let's just relax and enjoy each other's company. Besides, I think we're embarrassing him," Paul said, as he reached over and gave John a gentle hug.

Saturday afternoon both Joan and Mary arrived in a fairly new car that they had recently purchased. As they pulled up in front of Yorky's, John could hardly hold back his emotions, as Joan and Mary had written to him once a week without fail.

"John, you look great for all you've been through. Come on and give us a great big hug, and that goes for the rest of you guys. It's a little early but let's get started to The Golden Goose. Scott can't wait to see you, especially Gary," Mary said. "From what I've been hearing Gary and Scott have been seeing a lot of each other lately. Sounds like it might be leading to something more than friendship."

John looked over at the table where they usually sat and noticed that a large "Reserved" sign was on it to assure that it would be available when they arrived. Already there was a fairly large number of people gathered. Mainly the lunch crowd. No more had they sat down than Larry the bartender came rushing over with two pitchers of beer. "This is on Scott and so is anything you want to eat or drink." Larry returned to the bar only briefly to bring back glasses for everyone.

After all the glasses were filled, Joan offered the first toast. "Here's to John's safe return, and here's to the memory of David who I'm certain is here with us right now."

Next, Gary raised his glass: "Here's to our two good friends Mary and Joan. We love you kids."

Lastly, Steve raised his glass and said: "Here's to all our good health, our lasting friendship, and, of course, prosperity in our future."

"Hey, Mary, do me a favor," Larry asked, "and play my song. I'll turn the jukebox off for a minute."

Mary got up, walked over to the piano, and played "Bye, Bye, Blackbird" while many of the patrons sang along.

"After we eat and have a couple more beers, Joan and I have to head back. I have to work tomorrow and we wanna to be back in San Francisco before it gets dark."

Scott came over and took a seat next to Gary, placing his arm around Gary's shoulders while Gary placed his hand next to Scott's leg. There was no doubt about it, a romance of some sort was in the works.

After they had all eaten and finished drinking the remaining beer, they thanked Scott for everything and made their way to the car, after which they were driven back to Monterey to visit Rick for the remainder of the evening.

"Boy, am I glad to see you guys. What's say we party a bit?" With more drinking, laughing, and joking the evening passed rather quickly. Much to everyone's surprise, Gary consented to sleep over with Rick.

"I guess that Gary's just too horny to be totally faithful to anyone," Steve remarked, as he prepared to leave with the others.

The following morning John woke up with a headache which he attributed to drinking the night before. As the days progressed he began to feel weakness, a low grade fever, pallor, and chills, which caused him to visit one of the doctors at the hospital.

"Probably a virus," the doctor suggested. "No doubt it will go away shortly. Here, take these APCs. They should help the headache and the fever."

Within two more weeks John was experiencing labored breathing, fatigue, general malaise, tachycardia (or rapid heart rate) along with palpitations. With these symptoms, he was sent to Fort Ord for further diagnosis.

"You know what I suspect—I've seen these symptoms before. I bet this man has leukemia. I would like to do a bone marrow study and some blood work to confirm it or rule it out," Dr. Golden said following a rather thorough examination.

After the tests were performed and the results were finally in, Dr. Golden's diagnosis was confirmed. John did in fact have leukemia and the prognosis was poor.

Having been advised of the nature of his disease, John asked the doctor if he would contact General Allan and ask him if he would come to visit.

"Do you know the general, John?"

"Yes, doctor. I do, and he said if I should ever want to see him to just let him know."

The doctor contacted headquarters and within an hour the general arrived at John's room.

"I'm so sorry, Sergeant English. I was told the diagnosis and whatever I can do for you, I will."

"Well, sir, if my time is limited and I am dying, I'd like to receive a medical discharge so that I can be with a friend or with my parents. Can you arrange this, sir? I could be treated at the VA."

"What I'm going to do for you, John, is allow you to remain in the Army and be placed on an extended leave of absence until you recover. I am doing this because, in the event you should pass away, your parents will receive the ten thousand-dollar insurance policy you now hold, and all expenses toward a military funeral will be available. In the meantime you will receive an off-base living expense along with your regular Army paycheck, which I'm sure you'll definitely need. I'll see to it that your medical leave of absence is carried out immediately following your discharge from this hospital. However, you can stay here as long as you wish. Goddamn it, I just can't believe it. Such a good soldier. One of the Army's best and it has to end this way. At any rate, sergeant, or can I call you John?, it's been an honor and a pleasure to have known you. One thing's for certain, you can always call me and count on me wherever I am able to help. Incidentally, you will have to report back to this hospital every two weeks so as to maintain your medical leave of absence. I have to leave now, but I can't leave without wishing you good luck and, God willing, a cure."

"Thank you, sir, you're the finest gentleman I have ever known, sir," John said, as he shook the general's hand in a farewell gesture. With this said and done, the general left and John soon dozed off to sleep.

Later that afternoon Harold arrived to visit John as he had twice before. When he stopped at the nurse's station he was advised that John's condition was extremely serious.

"What's wrong with him?" Harold asked.

"I take it you're a friend of his. I really can't tell you anything other than what I've already said," the nurse answered.

"I'm his brother and I have a right to know."

"In that case, I'll have the doctor discuss it with you."

"Hi, I'm Dr. Golden. I've been following your brother's case since the beginning. What he has is leukemia. To be quite frank with you, it's difficult to guess just how long he'll last with this disease. He could have a period of remission but later it will return. It's always fatal. I'm so sorry. He's so young."

"Holy Christ, I can't believe it. After all my brother's been through and something like this has to happen. Damn it, I still can't believe it. If you don't mind doctor, I'll let his friends know. They'd want to know. They can visit, can't they?"

"Yes but they will have to wear masks as he is subject to infections. Actually, I would rather they didn't visit until he's feeling better."

A week later John felt well enough to leave and at first stayed with Niki and Maria. During this time Gary paid a visit.

"You know Gary, as much as I love Maria and Niki, what I think I need the most is to be with my own kind. Do you know anyone I could room with?"

"Matter of fact, I do. I have a friend named Vince who recently asked me if I knew anyone needing a roommate. I'll call him tonight. I'm sure he hasn't found anyone yet. You'll like Vince. He's around your age and actually quite good-looking. Not bad in bed either. You know me, I found that out already."

"Thanks, Gary, but sex is out of the question. First off, I'm not up to it and more importantly, David was my only lover. By the way, do me a favor and tell all my friends to never mention David to him. I don't think I could stand the pain of explaining my relationship with him. It's too painful to me. Promise me, OK?"

"Sure, John, you can count on all of us. He'll never know. Well, I have to get back to the ship, but you can be sure I'll call him and get back with you tonight."

"Thanks, Gary. I'll wait for your call and hope he still needs a room-mate." After Gary left, John dozed off and slept until Maria and Niki arrived back from work.

"What would you like to eat?" Maria asked, as she gave John a gentle hug.

"I'm really not hungry, Maria, but do you have any more of that really great soup you made yesterday?"

"Sure, John, I made plenty. How about some nice bread with the soup? It's really delicious"

"Thanks Maria, that sounds just fine."

Later that evening Gary called. "Guess what, John, I talked to Vince and he said he'd love to have you as a roommate. I told him you didn't have much money, and he said that wasn't a problem and could be worked out once he meets you. Do you feel well enough to pay him a visit tonight? Steve wants to go along, and, of course, he has a car."

"Sure, Gary, I've been feeling a little better every day. Do me a favor, though? Try to keep the visit as short as possible, OK?"

"No problem, John, I'll be back in about a half-hour with Steve, so be ready."

After John had explained that he was going out briefly with his two friends Gary and Steve, he got dressed, combed his hair and was ready to go.

As it turned out, Vince lived only about five blocks from Niki and Maria's. The house was much larger and had a swimming pool with a rather beautiful back yard. John was really impressed with the pool, as it could give him some exercise that wouldn't be too strenuous. Gary was right, Vince was a really handsome man and just as pleasant as he was good-looking. Vince and John seemed to have much in common and immediately liked each another.

"You know, Vince, I'd like to move in as soon as possible. I'll have to break the news to my parents, as they actually wanted me to stay with them. I love them, but I really need to be with someone who understands me as a gay man."

"Great, I'll be looking forward to you moving in soon then," Vince said, as he gave John a hug and thanked Gary for recommending him.

"Did Gary tell you that I have a medical problem?"

"Yes, matter of fact, he did, but we'll deal with that day by day. In the meantime, I plan on enjoying your company, and of course, that also means that I'll be seeing a lot more of Gary, which is one of the added benefits of this arrangement."

"Thanks again, Vince. I'm going to leave now, but you can be sure I'll be back again soon."

"Niki and Maria, you both know how much I love you, but I feel it best that I be allowed to room with a friend of Gary's. He only lives about five blocks away and you could still see me as much as you wanted. I really don't want to hurt you, but even though I'm sick I need my independence, and sleeping in that room alone is too painful for me without David."

"No, John, we understand perfectly. The only thing that we ask is that I can cook for you boys as frequently as possible. That way we can feel like we're still a part of the family. Also, we want to pay your room and board. Don't worry, we have the money and can well afford it. "

"It's a deal, and I love you both for being so understanding. I'll always love you. And I'll always be your son. Incidentally, I'm still in the Army and on a medical leave of absence. I will be receiving off-base living expenses in addition to my regular pay, so I probably won't need much help financially. But thanks, anyway, as I knew you would be willing to help me."

That evening Niki and Maria helped John pack his belongings and the following day they drove him to Vince's house, where they introduced themselves as John's parents.

"I made my son promise that I could cook most of your meals, if that's OK with you?"

"OK? Sure it's OK. I'm the world's worst cook and some good home cooking would sure be welcomed. By the way, feel free to stop by at any time, you'll always be welcome," Vince said, as he followed Niki and Maria to their car to unload John's belongings.

Later that evening Gary arrived for a visit and after a few drinks decided to spend the night with Vince. John was still unpacking when Gary suggested a swim in the pool after dark.

"I don't have a bathing suit," John said, "unless you have an extra one."

"Bathing suit? We're swimming in the raw. If it doesn't bother us it shouldn't bother you. What you say, John?" Gary asked.

"Sure, Gary, I'm game. I'm feeling a lot better right now and the exercise should do me good. By the way, I'll finally get to see what it is that drives all those men mad about you."

Not much later, Steve, Gary, Vince, and John all stripped down and entered the pool. From what John could see, it was more than obvious why Gary was so popular with so many men—and women for that matter. He was well-built and had the equipment to go along with it.

After an hour or so of swimming everyone dried off and went into the house for a few drinks. Steve left shortly after, and Vince and Gary retired to their room almost immediately thereafter. It had been a pleasant first evening and John soon dozed off to sleep.

Within the next couple months John steadily felt better. It was now becoming apparent that the leukemia was probably in remission. John and Vince were becoming closer and closer friends, and Niki and Maria brought over dinner every night without fail. Harold and all the guys either visited or John would visit them, but always in the back of his mind John worried when the sickness would return.

It was now six months since John had moved in with Vince, who had become far closer to John than he ever thought he would have. One morning as he went in to check on John, he noted that John had a very high fever and was holding a towel to his nose due to a rather bad nosebleed.

"John, are you OK? I think I had better take you to the emergency room to see a doctor." Vince now checked John's pulse, which was 120 beats per minute. "Do you feel like you can get up and walk to the car, John?"

"I'll try, Vince, but I feel so weak I'm not sure I can make it."

"In that case I'll call an ambulance. I'm really scared this time, because I've fallen in love you, John. I know you probably don't feel the same about me, but that's OK. Here, let me get you some aspirin, some nice cold water, and a cold wet towel to hold over your nose until the ambulance arrives."

About fifteen minutes later the ambulance pulled up to the front of the house. Vince accompanied John to the Army base hospital where, after having blood drawn and a quick examination, he was admitted for further evaluation and treatment.

"Are you John's roommate?" the doctor asked Vince.

"Yes doctor, I guess you could also say I'm his best friend."

"Well, Vince, I think you had better get hold of everyone who cares about him because he's dying, you know. I would guess that he might be gone today or possibly tomorrow."

Immediately, Vince started crying uncontrollably, but when he finally regained his composure he called Niki and Maria, then Harold, who in turn notified everyone that he could possibly get into contact with.

John became more and more lethargic and was barely able to answer questions. He remained in this condition for at least four more hours, by which time everyone who had been contacted had managed to arrive. One by one, each in turn took John's hand and let him know that they loved him.

Finally, in one last effort John raised his body slightly from the bed, and it was at this point that he said, "David, Oh David," and reached out to grab hold of that unseen hand before he breathed his last and passed away.

The day of the funeral, in accordance with John's wishes, the funeral service was held outside where all his many friends and acquaintances could attend. In addition many admirers and dignitaries attended the military funeral that was to take place.

Mary had requested that Maria and Niki allow her to compose and deliver the eulogy, as she had been such a close and good friend to John.

"We are most honored and pleased that you have offered to deliver the eulogy and we are certain that John would have been equally pleased as he wrote and spoke of both you and Joan quite often," Maria said, as she accepted the offer.

After everyone had gathered at the site, Mary took her place next to the casket which was draped with the American flag, and upon it was placed his military decorations with the Medal of Honor most prominently displayed. To one side of the casket stood a military escort from the Presidio, wearing a black armband, a symbol of mourning.

After a brief pause Mary started the delivery of the eulogy.

"I am deeply honored that John's parents have consented to allow me to speak on behalf of John who I came to consider as a brother as well as a very close and dear friend.

"I would like to start by saying that John was always faithful in his relationships with his many friends. My partner, Joan, and myself, have much to be thankful for as a result of John's willingness to go to any extreme to protect us at a time when we were both in a state of crisis.

"We are deeply sorrowed in his passing; however the one thing he has left behind is the many fond memories which we were honored to have shared with him.

"During the Korean conflict John showed an extraordinary willingness to do whatever was necessary to protect and defend his fellow soldiers during a time of extreme danger that could have otherwise ended in the loss of countless lives. This was done with a complete disregard to his personal safety in the interest of those whom he was sworn to care for. For his bravery on the field of battle he won this nation's highest military decoration, the Medal of Honor.

"Both his parents, Maria and Niki, have much to be proud of, inasmuch as John often spoke how dearly he respected, honored, and loved them. I would like to extend to his parents our deepest sympathy on behalf of the United States Army and his many, many friends and acquaintances.

"At this point I could not go on without mentioning David, who remained to the very end John's greatest love and the one man whom he never forgot even until the very end of his life. I would like to thank especially Niki and Maria for understanding this relationship from the very beginning and for their continued love of their two sons, John and David, regardless of the implications; never judging them, but rather always loving and supporting them.

"In closing, I should like to say that John remained a hero not only to my friend Joan and myself, but also to all his many friends and to the nation as a whole. It is my sincerest hope and prayer that in his passing, John and David will once again be reunited and bound in a state of perpetual love throughout eternity.

"God bless you, John, we shall miss you and will never forget you," Mary said as she wiped the tears from her eyes.

Immediately following the eulogy, Mary took her place next to Joan and among the others in preparation for the military funeral that was to continue.

A military honor guard from Fort Ord fired ten rounds, and this was followed by taps. Upon request of Harold, John's brother, a Scottish member of the Veteran's Club piped "Amazing Grace."

Shortly after, the medals were removed from the casket and placed on a black velvet board. The flag was likewise removed and folded in accordance with the prescribed regulations for doing so.

Bill Standish was given the honor of presenting the flag and the medals to John's adopted parents, Niki and Maria, who were so distraught that they had to remain seated during this procedure.

"On behalf of a grateful nation, I present to you, the parents and loved ones of the deceased John Earl English Nevski, this flag as a gesture of our deepest and sincerest sympathy." As he presented the flag and the medals, Bill could barely say the words and could not keep back the tears that he kept wiping from his eyes.

"I want you to have this," Maria said, as she presented the Medal of Honor to Harold. "He was your brother, and I know you were as proud of him as we were."Thank you Maria, but you came to John at a time when he needed you most. Both you and Niki are his parents and he really loved you. No, this medal belongs to the both of you, more than it belongs to me. I want you to have it and keep it in remembrance of him," Harold now offered the medal to Maria, who now proudly accepted it.

After everyone had left, the casket was placed within the hearse and taken to the crematorium, in accordance with John's last wishes. His ashes were to be later spread upon the ocean along with David's, near to The Presidio and not far from the Wharf.

The following week Mario, a Russian Orthodox Priest, Niki, Maria, and all of John's friends including Joan and Mary, boarded a medium-sized yacht provided by one of Niki's friends, and sailed the short distance from the Fisherman's Wharf, as planned. When they arrived at the designated area Maria removed from her purse a piece of folded paper and quietly asked Harold if he would read it prior to the burial at sea.

"John wrote this shortly after David died and gave it to me not long ago. I would appreciate it if you would read it for us at this time," Maria said, as she handed the paper to Harold.

Harold took the piece of paper from Maria, and after briefly looking at it, he said, "I would first like to say how deeply I miss my brother and I am sure that each of you here feels this loss as much as I. However, I am certain that no one feels the loss greater than David and John's adoptive parents, Maria and Niki, who first lost their son David and now their remaining son, John. To Maria and Niki, I extend my deepest and sincerest sympathy on behalf of myself and all here present.

"This is a poem written by my brother John to his closest and dearest friend, David, shortly after David's death, and it's only fitting that I read it at this time."

TO DAVID

Two men bound by God
One unto the other,
I was your very best of friends
And yet I was your lover.
Oh, how dearly have I loved you
And if I had a choice of when I'd die,
I would gladly had forfeit my life
And in your place I'd lie.
When at last my time has come
And life is gone from me,
Forever, together as we have lived
Bound by love we'll always be.
I miss you
I love you
John

After he had finished, Harold gently folded the paper as it was before, and returned it to Maria.

Following the reading of the poem, the priest then commenced to mix the ashes of John and David together by simultaneously emptying the cartons of their contents into the sea.

"I commit to the ocean the ashes of John Earl English Nevski, and David Eduardo Marconi Nevski, the sons of Princess Maria Anastasia Romanoff Nevski and General Nicholas Petr Aleksandr Nevski. In so doing, John and David are united together again as they had been in life.

"Both John, and David, had always retained the greatest and dearest love for one another even unto death. It is therefore, only fitting that their ashes are spread together here, and their spirits having left their bodies, shall know eternal life and love from this day forward."

About the Author

C.G.Mitchell was born in Hazel Park, Michigan in 1932. After his father died in 1939 he was placed in a children's home where he remained until the end of WWII. In 1949 at the age of seventeen, he joined the United States Army where he served as a Medic before, during and after the Korean War.

Mr. Mitchell has traveled extensively: however, has remained a resident of Michigan most of his life. Over the years he has enjoyed writing short stories, essays and poetry in addition to detailed monthly letters to his many friends. In addition to *Marching to an Angry Drum*, he has published several of his poems and a recent book, *Storytime Anytime*, consisting of twenty-two short stories, a revision of his first book, *I Quit—I Promise*.

In addition to writing, which is his principal interest and passion, he likewise enjoys cooking, gardening, museums, theaters, flea markets, art fairs, the zoo and strolls in the park. He also enjoys traveling, fishing, boating, hiking, swimming, art, antique collecting, lapidary and jewelry design and most especially being with and enjoying the company of his many friends and acquaintances.

0-595-00144-0

www.ingramcontent.com/pod-product-compliance
Lightning Source LLC
Chambersburg PA
CBHW061338280526
45784CB00001B/59